D0859781

301.8
W388

30036

The John J. Wright Library
LA ROCHE COLLEGE
Allison Park, Pennsylvania

THE METHODOLOGY

OF THE

Social
Sciences

MAX WEBER

301.8
W388

Translated and Edited by
EDWARD A. SHILS and HENRY A. FINCH

With a Foreword by EDWARD A. SHILS

THE FREE PRESS, *New York*

Copyright 1949 by The Free Press

Printed in the United States of America

All rights reserved. No part of this book may be reproduced or transmitted in any form or by any means, electronic or mechanical, including photocopying, recording, or by any information storage and retrieval system, without permission in writing from the Publisher.

Fourth printing February 1968

30036

The John J. Wright Library
LA ROCHE COLLEGE
Allison Park, Pennsylvania

Macmillan #4.95 ($4.21)

5/68

FOREWORD

I

The essays in this book were written, as all methodological essays should be written, in the closest intimacy with actual research and against a background of constant and intensive meditation on the substantive problems of the theory and strategy of the social sciences. They were written in the years between 1903 and 1917, the most productive years of Max Weber's life, when he was working on his studies in the sociology of religion and on the second and third parts of *Wirtschaft und Gesellschaft*. Even before the earliest of the three published here —" 'Objectivity' in Social Science and Social Policy"[1]— was written, Weber had achieved eminence in Germany in a variety of fields. He had already done important work in economic and legal history and had taught economic theory as the incumbent of one of the most famous chairs in Germany; on the basis of original investigations, he had acquired a specialist's knowledge of the details of German economic and social structure. His always vital concern for the political prosperity of Germany among the nations had thrust him deeply into the discussion of political ideals and programmes. Thus he did not come to the methodology of the social sciences as an outsider who seeks to impose standards on practices and problems of which he is ignorant. The interest which his methodology holds for us to-day is to a great extent a result of this feature of Weber's career just as some of its shortcomings from our present point of view may perhaps be attributed to the fact that some of the methodological problems which he treated could not be satisfactorily resolved prior to certain actual developments in research technique.

The essay on "Objectivity" had its immediate origins in his desire to clarify the implications of a very concrete problem. Weber, together

---

[1] First published in the *Archiv für Sozialwissenschaft und Sozialpolitik* in 1904.

iii

with Werner Sombart and Edgar Jaffé, was assuming the editorship of the *Archiv fur Sozialwissenschaft und Sozialpolitik* which was, from his assumption of editorial responsibility in 1904 until its suspension in 1933, probably the greatest periodical publication in the field of the social sciences in any language. He wished to make explicit the standards which the editors would apply and to which they would expect their contributors to conform. In doing so, his powerful mind, which strove restlessly for clarity at levels where his contemporaries were satisfied with ambiguities and clichés, drove through to the fundamental problems of the relationship between general sociological concepts and propositions on the one hand, and concrete historical reality on the other. Another problem which was to engage him until his death — the problem of the relationship between evaluative standpoints or normative judgments and empirical knowledge — received its first full statement in this essay.

"Critical Studies in the Logic of the Cultural Sciences" was published in the *Archiv* in 1905. It must have been in the process of production while he was also busy with a large scale investigation of certain aspects of German rural society and with *The Protestant Ethic and the Spirit of Capitalism*. The intricate task of explaining causally the emergence of an "historical individual" (in this instance, modern capitalism) finds its methodological reflection in this essay which treats of the nature of explanation of particular historical events in its relationship to general or universal propositions. At the same time, he continued, on this occasion much more specifically and with many illustrations, to examine, as he had in the essay on "Objectivity", the role of evaluative points of view in the selection of subject matters and problems and in the constructive application of categories. His efforts in this essay were partly a continuation of his long-standing, self-clarifying polemic against "objectivism" and "historicism" but its analysis drew its vividness and its realistic tone from the fact that he was continuously attempting to explain to himself the procedures which he (and other important historians and social scientists) were actually using in the choice of problems and in the search for solutions to them.

"The Meaning of 'Ethical Neutrality' in Sociology and Economics" was published in *Logos* in 1917, in the midst of the first World War.

It was a time when patriotic professors were invoking the authority
of their academic disciplines for the legitimation of their political
arguments, when Weber himself was engaged in a series of titanic
polemics against the prevailing political system and while he was still
working on the sociology of religion. (Perhaps he had already begun
by this time to work on the more rigorously systematic First Part of
Wirtschaft und Gesellschaft.[2]) The essay itself was a revision of a
memorandum, written about four years earlier to serve as the basis
of a private discussion in the *Verein fur Sozialpolitik* and never made
publicly accessible. A mass of particular, concrete interests underlie
this essay — his recurrent effort to penerate to the postulates of
economic theory,[3] his ethical passion for academic freedom, his fervent
nationalist political convictions and his own perpetual demand for
intellectual integrity. Max Weber's pressing need to know the grounds
for his own actions and his strong belief that man's dignity consists in
his capacity for rational self-determination are evident throughout
this essay—as well as his contempt for those whose confidence in the
rightness of their moral judgment is so weak that they feel the urge
to support it by some authority such as the "trend of history" or its
conformity with scientific doctrine in a sphere in which the powers of
science are definitely limited. On this occasion too, Weber worked his
way through to the most fundamental and most widely ramified
methodological problems in the attempt to reach clarity about the
bases of his own practical judgment. Here, of course, he was not
dealing primarily with the methodology of research, but his procedure
and his success illustrate the fruitfulness of methodological analysis
when it has actual judgments and observations to analyze rather than
merely a body of rules from which it makes deductions.

The three essays published here do not comprise all of Weber's
methodological writings—in the *Gesammelte Aufsätze zur Wissenschaftslehre* they constitute only one third of a volume of nearly six

---

[2] Recently published by Talcott Parsons under the title *The Theory of
Social and Economic Organization* (London 1947).

[3] Cf. his contribution to the discussion on "Die Produktivität der Volks-
wirtschaft" at the meeting of the Verein für Sozialpolitik in 1909 (*reprinted
in Gesammelte Aufsätze zur Soziologie und Sozialpolitik*) and "Die Grenzutz-
lehre und das psychophysische Grundgesetz" (1908) (reprinted in *Gesammelte
Aufsätze zur Wissenschaftslehre*).

hundred pages. One of the most important of his methodological essays — "Roscher und Knies und die logischen Problems der historischen National ökonomie" has not been included in the present collection, while another important section of the German edition — "Methodische Grundlagen der Soziologie" — has already been published in English.[4] Yet except for the analysis of the procedure involved in the *verstehende* explanation of behaviour which is contained in the latter essay and in an earlier and less elaborate version, in the essay "Über einige Kategorien der verstehenden Soziologie,"[5] the main propositions of Weber's methodology are fully contained here.

II.

In many respects, social science to-day is unrecognizably different from what it was in the years when these essays were written. Particularly in the United States and Great Britain, the social sciences have developed a whole series of techniques of observation and analysis and have on the basis of these, proceeded to describe the contemporary world with a degree of concreteness and accuracy which only a few optimists could have expected in Weber's time. The number of social scientists engaged in research has increased by a large multiple and the resources available for financing research have likewise multiplied many times over. The success of the social sciences in devising procedures of convincing reliability have led to their marriage with policy to an extent which could have been conceived only in principle in Weber's time.

The turn of events and the passage of years have not however reduced the relevance of these essays. The concrete incidents have changed — we are no longer concerned to refute the errors of "objectivism" and "professorial prophets" are not a very important problem for us — but the relationship between concrete research, whether it be descriptive concrete research or explanatory concrete research, and general theory has become a problem more pressing than ever, even

---

[4] *The Theory of Social and Economic Organization.* Chapter I.

[5] First published in *Logos* (1913). Reprinted in *Gesammelte Aufsätze zur Wissenschaftslehre.*

though awareness of it is much less than universal. Many of our current advances in research are made in ways which seem to avoid raising the problem—so many of our successes are successes in accurate description in investigations in which the problem of explanation is left to those who requested the investigation or who are to "use" the results. Sometimes our desire for accurate description is so great that we feel that our intellectual needs are exhausted when that end has been achieved. Moreover much of the acceptance and appreciation of the utility of social science in the circles with the power to finance it and use it, extends largely to just those aspects of social science research which are almost exclusively descriptive or in which the task of explanation is disposed of by correlations of indices of ambiguous analytical meaning or by *ad hoc* common sense interpretations. The fact that the correlations among the indices of ambiguous analytical meaning is often high and that the possibilities of successful practical manipulation are thus enhanced constitutes a barrier to our perception of the need for theory. Here, these essays of Max Weber can perform a very useful service. The substantive theory itself will not be found here — that must be sought in part in the other writings of Max Weber, in part it must be sought in other writers, and in largest part it is still to be created — but the rigorous and convincing demonstration of the indispensability of theory in any explanation of concrete phenomena will be found here. Although the content of the theory will have to be sought elsewhere, Weber's methodological writings also raise important questions regarding the structure of a theoretical system, and the possibilities of a variety of theoretical systems constructed around their central problems and ultimately "related to values".

In the period of his life when he wrote "Objectivity in Social Science and Social Policy," Weber still, under Rickert's influence, regarded the particular and the concrete as the really "value-relevant" phenomenon which the social scientist must understand and seek to explain in the appropriate manner. For him, at this stage, a system of general concepts and a general theory was simply an instrument. It is really irrelevant as to whether we agree with Weber that it is the "value relevance" of concrete events which distinguishes the social from the natural sciences — the important point was that he saw the possibility and significance of a general theory. It is most unfortunate that when he began to elaborate the general conceptual system which was to form the first four chapters of *Wirtschaft and Gesellschaft,* and which must have been intended by him as part of a general theory which would have explanatory value, he did not write a methodological essay on the problems of theory-construction and systematization in the social sciences. " 'Objectivity' in Social Science and Social Policy" brings the problem before us in a most intriguing way but leaves it unsolved. In doing so however, it raises issues which contemporary social scientists must face if our knowledge is to rise into a systematic scientific theory and not merely pile up in a chaos of unrelated monographs and articles.

The impressive improvement of social science over the three decades since Weber's death has been accompanied by a vast sprawl of interest over a multitude of subject matters which cannot readily be coordinated intellectually into a unified body of knowledge. In some measure this has been the outcome of random curiosity, in some instances it has been the result of immediate practical problems. But it is now appropriate to begin to pay more attention to the criteria by which problems are to be selected. A healthy science, developing in a balanced way, would not normally have to concern itself with this matter. But it does seem that in the present state of social science in which theory and observation have tended to run apart from one another, and in which there has been a scatter of attention over a large number of unconnected particular problems, some serious consideration of the criteria of problem-selection would be fruitful. Here Weber's discussion of "value-relevance" can help to bring order into the social sciences. His discussion can heighten our self-consciousness regarding the grounds on which we choose problems for investigation. More self-consciousness about this process and more discussion about it might also increase the amount of consensus about the substantive as well as the formal criteria of problem-selection. And if this is coupled with an intensified awareness of the theoretical necessities entailed in concrete empirical investigation, the chances for a growth of knowledge about certain crucial problems' would appear, in the light of our constantly improving technical resources, to be very good.

Weber's appositeness to the present situation of social science emerges again when we turn to still another problem. In Weber's own life-time social scientists were scarcely ever found in the employ-ment of governments. "The Meaning of 'Ethical Neutrality' in Sociol-ogy and Economics" was directed towards the social scientists in universities who made assertions about the right ends of policy in the name of their scientific or scholarly disciplines; it was intended to clarify the ways and the extent to which statements about policy could be based on scientific knowledge. The situation has changed greatly since then. In both the United States and Great Britain very large numbers of social scientists are employed in Governmental service, and outside the Government social scientists are becoming increasingly concerned with "applied social research". In most instances the ends of policy are taken for granted, the social scientists working to provide data about the present situation from which the policy is to take its departure, or to provide estimates of the consequences of alternative policies. In a smaller proportion of cases, social scientists believe that the right ends of policy can be determined by social science research. (This "scientistic" attitude seems to have become more pronounced with the scientifically right and necessary ascent to pre-eminence of the theory of personality, but it is by no means limited to social scien-tists trained in psychology.) Weber's treatment of the relationship between social science and the ends of action and therewith of policy should aid social scientists to see both their possibilities and their limitations. It should dissolve the false identification of an apolitical attitude with scientific integrity, and it should help to refute the baseless accusation that the social sciences are ethically relativistic or nihilistic either in their logical implications or in their empirical con-sequences. If it helps social scientists to think better about the way in which social science can clarify the assumptions of policy, it will also help them in the clarification of the criteria of value-relevance. By tracing the assumptions of any policy back to its postulates, the establishment of the "value-relevance" of a subject matter or problem will also be carried out on a more general or theoretical plane. Problems for research will therefore themselves tend to be formulated with closer regard for their theoretical assumptions; and the move-ment of research interest on to a more abstract plane, where theory and research will be fused, will become more likely.

But these are only a few of the many lines which connect Max Weber's methodological analysis to the main issues of contemporary social science.[6]

EDWARD A. SHILS.

London, April 1949

---

[6] The most accurate and elaborate studies of Max Weber's methodology are Alexander von Schelting: *Max Weber's Wissenschaftslehre* (Tübingen 1934) and Talcott Parsons: *The Structure of Social Action* (Glencoe, Illinois, 1949) (Chapter XVI). Useful analyses of some of Max Weber's methodological problems will be found in F. A. Hayek. "Scientism and the Study of Society": *Economica*: N.S.I. (1942) II. (1943), III (1944) and Karl Popper: "The Poverty of Historicism": *Economica* I & II (1944), III (1945).

TABLE OF CONTENTS

With an Analytical Summary

by

HENRY A. FINCH

investigations—the "understanding" knowledge of human conduct and culture involves conventional rather than normative validity; P. 41-2, The truth value of ideas is the guiding value in the writing of intellectual history—an illustration from military history of the possible study of causal effects of erroneous thoughts and calculation—ideal types even of incorrect and self-defeating thought necessary for the determining of causation of empirical events; P. 43, The normative correctness of the ideal type not necessary for its use—the function of ideal-types *vis-a-vis* empirical reality; P. 43-6, Nature of pure economic theory—its idealtypical character — it is apolitical, asserts no moral evaluations but is indispensible for analysis—critique of theses of opponents of pure economics—relationship of mean-end propositions to causeeffect propositions which economic science can supply—other problems of economics; P. 46, Factual importance of the state in the modern social scene does not establish the state as an ultimate value—the view that the state is a means to value is defensible.

II. "Objectivity" in Social Science and Social Policy 50

P. 50, Introductory note on the responsibility for and content of the essay; P. 50-1, Problem of relationship of practical social criticism to scientific social research; P. 51-2, Points of view hampering logical formulation of difference between "existential" and "normative" knowledge in social-economic science; P. 52, Rejection of view that empirical science provides norms and ideals—however, criticism *vis-a-vis* "value-judgments" is not to be suspended; P. 52-3, Appropriateness of means to, and chance of achieving, a given end are accessible to scientific analysis; P. 53, Scientific analysis can predict "costs" of unintended or incidental consequences of action; P. 53-4, Scientific treatment of "valuejudgment" can reveal "ideas" and ideals underlying concrete ends; P. 55, The judgment of the validity of values is a matter for faith or possibly for speculative philosophy, but not within province of empirical science—the distinction between empirical and normative not obliterated by the fact of cultural change; P. 55-7, Illusory self-evidence of consensus on certain goals— problems of social policy are not merely technical—naive belief in the scientific deducibility of normatively desirable cultural values—cultural values are ethical imperatives only for dogmatically bound religious sects; P. 57-8, The *via media* of the practical politician or syncretic relativism is not warranted as correct by science; P. 58, The inexpugnable difference between arguments appealing to (1) enthusiasm and feeling (2) ethical conscience (3) capacity as a scientific knower; P. 58-9, Scientifically valid social science analysis can strive for supra-cultural validity; P. 59-60, Reasons for expressing "value-judgments" if they are clearly formulated as such and distinguished from scientific statements; P. 61-2, The recognition of social problems is value-oriented—character of the *Archiv* in the past, in the future; P. 63, What is the meaning of objectively valid truth in the social sciences; P. 63-4, Scarcity of means is the basic characteristic of socio-economic subject matter—what a social science problem is; P. 64-6, Distinction between "economic", "economically rele-

I. A critique of Eduard Meyer's methodological views.

II. Objective possibility and adequate causation in historical explanation.

for an individual effect; P. 171-2, Account, with an illustration, of logical operations which establish historical causal relations; P. 172-3, Historians ought not to be reluctant to admit objective possibility; P. 173-4, Isolations and generalizations required to secure "judgment of possibility"—category of objective possibility not an expression of ignorance or incomplete knowledge—such judgments presuppose known empirical rules—instance of the Battle of the Marathon; P. 175, Meaning of "adequate causes"; P. 175, The simplest historical judgment is not simple registration of something found and finished, rather does it presuppose the use of a forming category and a whole body of empirical knowledge; P. 175-77, Psychological processes of historical discovery not to be confused with its logical structure; P. 177-80, The causal analysis of personal actions must also distinguish between categorically formed constructs and immediate experience; P. 180, Recognition of possibility in causal inquiry does not imply arbitrary historiography, for category of objective possibility enables the assessment of the causal significance of a historical fact; P. 181, The certainty of judgments of objective possibility may vary in degree—objective historical possibility is an analogue, with important differences, of the kind of probability that is determined from observed frequencies; P. 184-5, Definition of "adequate causation"—application to Battle of Marathon, the March Revolution, the unification of Germany—reiteration of constructive nature of historian's conceptualization; P. 186-7, Binding's "anthropomorphic" misunderstanding of objective possibility—real meaning of "favoring" and "obstructing" conditions—the special character of causality when adequacy of causation is concerned needs further study.

The Meaning of "Ethical Neutrality" in Sociology and Economics

B Y "VALUE-JUDGMENTS" are to be understood, where nothing else is implied or expressly stated, practical evaluations of the unsatisfactory or satisfactory character of phenomena subject to our influence. The problem involved in the "freedom" of a given science from value-judgments of this kind, i.e., the validity and the meaning of this logical principle, is by no means identical with the question which is to be discussed shortly, namely, whether in teaching one should or should not declare one's acceptance of practical value-judgments, deduced from ethical principles, cultural ideals or a philosophical outlook. This question cannot be discussed scientifically. It is itself entirely a question of practical valuation, and cannot therefore be definitively settled. With reference to this issue, a wide variety of views is held, of which we shall only mention the two extremes. At one pole we find (*a*) the standpoint that the distinction between purely logically deducible and empirical factual assertions on the one hand, and practical, ethical or philosophical value-judgments on the other, is correct, but that, nevertheless (or perhaps, precisely because of this), both classes of problems properly belong within the area of instruction. At the other pole we encounter (*b*) the proposition that even when the distinction cannot be made in a logically complete manner, it is nevertheless desirable that the assertion of value-judgments should be held to a minimum.

The latter point of view seems to me to be untenable. Especially untenable is the distinction which is rather often made in our field between value-judgments of a partisan character and those which are non-partisan. This distinction only obscures the practical implications of the preferences which are suggested to the audience. Once the assertion of value-judgments from the academic platform is admitted, the contention that the university teacher should be entirely devoid of "passion" and that he should avoid all subjects which threaten to arouse over-heated controversies constitutes a narrow-minded, bureaucratic opinion which every independent teacher must reject. Of the scholars who believed that they should not renounce the assertion of practical value-judgements in empirical discussions, it was the most passionate of them — such as Treitschke — and in his own way, Mommsen, who were the most tolerable. As a result of their intensely emotional tone, their audiences were enabled to discount the influence of their evaluations in whatever distortion was introduced into their factual assertions. Thereby the audiences did for themselves what the lecturers were temperamentally prevented from doing. The effect on the minds of the students was thus guaranteed the same depth of moral feeling which, in my opinion, the proponents of the assertion of practical value-judgments in teaching want to protect, without the audience's being confused as to the logical disjunction between the different spheres. This confusion must of necessity occur whenever the exposition of empirical facts and the exhortation to take an evaluative position on important issues are both done with the same cool dispassionateness.

The first point of view (a) is acceptable and, can indeed be acceptable from the standpoint of its own proponents, only when the teacher sets as his unconditional duty, in every single case, even to the point where it involves the danger of making his lecture less lively or attractive, to make relentlessly clear to his audience, and especially to himself, which of his statements are statements of logically deduced or empirically observed facts and which are statements of practical evaluations. Once one has acknowledged the logical disjunction between the two spheres, it seems to me that the assumption of this attitude is an imperative requirement of intellectual honesty; in this case it is the absolutely minimal requirement.

On the other hand, the question whether one should in general assert practical value-judgments in teaching (even with this reservation) is one of practical university policy. On that account, it must in the last analysis, be decided only with reference to those tasks which the individual, according to his own value-system, assigns to the universities. Those who on the basis of their qualifications as teachers assign to the universities and thereby to themselves the universal role of moulding human beings, of inculcating political, ethical, æsthetic, cultural or other attitudes, will take a different position than those who believe it necessary to affirm the fact (and its consequences) that the academic lecture-hall achieves a really valuable influence only through specialized training by specially qualified persons. For the latter, therefore, "intellectual integrity" is the only specific virtue which it should seek to inculcate. The first point of view can be defended from as many different ultimate value-positions as the second. The second (which I personally accept) can be derived from a most enthusiastic as well as from a thoroughly modest estimate of the significance of specialized training (*Fachbildung*). In order to defend this view, one need not be of the opinion that everyone should become as specialized as possible. One may, on the contrary, hold the view in question because one does not wish to see the ultimate and highest personal decisions which a person must make regarding his life, confounded with specialized training — however highly one may estimate the significance of specialized training not only for general intellectual training but indirectly also for the self-discipline and ethical attitude of the young person. One may hold the latter view because one does not wish to see the student so influenced by the teacher's suggestions that he is prevented from solving his problems on the basis of his own conscience.

Professor Schmoller's favorable disposition towards the teacher's assertion of his own value-judgments in the classroom is thoroughly intelligible to me personally as the echo of a great epoch which he and his friends helped to create. But even he cannot deny the fact that for the younger generation the objective situation has changed considerably in one important respect. Forty years ago there existed among the scholars working in our discipline, the widespread belief that of the various possible points of view in the domain of practical-political preferences, ultimately only one was the correct one. (Schmoller himself to be sure took this position only to a limited extent). Today this is no longer the case among the proponents of the assertion of professorial evaluations — as may easily be demonstrated. The legitimacy of the assertion of professorial evaluations is no longer defended in the name of an ethical imperative whose comparatively simple postulate of justice, both in its ultimate foundations as well as in its consequences, partly was, and partly seemed to be, relatively unambiguous and above all relatively impersonal (due to its specifically suprapersonal character). Rather, as the result of an inevitable development, it is now done in the name of a patchwork of cultural values, i.e., actually subjective demands on culture, or quite openly, in the name of the alleged "rights of the teacher's personality." One may well wax indignant over this, but one cannot — because it is a value-judgment — refute this point of view. Of all the types of prophecy, this "personally" tinted professorial type of prophecy is the only one which is altogether repugnant. An unprecedented situation exists when a large number of officially accredited prophets do not do their preaching on the streets, or in churches or other public places or in sectarian conventicles, but rather feel themselves competent to enunciate their evaluations on ultimate questions "in the name of science" in governmentally privileged lecture halls in which they are neither controlled, checked by discussion, nor subject to contradiction. It is an axiom of long standing, which Schmoller on one occasion vigorously espoused that what took place in the lecture hall should be held separate from the arena of public discussion. Although it is possible to contend that even scientifically this may have its disadvantages, I take the view that a "lecture" should be different from a "speech." The calm rigor, matter-of-factness and sobriety of the lecture declines with definite pedagogical losses, when the substance and manner of public discussion are introduced, in the style of the press. This privilege of freedom from outside control seems in any case to be appropriate only to the sphere of the specialized qualifications of the professor. There is, however, no specialized qualification for personal prophecy, and for this reason it is not entitled to that privilege of freedom from external control. Furthermore, there should be no exploitation of the fact that the student, in order to make his way, must attend certain educational institutions and take courses with certain teachers, with the result that in addition to what is required, i.e., the stimulation and cultivation of his capacity for observation and reasoning, and a certain body of factual information, the teacher slips in his own uncontradict-able evaluations, which though sometimes of considerable interest, are often quite trivial.

Like everyone else, the professor has other facilities for the diffusion of his ideals. When these facilities are lacking, he can easily create them in an appropriate form, as experience has shown in the case of every honest attempt. But the professor should not demand the right as a professor to carry the marshal's baton of the statesman or reformer in his knapsack. This is just what he does when he uses the unassailability of the academic chair for the expression of political (or cultural-political) evaluations. In the press, in public meetings, in associations, in essays, in every avenue which is open to every other citizen, he can and should do what his God or dæmon demands. Today the student should obtain, from his teacher in the lecture hall, the capacity: (1) to fulfill a given task in a workmanlike fashion; (2) definitely to recognize facts, even those which may be personally uncomfortable, and to distinguish them from his own evaluations; (3) to subordinate himself to his task and to repress the impulse to exhibit his personal tastes or other sentiments unnecessarily. This is vastly more important today than it was forty years ago when the problem did not even exist in this form. It is not true — as many people have insisted — that the "personality" is and should be a "whole" in the sense that it is injured when it is not exhibited on every possible occasion.

Every professional task has its own "inherent norms" and should be fulfilled accordingly. In the execution of his professional responsibility, a man should confine himself to it alone and should exclude whatever is not strictly *proper to it* — particularly his own loves and hates. The powerful personality does not manifest itself by trying to give everything a "personal touch" at every possible opportunity. The generation which is now growing up should, above all, again become used to the thought that "being a personality" is something that cannot be deliberately striven for and that there is only one way by which it can (perhaps!) be achieved: namely, the whole-hearted devotion to a "task" whatever it (and its derivative "demands of the hour") may be. It is poor taste to mix personal questions with specialized factual analyses. We deprive the word "vocation" of the only meaning which still retains ethical significance if we fail to carry out that specific kind of self-restraint which it requires. But whether the fashionable "cult of the personality" seeks to dominate the throne, public office or the professorial chair — its impressiveness is superficial. Intrinsically, it is very petty and it always has prejudicial consequences. Now I hope that it is not necessary for me to emphasize that the proponents of the views against which the present essay is directed can accomplish very little by this sort of cult of the "personality" for the very reason that it is "personal." In part they see the responsibilities of the professorial chair in another light, in part they have other educational ideals which I respect but do not share. For this reason we must seriously consider not only what they strive to achieve but also how the views which they legitimate by their authority influence a generation with an already extremely pronounced predisposition to overestimate its own importance.

Finally, it scarcely needs to be pointed out that many ostensible opponents of the assertion of political value-judgments from the academic chair are by no means justified when, in seeking to discredit cultural and social-political discussions which take place in public, they invoke the postulate of "ethical neutrality" which they often misunderstand so gravely. The indubitable existence of this spuriously "ethically neutral" tendentiousness, which (in our discipline) is manifested in the obstinate and deliberate partisanship of powerful interest groups, explains why a significant number of intellectually honest scholars still continue to assert their personal evaluations from their chair. They are too proud to identify themselves with this pseudo-ethical neutrality. Personally I believe that, in spite of this, what is right (in my opinion) should be done and that the influence of the value-judgments of a scholar who confines himself to championing them at appropriate occasions outside the classroom, will increase when it becomes known that he does only his "task" inside the classroom. But these statements are in their turn, all matters of evaluation, and hence scientifically undemonstrable.

In any case the fundamental principle which justifies the practice of asserting value-judgments in teaching can be consistently held only when its proponents demand that the spokesman for all party-preferences be granted the opportunity of demonstrating their validity on the academic platform.[1] But in Germany, insistence on the right of professors to state their evaluations has been associated with the opposite of the demand for the equal representation of all (even the most "extreme") tendencies. Schmoller thought that he was being entirely consistent from - his own premises when he declared that "Marxists and Manchesterites" were disqualified from holding academic positions although he was never so unjust as to ignore their scientific accomplishments. It is exactly on these points that I could never agree with our honored master. One obviously ought not justify the expression of evaluations in teaching — and then when the conclusions are drawn therefrom, point out that the university is a state institution for the training of "loyal" administrators. Such a procedure makes the university, not into a specialized technical school (which appears to be so degrading to many teachers) but rather into a theological seminary — except that it does not have the latter's religious dignity.

Attempts have been made to set up certain purely "logical" limits to the range of value-judgments which should be allowed from the academic chair. One of our foremost jurists once explained, in discussing his opposition to the exclusion of socialists from university posts, that he too would not be willing to accept an "anarchist" as a teacher of law since anarchists deny the validity of law in general — and he regarded his argument as conclusive. My own opinion is exactly the opposite. An anarchist can surely be a good legal scholar. And if he is such, then indeed the Archimedean point of his convictions, which is outside the conventions and presuppositions which are so self-evident to us, can equip him to perceive problems in the fundamental postulates of legal theory which escape those who take them for granted. Fundamental doubt is the father of knowledge. The jurist is no more responsible for "proving" the value of

---

[1]Hence we cannot be satisfied with the Dutch principle: i.e., emancipation of even theological faculties from confessional reuirements, together with the freedom to found universities as long as the following conditions are observed: guarantee of finances, maintenance of standards as to qualifications of teachers and the private right to found chairs as a patron's gift to the university. This gives the advantage to those with large sums of money and to groups which are already in power. Only clerical circles have, as far as we know, made use of this privilege.

those cultural objects which are relevant to "law" than the physician is responsible for demonstrating that the prolongation of life is desirable under all conditions. Neither of them is in a position to do this with the means at their disposal. If, however, one wishes to turn the university into a forum for the discussion of values, then it obviously becomes a duty to permit the most unrestrained freedom of discussion of fundamental questions from all value-positions. Is this possible? Today the most decisive and important questions of practical and political values are *excluded* from German universities by the very nature of the present political situation. For all those to whom the interests of the nation are more important than any of its particular concrete institutions, a question of central importance is whether the conception which prevails today regarding the position of the monarch in Germany is reconcilable with the world-interests of the nation, and with the instruments (war and diplomacy) through which these are expressed. It is not always the worst patriots nor even anti-monarchists who give a negative answer to this question and who doubt the possibility of lasting success in both these spheres as long as very basic changes are not made. Everyone knows, however, that these vital questions of our national life cannot be discussed with full freedom in German universities.[2] In view of the fact that certain value-questions which are of decisive political significance are permanently banned from university discussion, it seems to me to be only in accord with the dignity of a representative of science *to be silent* as well about such value-problems as he is allowed to treat.

But in no case, however, should the unresolvable question — unresolvable because it is ultimately a question of evaluation — as to whether one may, must, or should champion certain practical values in teaching, be confused with the purely logical discussion of the relationship of value-judgments to empirical disciplines such as sociology and economics. Any confusion on this point will impede the thoroughness of the discussion of the actual logical problem. Its solution will, however, not give any directives for answering the other

---

[2]This is by no means peculiar to Germany. In almost every country there exist, openly or hidden, actual restraints. The only differences are in the character of the particular value-questions which are thus excluded.

question beyond two purely logical requirements, namely: clarity and an explicit separation of the different types of problems. Nor need I discuss further whether the distinction between empirical statements of fact and value-judgments is "difficult" to make. It is. All of us, those of us who take this position as well as others, encounter the subject time and again. But the exponents of the so-called "ethical economics" particularly should be aware that even though the moral law is perfectly unfulfillable, it is nonetheless "imposed" as a duty. The examination of one's conscience would perhaps show that the fulfillment of our postulate is especially difficult, just because we reluctantly refuse to enter the very alluring area of values without a titillating "personal touch." Every teacher has observed that the faces of his students light up and they become more attentive when he begins to set forth his personal evaluations, and that the attendance at his lectures is greatly increased by the expectation that he will do so. Everyone knows furthermore that in the competition for students, universities in making recommendations for advancement, will often give a prophet, however minor ,who can fill the lecture halls, the upper hand over a much superior scholar who does not present his own preferences. Of course, it is understood in those cases that the prophecy should leave sufficiently untouched the political or conventional preferences which are generally accepted at the time. The pseudo-"ethically-neutral" prophet who speaks for the dominant interests has, of course, better opportunities for ascent due to the influence which these have on the political powers-that-be. I regard all this as very undesirable, and I will also therefore not go into the proposition that the demand for the exclusion of value-judgments is "petty" and that it makes the lectures "boring." I will not touch upon the question as to whether lecturers on specialized empirical problems must seek above all to be "interesting." For my own part, in any case, I fear that a lecturer who makes his lectures stimulating by the insertion of personal evaluations will, in the long run, weaken the students' taste for sober empirical analysis.

I will acknowledge without further discussion that it is possible, under the semblance of eradicating all practical value-judgments, to suggest such preferences with especial force by simply "letting the facts speak for themselves." The better kind of our parliamentary and electoral speeches operate in this way — and quite legitimately, given their purposes. No words should be wasted in declaring that all such procedures on the university lecture platform, particularly from the standpoint of the demand for the separation of judgments of fact from judgments of value, are, of all abuses, the most abhorrent. The fact, however, that a dishonestly created illusion of the fulfillment of an ethical imperative can be passed off as the reality, constitutes no criticism of the imperative itself. At any rate, even if the teacher does not believe that he should deny himself the right of asserting value-judgments, he should make them absolutely *explicit* to the students and to himself.

Finally, we must oppose to the utmost the widespread view that scientific "objectivity" is achieved by weighing the various evaluations against one another and making a "statesman-like" compromise among them. Not only is the "middle way" just as undemonstrable scientifically (with the means of the empirical sciences) as the "most extreme" evaluations; rather, in the sphere of evaluations, it is the least unequivocal. It does not belong in the university — but rather in political programs and in parliament. The sciences, both normative and empirical, are capable of rendering an inestimable service to persons engaged in political activity by telling them that (1) these and these "ultimate" positions are conceivable with reference to this practical problem; (2) such and such are the facts which you must take into account in making your choice between these positions. And with this we come to the real problem.

Endless misunderstanding and a great deal of terminological — and hence sterile — conflict have taken place about the term "value-judgment." Obviously neither of these has contributed anything to the solution of the problem. It is, as we said in the beginning, quite clear that in these discussions, we are concerned with *practical* evaluations regarding the desirability or undesirability of social facts from ethical, cultural or other points of view. In spite of all that I have said,[3] the following "objections" have been raised in all seriousness:

---

[3] I must refer here to what I have said in other essays in this volume (the possible inadequacies of particular formulations on certain points do not

science strives to attain "valuable" results, meaning thereby logically and factually correct results which are scientifically significant; and that further, the selection of the subject-matter already involves an "evaluation." Another almost inconceivable misunderstanding which constantly recurs is that the propositions which I propose imply that empirical science cannot treat "subjective" evaluations as the subject-matter of its analysis — (although sociology and the whole theory of marginal utility in economics depend on the contrary assumption).

What is really at issue is the intrinsically simple demand that the investigator and teacher should keep unconditionally separate the establishment of empirical facts (including the "value-oriented" conduct of the empirical individual whom he is investigating) and *his* own practical evaluations, i.e., his evaluation of these facts as satisfactory or unsatisfactory (including among these facts evaluations made by the empirical persons who are the objects of investigation.) These two things are logically different and to deal with them as though they were the same represents a confusion of entirely heterogeneous problems. In an otherwise valuable treatise, an author states "an investigator can however take his own evaluation as a 'fact' and then draw conclusions from it." What is meant here is as indisputedly correct as the expression chosen is misleading. Naturally it can be agreed before a discussion that a certain practical measure: for instance, the covering of the costs of an increase in the size of the army from the pockets of the propertied class should be presupposed in the discussion and that what are to be discussed are means for its execution. This is often quite convenient. But such a commonly postulated practical goal should not be called a "fact" in the ordinary sense but an " a priori end." That this is also of two-fold significance will be shown very shortly in the discussion of "means" even if the end which is postulated as "indiscussible" were as concrete as the act of lighting a cigar. In such cases, of course, discussion of the means is seldom necessary. In almost every case of a generally formulated purpose, as in the illustration chosen above, it

affect any essential aspects of the issue), As to the "irreconcilability" of certain ultimate evaluations in a certain sphere of problems, cf. G. Radbruch's *Einfuhrung in die Rechtwissenschaft* (2d ed., 1913). I diverge from him on certain points but these are of no significance for the problem discussed here.

is found that in the discussion of means, each individual understood something quite different by the ostensibly unambiguous end. Furthermore, exactly the same end may be striven after for very divergent ultimate reasons, and these influence the discussion of means. Let us however disregard this. No one will dispute the idea that a certain end may be commonly agreed on, while only the means of attaining it are discussed. Nor will anyone deny that this procedure can result in a discussion which is resolved in a strictly empirical fashion. But actually the whole discussion centers about the choice of ends (and not of "means" for a given end); in other words, in what sense can the evaluation, which the individual asserts, be treated, not as a fact but as the object of scientific criticism. If this question is not clearly perceived then all further discussion is futile.

We are not concerned with the question of the extent to which different types of evaluations may claim different degrees of normative dignity — in other words, we are not interested in the extent to which ethical evaluations, for example, differ in character from the question whether blondes are to be preferred to brunettes or some similar judgment of taste. These are problems in axiology, not in the methodology of the empirical disciplines. The latter are concerned only with the fact that the validity of a practical imperative *as a norm* and the truth-value of an empirical proposition are absoluetely heterogeneous in character. Any attempt to treat these logically different types of propositions as identical only reduces the particular value of each of them. This error has been committed on many occasions, especially by Professor von Schmoller.[4] Respect for our master forbids me to pass over these points where I find myself unable to agree with him.

At first, I might make a few remarks against the view that the mere existence of historical and individual variations in evaluations proves the necessarily "subjective" character of ethics. Even propositions about empirical facts are often very much disputed and there might well be a much greater degree of agreement as to whether someone is to be considered a scoundrel than there would be (even

---

[4]In his essay on "Volkswirtschaftslehre" in the *Handworterbuch der Staatswissenschaften.*

among specialists) concerning, for instance, the interpretation of a mutilated inscription. I have not at all perceived the growing unanimity of all religious groups and individuals with respect to value-judgments which Schmoller claims to perceive. But in any case it is irrelevant to our problem. What we must vigorously oppose is the view that one may be "scientifically" contented with the conventional self-evidentness of very widely accepted value-judgments. The specific function of science, it seems to me, is just the opposite: namely, to ask questions about these things which convention makes self-evident. As a matter of fact, Schmoller and his associates did exactly this in their time. The fact that one investigates the influence of certain ethical or religious convictions on economic life and estimates it to be large under certain circumstances does not, for instance, imply the necessity of sharing or even esteeming those casually very significant convictions. Likewise, the imputation of a highly positive value to an ethical or religious phenomenon tells us nothing at all about whether its consequences are also to be positively valued to the same extent. Factual assertions tell us nothing about these matters, and the individual will judge them very differently according to his own religious and other evaluations. All this has nothing to do with the question under dispute. On the contrary, I am most emphatically opposed to the view that a realistic "science of ethics," i.e., the analysis of the influence which the ethical evaluations of a group of people have on their other conditions of life and of the influences which the latter, in their turn, exert on the former, can produce an "ethics" which will be able to say anything about what *should* happen. A "realistic" analysis of the astronomical conceptions of the Chinese, for instance — which showed the practical motives of their astronomy and the way in which they carried it on, at which results they arrived and why — would be equally incapable of demonstrating the correctness of this Chinese astronomy. Similarly the fact that the Roman surveyors or the Florentine bankers (the latter even in the division of quite large fortunes) often came to results which were irreconcilable with trigonometry or the multiplication table, raises no doubts about the latter.

The empirical-psychological and historical analysis of certain evaluations with respect to the individual social conditions of their emergence and continued existence can never, under any circumstances, lead to anything other than an *"understanding" explanation*. This is by no means negligible. It is desirable not only because of the incidental personal (and non-scientific) effect: namely, being able "to do justice" more easily to the person who really or apparently thinks differently. It also has high scientific importance: (1) for purposes of an empirical causal analysis which attempts to establish the really decisive motives of human actions, and (2) for the communication of really divergent evaluations when one is discussing with a person who really or apparently has different evaluations from one's self. The real significance of a discussion of evaluations lies in its contribution to the understanding of what one's opponent — or one's self — really means — i.e., in understanding the evaluations which really and not merely allegedly separate the discussants and consequently in enabling one to take up a position with reference to this value. We are far removed, then, from the view that the demand for the exclusion of value-judgments in empirical analysis implies that discussions of evaluations are sterile or meaningless. For the recognition of their evaluative character is indeed the presupposition of all useful discussions of this sort. Such discussions assume an insight into the possibility of, in principle, unbridgeably divergent ultimate evaluations. "Understanding all" does not mean "pardoning all" nor does mere understanding of another's viewpoint as such lead, in principle, to its approval. Rather, it leads, at least as easily, and often with greater probability to the awareness of the issues and reasons which prevent agreement. This is a true proposition and it is certainly advanced by "discussions of evaluations." On the other hand, this method because it is of a quite different character, cannot create either a normative ethic or in general the binding force of an ethical "imperative." Everyone knows, furthermore, that the attainment of such an ethic is externally, at least, impeded by the relativizing effects of such discussions. This does not imply that they should be avoided on that account. Quite the contrary. An "ethical" conviction which is dissolved by the psychological "understanding" of other values is about as valuable as religious beliefs which are destroyed by scientific knowledge, which is of course a quite frequent occurrence. Finally, when Schmoller asserts that the exponents of "ethical neutrality" in the empirical disciplines can acknowledge only "formal" ethical truths (in the sense of the *Critique of Practical Reason*) a few comments are called for even though the problem, as such, is not integral to the present issue.

First, we should reject Schmoller's implication that ethical imperatives are identical with "cultural values" — even the highest of them. For, from a certain standpoint, "cultural values" are "obligatory"— even where they are in inevitable and irreconcilable conflict with every sort of ethics. Likewise, an ethic which rejects all cultural values is possible without any internal contradictions. In any case, these *two* value-spheres are not identical. The assertion that "formal" propositions, for example, those in the Kantian ethics, contain no material directives, represents a grave but widespread misunderstanding. The possibility of a normative ethics is not brought into question by the fact that there are problems of a practical sort for which it cannot, by itself, offer unambiguous directives. (Among these practical problems, I believe, are included in a particular manner, certain institutional, i.e., "social-political" problems.) Nor is the possibility of normative ethics placed in doubt by the fact that ethics is not the only thing in the world that is "valid"; rather it exists alongside of other value-spheres, the values of which can, under certain conditions, be realized only by one who takes ethical "responsibility" upon himself. This applies particularly to political action. It would be pusillanimous, in my opinion, to attempt to deny this conflict. This conflict moreover is not peculiar to the relations between politics and ethics, as the customary juxtaposition of "private" and "political" morality would have it. Let us investigate some of the "limits" of ethics referred to above.

The implications of the postulate of "justice" cannot be decided unambiguously by any ethic. Whether one, for example — as would correspond most closely with the views expressed by Schmoller — owes much to those who achieve much or whether one should demand much from those who can accomplish much; whether one should, e.g., in the name of justice (other considerations — for instance, that of the necessary "incentives" — being disregarded for the moment) accord great opportunities to those with eminent talents or whether on the contrary (like Babeuf) one should attempt to equalize the injustice of the unequal distribution of mental capacities through the rigorous provision that talented persons, whose talent gives them prestige, must not utilize their better opportunities for their own benefit — these questions cannot be definitely answered. The ethical problem in most social-political issues is, however, of this type.

But even in the sphere of personal conduct there are quite specific ethical problems which ethics cannot settle on the basis of its own presuppositions. These include above all, the basic questions: (a) whether the intrinsic value of ethical conduct — the "pure will" or the "conscience" as it used to be called — is sufficient for its justification, following the maxim of the Christian moralists: "The Christian acts rightly and leaves the consequences of his action to God"; or (b) whether the responsibility for the predictable consequences of the action is to be taken into consideration. All radical revolutionary political attitudes, particularly revolutionary "syndicalism," have their point of departure in the first postulate; all *Realpolitik* in the latter. Both invoke ethical maxims. But these maxims are in eternal conflict — a conflict which cannot be resolved by means of ethics alone.

Both these ethical maxims are of a strictly "formal" character. In this they resemble the well-known axioms of the *Critique of Practical Reason*. It is widely believed that as a result of this formalism, the latter did not generally contain substantive indications for the evaluation of action. This however is by no means true. Let us purposely take an example as distant as possible from politics to clarify the meaning of the much-discussed "merely formal" character of this type of ethics. If a man says of his erotic relationships with a woman, "At first our relationship was only a passion, but now it represents a value," — the cool matter-of-factness of the Kantian *Critique* would express the first half of this sentence as follows: "At first, each of us was a means for the other" and would therewith claim that the whole sentence is a special case of that well-known principle, which people have been singularly willing to view as a strictly historically conditioned expression of an "individualistic" attitude, whereas it was, in truth, a brilliant formulation which covered an immeasurably large number of ethical situations, which must however be correctly understood. In its negative form and excluding any statement as to what would be the opposite of treating another person "as a means," it obviously contains: (1) the recognition of autonomous, extra-ethical spheres, (2) the delimitation of the ethical sphere from these, and finally, (3) the determination of the sense in which different degrees of ethical status may be imputed to activity oriented towards extra-ethical values. Actually, those value-spheres which permit or prescribe the treatment of the other "only as a means" are quite heterogeneous vis-a-vis ethics. This cannot be carried any further here; it shows, in any case, that the "formal" character of that highly abstract ethical proposition is not indifferent to the substantive content of the action. But the problem becomes even more complicated. The negative predicate itself, which was expressed in the words "only a passion," can be regarded as a degradation of what is most genuine and most appropriate in life, of the only, or, at any rate, the royal road away from the impersonal or supra-personal "value"-mechanisms which are hostile to life, away from enslavement to the lifeless routine of everyday existence and from the pretentiousness of unrealities handed down from on high. At any rate, it is possible to imagine a conception of this standpoint which — although scorning the use of the term "value" for the concrete facts of experience to which it refers — would constitute a sphere claiming its own "immanent" dignity in the most extreme sense of the word. Its claim to this dignity would not be invalidated by its hostility or indifference to everything sacred or good, to every ethical or aesthetic law, and to every evaluation of cultural phenomena or personality. Rather its dignity might be claimed just because of this hostility or indifference. Whatever may be our attitude towards this claim, it is still not demonstrable or "refutable" with the means afforded by any "science."

Every empirical consideration of this situation would, as the elder Mill remarked, lead to the acknowledgment of absolute polytheism as the only appropriate metaphysic. A non-empirical approach oriented to the interpretation of meaning, or in other words, a genuine axiology could not, on proceeding further, overlook the fact that a system of "values," be it ever so well-ordered, is unable to handle the situation's crucial issue. It is really a question not only of alternatives between values but of an irreconcilable death-struggle, like that between "God" and the "Devil." Between these, neither relativization nor compromise is possible. At least, not in the true sense. There are, of course, as everyone realizes in the course of his life, compromises, both in fact and in appearance, and at every point. In almost every important attitude of real human beings, the value-spheres cross and interpenetrate. The shallowness of our routinized daily existence in the most significant sense of the word consists indeed in the fact that the persons who are caught up in it do not become aware, and above all do not wish to become aware, of this partly psychologically, part pragmatically conditioned motley of irreconcilably antagonistic values. They avoid the choice between "God" and the "Devil" and their own ultimate decision as to which of the conflicting values will be dominated by the one, and which by the other. The fruit of the tree of knowledge, which is distasteful to the complacent but which is, nonetheless, inescapable, consists in the insight that every single important activity and ultimately life as a whole, if it is not to be permitted to run on as an event in nature but is instead to be consciously guided, is a series of ultimate decisions through which the soul — as in Plato — chooses its own fate, i.e., the meaning of its activity and existence. Probably the crudest misunderstanding which the representatives of this point of view constantly encounter is to be found in the claim that this standpoint is "relativistic" — that it is a philosophy of life which is based on a view of the interrelations of the value-spheres which is diametrically opposite to the one it actually holds, and which can be held with consistency only if it is based on a very special type of ("organic") metaphysics.

Returning to our special case, it may be asserted without the possibility of a doubt that as soon as one seeks to derive concrete directives from practical political (particularly economic and social-political) evaluations, (1) the indispensable means, and (2) the inevitable repercussions, and (3) the thus conditioned competition of numerous possible evaluations in their *practical* consequences, are all that an *empirical* discipline can demonstrate with the means at its disposal. Philosophical disciplines can go further and lay bare the "meaning" of evaluations, i.e., their ultimate meaningful structure and their meaningful consequences, in other words, they can indicate their "place" within the totality of all the possible "ultimate" evaluations and delimit their spheres of meaningful validity. Even such simple questions as the extent to which an end should sanction un-avoidable means, or the extent to which undesired repercussions should be taken into consideration, or how conflicts between several concretely conflicting ends are to be arbitrated, are entirely matters of choice or compromise. There is no (rational or empirical) scien-tific procedure of any kind whatsoever which can provide us with a decision here. The social sciences, which are strictly empirical sciences, are the least fitted to presume to save the individual the difficulty of making a choice, and they should therefore not create the impression that they can do so.

Finally it should be explicitly noted that the recognition of the existence of this situation is, as far as our disciplines are concerned, completely independent of the attitude one takes toward the very brief remarks made above regarding the theory of value. For there is, in general, no logically tenable standpoint from which it could be denied except a hierarchical ordering of values unequivocally pre-scribed by *ecclesiastical* dogmas. I need not consider whether there really are persons who assert that such problems as (*a*) does a con-crete event occur thus and so or otherwise, or (*b*) why do the concrete events in question occur thus and so and not otherwise, or (*c*) does a given event ordinarily succeed another one according to a certain law and with what degree of probability — are not basically differ-ent from the problems: (*a₁*) what should one do in a concrete situa-tion, or (*b₁*) from which standpoints may those situations be satisfac-tory or unsatisfactory, or (*c₁*) whether they are — whatever their form — generally formulatable propositions (axioms) to which these standpoints can be reduced. There are many who insist further that there is no logical disjunction between such equiries as, (*a*) in which direction will a concrete situation (or generally, a situation of a cer-tain type) develop and with what greater degree of probability in which particular direction than in any other and (*b*) a problem which investigates whether one *should* attempt to influence the de-velopment of a certain situation in a given direction — regardless of whether it be the one in which it would also move if left alone, or the opposite direction or one which is different from either. There are those who assert that (*a*) the problem as to which attitudes towards any given problem specified persons or an unspecified number of persons under specified conditions will probably or even certainly take and (*b*) the problem as to whether the attitude which emerged in the situation referred to above is *right* — are in no way different from one another. The proponents of such views will resist any statement to the effect that the problems in the above-cited jutxapositions do not have even the slightest connection with one another and that they really are "to be separated from one another." These persons will insist furthermore that their position is not in contradiction with the requirements of scientific thinking. Such an attitude is by no means the same as that of an author who conceding the absolute heterogeneity of both types of problems, nevertheless, in one and the same book, on one and the same page, indeed in a principal and subordinate clause of one and the same sentence, makes statements bearing on each of the two heterogeneous problems referred to above. Such a procedure is strictly a matter of choice. All that can be demanded of him is that he does not unwittingly (or just to be clever) deceive his readers concerning the absolute heterogeneity of the problems. Personally I am of the opinion that nothing is too "pedantic" if it is useful for the avoidance of confusions.

Thus, the discussion of value-judgments can have only the following functions:

a) The elaboration and explication of the ultimate, internally "consistent" value-axioms, from which the divergent attitudes are derived. People are often in error, not only about their opponent's evaluations, but also about their own. This procedure is essentially an operation which begins with concrete particular evaluations and analyzes their meanings and then moves to the more general level of irreducible evaluations. It does not use the techniques of an empirical discipline and it produces no new knowledge of facts. Its "validity" is similar to that of logic.

b) The deduction of "implications" (for those accepting certain value-judgments) which follow from certain irreducible value-axioms, when the practical evaluation of factual situations is based on these axioms alone. This deduction depends on one hand, on logic, and on the other, on empirical observations for the completest possible casuistic analyses of all such empirical situations as are in principle subject to practical evaluation.

c) The determination of the factual consequences which the realization of a certain practical evaluation must have: (1) in consequence of being bound to certain indispensable means, (2) in consequence of the inevitability of certain, not directly desired repercussions. These purely empirical observations may lead us to the conclusion that (a) it is absolutely impossible to realize the object of the preference, even in a remotely approximate way, because no means of carrying it out can be discovered; (b) the more or less considerable improbability of its complete or even approximate realization, either for the same reason or because of the probable appearance of undesired repercussions which might directly or indirectly render the realization undesirable; (c) the necessity of taking into account such means or such repercussions as the proponent of the practical postulate in question did not consider, so that his evaluation of end, means, and repercussions becomes a new problem for him. Finally: *d*) the uncovering of new axioms (and the postulates to be drawn from them) which the proponent of a practical postulate did not take into consideration. Since he was unaware of those axioms, he did not formulate an attitude towards them although the execution of his own postulate conflicts with the others either (1) in principle or (2) as a result of the practical consequences, (i.e., logically or actually). In (1) it is a matter in further discussion of problems of type (*a*); in (2), of type (*c*).

Far from being meaningless, value-discussions of this type can be of the greatest utility as long as their potentialities are correctly understood.

The utility of a discussion of practical evaluations at the right place and in the correct sense is, however, by no means exhausted with such direct "results." When correctly conducted, it can be extremely valuable for empirical research in the sense that it provides it with problems-for investigation.

The problems of the empirical disciplines are, of course, to be solved "non-evaluatively." They are not problems of evaluation. But the problems of the social sciences are selected by the value-relevance of the phenomena treated. Concerning the significance of the expression "relevance to values" I refer to my earlier writings and above all to the works of Heinrich Rickert and will forbear to enter upon that question here. It should only be recalled that the expression "relevance to values" refers simply to the philosophical interpretation of that specifically scientific "interest" which determines the selection of a given subject-matter and the problems of an empirical analysis.

In empirical investigation, no "practical evaluations" are legitimated by this strictly logical fact. But together with historical experience, it shows that cultural (i.e., evaluative) interests give purely empirical scientific work its direction. It is now clear that these evaluative interests can be made more explicit and differentiated by the analysis of value-judgments. These considerably reduce, or at any rate lighten, the task of "value-interpretation" — an extremely important preparation for empirical work — for the scientific investigator and especially the historian.[5]

Instead of entering once more on this basic methodological problem of value-relation, I will deal in greater detail with certain issues which are of practical importance for our disciplines.

The belief is still widespread that one should, and must, or at any rate, can derive value-judgments from factual assertions about "trends." But even from the most unambiguous "trends," unambiguous norms can be derived only with regard to the prospectively most appropriate means — and then only when the irreducible evaluation is already given. The evaluations themselves cannot be derived from these "tendencies." Here, of course, the term "means" is being used in the broadest sense. One whose irreducible value is, for instance, the power of the state, may view an absolutistic or a radical democratic constitution as the relatively more appropriate means, depending on the circumstances. It would be highly ludicrous to interpret a change from a preference for one of these types of con-

---

[5]Since not only the distinction between evaluation and value-relations but also the distinction between evaluation and value-interpretation (i.e., the elaboration of the various possible meaningful attitudes towards a given phenomena) is very often not clearly made and since the consequent ambiguities impede the analysis of the logical nature of history, I will refer the reader to the remarks in "Critical Studies in the Logic of the Cultural Sciences." These remarks are not, however, to be regarded as in any way conclusive.

stitutions to another as a change in the "ultimate" evaluation itself. Obviously, however, the individual is constantly being faced with the problem as to whether he should give up his hopes in the realizability of his practical evaluations if he is aware of a clear-cut developmental tendency (*a*) which necessitates, if the goal is to be realized, the application of new means which are ethically or otherwise dubious; or (*b*) which requires the taking into account of repercussions which are abhorrent to him, or (*c*) which finally renders his efforts quixotic as far as their success is concerned. But the perception of such "developmental tendencies" which are modifiable only with more or less difficulty by no means represents a unique case. Each new fact may necessitate the re-adjustment of the relations between end and indispensable means, between desired goals and unavoidable subsidiary consequences. But whether this readjustment *should* take place and what *should* be the practical conclusions to be drawn therefrom is not answerable by empirical science — in fact it can not be answered by any science whatsoever. One may, for example, demonstrate ever so concretely to the convinced syndicalist that his action is socially "useless" i.e., it is not likely to be successful in the modification of the external class position of the proletariat, and that he even weakens this greatly by generating "reactionary" attitudes, but still — for him — if he is really faithful to his convictions — this proves nothing. And this is so, not because he is mad but because from his point of view, he can be "right" — as we shall discuss shortly. On the whole, people are strongly inclined to adapt themselves to what promises success, not only — as is self-evident — with respect to the means or to the extent that they seek to realize their ideals, but even to the extent of giving up these very ideals. In Germany this mode of behavior is glorified by the name *Realpolitik*. In any case, it is not easily intelligible why the practitioners of an empirical science should feel the need of furthering this kind of behavior by providing their salute of approval for existing "trends." Nor do we see why empirical scientists should transform the adaptation to these "trends" from an ultimate value-problem, to be solved only by the individual as his conscience dictates with reference to each particular situation, into a principle ostensibly based on the authority of a "science."

In a sense, successful political action is always the "art of the possible." Nonetheless, the possible is often reached only by striving to attain the impossible that lies beyond it. Those specific qualities of our culture, which, despite our differences in viewpoint, we all esteem more or less positively, are not the products of the only consistent ethic of " 'adaptation' to the possible," namely, the bureaucratic morality of Confucianism. I, for my part, will not try to dissuade the nation from the view that actions are to be judged not merely by their instrumental value but by their intrinsic value as well. In any case, the failure to recognize this fact impedes our understanding of reality. To cite the syndicalist again: it is senseless even logically to criticize in terms of its "instrumental value" an action which — if consistent — must be guided by its "intrinsic value." The central concern of the really consistent syndicalist must be to preserve in himself certain attitudes which seem to him to be absolutely valuable and sacred, as well as to induce them in others, whenever possible. The ultimate aim of his actions which are, indeed, doomed in advance to absolute failure, is to give him the subjective certainty that his attitudes are "genuine," i.e., have the power of "proving" themselves in action and of showing that they are not mere swagger. For this purpose, such actions are perhaps the only means. Aside from that — if it is consistent — its kingdom, like that of every "absolute value" ethics, is not of this world. It can be shown strictly "scientifically" that this conception of his ideal is the only internally consistent one and cannot be refuted by external "facts." I think that a service is thereby rendered to the proponents as well as the opponents of syndicalism — one which they can rightly demand of science. Nothing is ever gained in any scientific sense whatever by "on the one hand," and "on the other," by seven reasons "for" and six "against" a certain event (for instance, the general strike) and by weighing them off against one another in cameralistic fashion or like modern Chinese administrative memoranda. The task of an ethically neutral science in the analysis of syndicalism is completed when it has reduced the syndicalistic standpoint to its most rational and internally consistent form and has empirically investigated the pre-conditions for its existence and its practical consequences. Whether one should or should not be a syndicalist can never be proved without reference to very definite metaphysical premises which are never demonstrable by science. If an officer blows himself up with his fortifications rather than surrender, his action may, in a given case, be absolutely futile in every respect, but the existence or non-existence of the attitude which impels such an action without inquiring into its utility is not a matter of indifference. In any case, it would be just as incorrect to designate it as "meaningless" as would be such a designation of the consistent syndicalist's action. It is not particularly appropriate for a professor to recommend such Cato-like acts of courage from the comfortable heights of a university chair. But he is also not required to laud the opposite extreme and to declare that it is a duty to accommodate one's ideals to the opportunities which are rendered available by existing "trends" and situations.

We have been making repeated use of the expression "adaptation" (*Anpassung*) in a meaning which has been sufficiently clear in each context. But actually it has two meanings: (1) the adaptation of the means for attaining a given ultimate goal in a particular situation (*Realpolitik* in the narrower sense), and (2) adaptation to the chances, real or imaginary, for immediate success in the selection of one's ultimate value-standpoint from among the many possible ultimate value-standpoints (this is the type of *Realpolitik* which our government has followed for the last 27 years with such notable success!). But its connotations are by no means exhausted with these two. For this reason, I think that it is advisable to drop this widely misused term entirely when we discuss our problem — evaluative problems as well as others. It is entirely ambiguous as a scientific term, although it perpetually recurs both as an "explanation" (of the occurrence of certain ethical views in certain social groups under certain conditions) and as an "evaluation" (e.g., of these factually existing ethical views which are said to be objectively "appropriate" and hence objectively "correct" and valuable).

It is not very helpful in any of these usages since it must always be interpreted in order for the propositions in which it is used to be understood. It was originally used in biology and if it is understood in its biological meaning, i.e., as the relatively determinable chance, given by the environment, for a social group to maintain its own psycho-physical heritage through reproduction, then the social strata which are economically the best provided for and whose lives are the most rationally regulated, are according to birth statistics, the worst adapted. The few Indians who lived in the Salt Lake area before the Mormon migration were in the biological sense — as well as in all the other of its many conceivable empirical meanings — just as well or poorly "adapted" as the later populous Mormon settlements. This term adds absolutely nothing to our empirical understanding, although we easily delude ourselves that it does. Only in the case of two otherwise absolutely identical organizations, can one assert that a particular concrete difference is more conducive to the continued existence of the organization which has that characteristic, and which is therefore "better adapted" to the given conditions. But as regards the evaluation of the above situation, one person may assert that the greater numbers and the material and other accomplishments and characteristics which the Mormons brought there and developed, are a proof of the superiority of the Mormons over the Indians, while another person who abominates the means and subsidiary effects involved in the Mormon ethics which are responsible at least in part for those achievements, may prefer the desert and the romantic existence of the Indians. No science of any kind can purport to be able to dissuade these persons from their respective views. Here we are already confronted with the problem of the unarbitratable reconciliation of end, means, and subsidiary consequences.

Strictly and exclusively empirical analysis can provide a solution only where it is a question of a means adequate to the realization of an absolutely unambiguously given end. The proposition: x is the only means by which y can be attained, is in fact merely the reverse of the proposition: y is the effect of x. The term "adaptedness" (and all other related terms) do not provide — and this is the main thing — even the slightest hint about the value-judgments which they contain and which they actually obscure — just as does for example, the recently favored term "human economy" (*Menschenökonomie*) which in my opinion is fundamentally confused. Depending on how one uses the term, either everything or nothing in society is "adapted." Conflict cannot be excluded from social life. One can change its means, its object, even its fundamental direction and its bearers, but it cannot be eliminated. There can be, instead of an external struggle of antagonistic persons for external objects, an inner struggle of mutually loving persons for subjective values and therewith, instead of external compulsion, an inner control (in the form of erotic or charitable devotion). Or it can take the form of a subjective conflict in the individual's own mind. It is always present and its influence is often greatest when it is least noticed, i.e., the more its course takes the form of indifferent or complacent passivity or self-deception, or when it operates as "selection." "Peace" is nothing more than a change in the form of the conflict or in the antagonists or in the objects of the conflict, or finally in the chances of selection. Obviously, absolutely nothing of a general character can be said as to whether such shifts can withstand examination according to an ethical or other value-judgment. Only one thing is indisputable: every type of social order, without exception, must, if one wishes to *evaluate* it, be examined with reference to the opportunities which it affords to *certain types of persons* to rise to positions of superiority through the operation of the various objective and subjective selective factors. For empirical investigation is not really exhaustive nor does there exist the necessary factual basis for an evaluation, regardless of whether it is consciously subjective or claims objective validity. This should at least be borne in mind by our many colleagues who believe that they can analyze social change by means of the concept of "progress." This leads to a closer consideration of this important concept.

One can naturally use the term "progress" in an absolutely non-evaluative way if one identifies it with the "continuation" of some concrete process of change viewed in isolation. But in most cases, the situation is more complicated. We will review here a few cases from different fields, in which the entanglement with value-judgments is most intricate.

In the sphere of the emotional, affective content of our own subjective behavior, the quantitative increase and — what is usually bound up with it — the qualitative diversification of the possible modes of response can be designated as the progress of psychic "differentiation" without reference to any evaluations. This usually implies the preference for an increase in the "scope" or "capacity" of a concrete "mind" or — what is already an ambiguous term — of an "epoch" (as in Simmel's *Schopenhauer und Nietzche*).

Undoubtedly such a "progressive differentiation" does exist. Of course, it must be recognized that it is not always really present when it is believed to be. An increased *responsiveness* to nuances — due sometimes to the increased rationalization and intellectualization of life and sometimes to the increase in the amount of importance which the individual attributes to all his actions (even the least significant) — can very often lead to the illusion of progressive differentiation. This responsiveness can, of course, either indicate or promote this progressive differentiation. Appearances are deceitful, however, and I think that the range of this illusion is rather considerable. Be that as it may, it exists, and whether one designates progressive differentiation as "progress" is a matter of terminological convenience. But as to whether one should evaluate it as "progress" in the sense of an increase in "inner richness" cannot be decided by any empirical discipline. The empirical disciplines have nothing at all to say about whether the various possibilities in the sphere of feeling which have just emerged or which have been but recently raised to the level of consciousness and the new "tensions" and "problems" which are often associated with them are to be *evaluated* in one way or another. But whoever wishes to state a value-judgment regarding the fact of differentiation as such — which no empirical discipline can forbid — and seeks a point of view from which this can be done, will come upon the question as to the price which is "paid" for this process (insofar as it is more than an intellectualistic illusion). We should not overlook the fact that the pursuit of "experience" — which has been having a great vogue in Germany — might, to a large extent, be the product of a diminishing power to stand the stress of everyday life and that the publicity which the individual feels the increasing need of giving to his "experience," can perhaps be evaluated as a loss in the sense of privacy and therewith in the sense of propriety and dignity. At any rate, in the sphere of the evaluation of subjective experience, "progressive differentiation" is to be identified with an increase in "value" only in the intellectualistic sense of an increase in self-awareness or of an increasing capacity for expression and communication.

The situation is somewhat more complicated if we consider the applicability of the concept of "progress" (in the evaluative sense) in the sphere of art. It is from time to time energetically disputed, rightly or wrongly, depending on the sense in which it is meant. There has never been an evaluative approach to art for which the dichotomy between "art" and "non-art" has sufficed. Every approach distinguishes between "attempt" and "realization," between the values of various realizations and between the complete fulfillment and that which was abortive in one or more points but which was not nevertheless entirely worthless. This is true for the treatment not only of a concrete, individual creative action, but also for the artistic strivings of whole epochs. The concept of "progress" when applied to such situations is of trivial significance because of its usual utilization for purely technical problems. But in itself it is not meaningless.

The problem is quite different as far as the purely empirical *history* of art and the empirical *sociology* of art are concerned. For the first, there is naturally no "progress" in art with respect to the aesthetic evaluation of works of art as meaningful realizations. An aesthetic evaluation cannot be arrived at with the means afforded by an empirical approach and it is indeed quite outside its province. The empirical history of art can use only a technical, rational concept of "progress," the utility of which follows from the fact that it limits itself entirely to the establishment of the technical means which a certain type of artistic impulse applies when the end is definitely given. The significance of these unpretentious investigations is easily underestimated or else they are misinterpreted in the fashion of the modish but quite unconsequential and muddle-headed type of "connoisseur" who claims to have "understood" an artist as a result of having peered through the blinds of the artist's studio and examined what is obvious in his style, i.e., his "manner." "Technical" progress, correctly understood, does indeed belong to the domain of art history, because it (and its influence on the artistic impulse) is a type of phenomenon which is determinable in a strictly empirical way, i.e., without aesthetic evaluation. Let us cite certain illustrations which will clarify the meaning of "technical" as used in the history of art.

The origin of the Gothic style was primarily the result of the technically successful solution of an architectural problem, namely, the problem of the technical optimum in the construction of abutments for the support of the cross-arched vault, in connection with certain details which we shall not discuss here. Quite concrete architectural problems were solved. The knowledge that in this way a certain type of vaulting of non-quadratic areas was also made possible awakened the passionate enthusiasm of the early and perhaps forever unknown architects to whom we owe the development of the new architectural style. Their technical rationalism applied the new principle with a thoroughgoing consistency. Their artistic impulse used it as a means for fulfilling artistic tasks which had until then been scarcely suspected and swung sculpture in the direction of a "feeling for the body" which was stimulated primarily by the new methods of treating space and surface in architecture. The convergence of this primarily technically conditioned revolution with certain largely socially and religiously conditioned feelings supplied most of those problems on which the artists of the Gothic epoch worked. When the history and sociology of art have uncovered these purely factual technical, social, and psychological conditions of the new style, they have exhausted their purely empirical task. In doing so, they do not "evaluate" the Gothic style in relation, for instance, to the Romanesque or the Renaissance style, which, for its own part, was very strongly oriented towards the technical problems of the cupola and therewith toward the socially conditioned changes in the architectural problem-complex. Nor, as long as it remains empirical, does art-history "evaluate" the individual building esthetically. The interest in works of art and in their æsthetically relevant individual characteristics is heteronomously given. It is given by the æsthetic value of the work of art, which cannot be established by the empirical disciplines with the means which they have at their disposal.

The same is true in the history of music. From the standpoint of the interests of the modern European ("value-relevance"!) its central problem is: why did the development of harmonic music from the universally popularly developed folk polyphony take place only in Europe and in a particular epoch, whereas everywhere else the rationalization of music took another and most often quite opposite direction: interval development by division (largely the fourth) instead of through the harmonic phrase (the fifth). Thus at the center stands the problem of the origin of the third in its harmonic meaningful interpretation, i.e., as a unit in the triad; further: the harmonic chromatics; and beyond that, the modern musical rhythm (the heavy and light beats) — instead of purely metronomic measuring — a rhythm without which modern instrumental music is inconceivable. Here again we are concerned primarily with problems of purely technical "progress." The fact, for example, that chromatic music was known long before harmonic music as a means of expressing "passion" is shown by the ancient chromatic (apparently homophonous) music for the passionate dochmiacs in the recently discovered Euripides fragments. The difference between ancient music and the chromatic music which the great musical experimenters of the Renaissance created in a tremendous rational striving for new musical discoveries and indeed for the purpose of giving musical form to "passion," lay not in the impulse to artistic expression but rather in the technical means of expression. The technical innovation, however, was that this chromatic music developed into our harmonic interval and not into the Hellenic melodic half and quarter tone distance. This development, in its turn, had its causes in the preceding solutions of technical problems. This was the case in the creation of rational notation (without which modern composition would not even be conceivable); even before this, in the invention of certain instruments which were conducive to the harmonic interpretation of musical intervals; and above all, in the creation of rationally polyphonous vocal music. In the early Middle Ages, the monks of the northern Occidental missionary area had a major share in these accomplishments without even a suspicion of the later significance of their action. They rationalized the popular folk polyphony for their own purposes instead of following the Byzantine monks in allowing the music to be arranged for them by the Hellenically trained *melopoios*. Certain socially and religiously conditioned characteristics of the internal and external situation of the Occidental Christian church enabled this musical problem-complex which was essentially "technical" in nature, to emerge from the rationalism peculiar to Occidental monasticism. On the other hand, the adoption and rationalization of the dance measure, which is the source of the musical form expressed in the sonata, was conditioned by certain forms of social life in the Renaissance. Finally the development of the pianoforte — one of the most important technical instruments of modern musical development — and its dissemination in the bourgeois class, was rooted in the specific character of the rooms in the buildings in the North European culture area. All these are "progressive" steps in musical technique and they have greatly influenced the history of music. The empirical history of music can and must analyze these features of its development without undertaking, on its own part, an *aesthetic* evaluation of the worth of musical art. Technical "progress" has quite often led to achievements which, when evaluated æsthetically, were highly imperfect. The focus of *interest,* i.e., the *object* which is to be historically explained, is heteronomously given to the history of music by its æsthetic significance.

In the field of painting, the elegant unpretentiousness of the formulation of the problem in Wölfflin's *Klassische Kunst* is a quite outstanding example of the possibilities of empirical work.

The complete distinction between the evaluative sphere and the empirical sphere emerges characteristically in the fact that the application of a certain particularly "progressive" technique tells us nothing at all about the æsthetic value of a work of art. Works of art with an ever so "primitive" technique — for example, paintings made in ignorance of perspective — may æsthetically be absolutely equal to those created completely by means of a rational technique, assuming of course that the artist confined himself to tasks to which "primitive" technique was adequate. The creation of new techniques signifies primarily increasing differentiation and merely offers the *possibility* of increasing the "richness" of a work of art in the sense of intensifying its value. Actually it has often had the reverse effect of "impoverishing" the feeling for form. Empirically and causally speaking, however, changes in "technique" (in the highest sense of the word) are indeed the most important factors in the development of art.

Not only art-historians, but historians in general usually declare that they will not allow themselves to be deprived of the right of asserting political, cultural, ethical, and æsthetic value-judgments. They even claim that they cannot do their work without them. Methodology is neither able nor does it aim to prescribe to anyone what he should put into a literary work. It claims for itself only the right to state that certain problems are logically different from certain other problems and that their confusion in a discussion results in the mutual misunderstanding of the discussants. It claims furthermore that the treatment of one of these types of problems with the means afforded by empirical science or by logic is meaningful, but that the same procedure is impossible in the case of the other. A careful examination of historical works quickly shows that when the historian begins to "evaluate," causal analysis almost always ceases — to the prejudice of the scientific results. He runs the risk, for example, of "explaining" as the result of a "mistake" or of a "decline" what is perhaps the consequence of ideals different from his own, and so he fails in his most important task, that is, the task of "understanding." The misunderstanding may be explained by reference to two factors. The first, to remain in the sphere of art, derives from the fact the artistic works may be treated, aside from the purely æsthetically evaluative approach and the purely empirical-causal approach, by still a third, i.e., the value-*interpretative* approach. There cannot be the least doubt as to the intrinsic value of this approach and its indispensability for every historian. Nor is there any doubt that the ordinary reader of historical studies of art also expects this sort of treatment. It must, however, be emphasized that in its logical structure, it is not identical with the empirical approach.

Thus it may be said: whoever wishes to do empirical research in the history of art must be able to "understand" artistic productions. This is, obviously enough, inconceivable without the *capacity* for evaluating them. The same thing is true, obviously, for the political historian, the literary historian, the historian of religion, or of philosophy. Of course, this is completely irrelevant to the logical structure of historical study.

We will treat of this later. Here we should discuss only the sense in which, apart from æsthetic evaluation, one can speak of "progress" in the history of art. It has been seen that this concept has a technical and rational significance, referring to the means used for the attainment of an artistic end. In this sense it is relevant to the empirical analysis of art. It is now time to examine this concept of "rational" progress and to analyze its empirical or non-empirical character. For what has been said above is only a particular case of a universal phenomenon.

THE JOHN J. WRIGHT LIBRARY

Windelband's definition of the subject-matter of his *History of Philosophy* (Tuft's translation, p. 9, 2nd edition) as ". . . the process in which European humanity has embodied in scientific conceptions its views of the world . . ." conditions the practical use in his own brilliant work of a specific conception of "progress" which is derived from this cultural value-relevance. This concept of progress which, although by no means imperative for every "history" of philosophy, applies, given the same cultural value-relevance, not only to a history of philosophy and to the history of any other intellectual activity but (here I differ from Windelband [p. 7, No. 1, Section 2]) to every kind of history. Nonetheless, in what follows we will use the term, rational "progress" in the sense in which it is employed in sociology and economics. European and American social and economic life is "rationalized" in a specific way and in a specific sense. The explanation of this rationalization and the analysis of related phenomena is one of the chief tasks of our disciplines. Therewith there re-emerges the problem, touched on, but left open in our discussion of the history of art: namely, what is really meant when we designate a series of events as "rational progress"?

There is a recurrence here of the widespread confusion of the three following meanings of the term "progress": (1) merely "progressive" differentiation, (2) progress of *technical* rationality in the utilization of means and, finally (3) increase in value. A *subjectively* "rational" action is not identical with a rationally "correct" action, i.e., one which uses the objectively correct means in accord with scientific knowledge. Rather, it means only that the *subjective* intention of the individual is planfully directed to the means which are *regarded* as correct for a given end. Thus a progressive subjective rationalization of conduct is not necessarily the same as progress in the direction of rationally or technically "correct" behavior. Magic, for example, has been just as systematically "rationalized" as physics. The earliest intentionally rational therapy involved the almost complete rejection of the cure of empirical symptoms by empirically tested herbs and potions in favor of the exorcism of (what was thought to be) the "real" (magical, dæmonic) cause of the ailment. Formally, it had exactly the same highly rational structure as many of the most important developments in modern therapy. But we do not look on these priestly magical therapies as "progress" towards a "correct" mode of action as contrasted with rule-of-thumb empiricism. Furthermore, not every "progressive" step in the use of "correct" means is achieved by "progress" in subjective rationality. An increase in subjectively rational conduct can lead to objectively more "efficient" conduct but it is not inevitable. But if, in a single case, the proposition is correct that measure x is, let us say, the only means of attaining the result y[6] and if this proposition — which is empirically establishable — is consciously used by people for the orientation of their activity to attain the result y, then their conduct is oriented in a "technically correct" manner. If any aspect of human conduct (of any sort whatsoever) is oriented in a technically more correct manner than it was previously, *technical progress* exists. Only an empirical discipline, which accepts the standard as unambiguously given, can determine whether "technical progress" exists.

Given a specified end, then it is possible to use the terms "technical correctness" and "technical progress" in the application of means, without any insuperable dangers of ambiguity. ("Technique" is used here in its broadest sense, as rational action in general: in all spheres, including the political, social, educational, and propagandist manipulation and domination of human beings.) Only when a specified condition is taken as a standard can we speak of progress in a given sphere of technique, for example, commercial technique or legal technique. We should make explicit that the term "progress" even in this sense is usually only approximately precise because the various technically rational principles conflict with one another and a compromise can never be achieved from an "objective" standpoint but only from that of the concrete interests involved at the time. We may also speak of "economic" progress towards a relative optimum of want-satisfaction under conditions of given resources — if it is assumed that there are given wants, that all these wants and their rank order are accepted, and that finally a given type of economic order exists — and with the reservation that preferences regarding the duration, certainty and exhaustiveness, respectively, of the satis-

---

[6]This is an empirical statement and nothing but a simple inversion of the causal proposition: y is an effect of x.

faction of these wants may often conflict with each other.

Attempts have been made to derive the possibility of unambiguous and thereby purely *economic* evaluations from this. A characteristic example of this is the case cited by Professor Liefmann concerning the intentional destruction of goods in order to satisfy the profit-interests of the producers when the price has fallen below cost. This action is then "objectively" evaluated as "economically correct." But the flaw in this assertion is that it — and every smiliar statement — treats a number of presuppositions as self-evident when they really are not self-evident: first, that the interests of the individual not only often do continue beyond his death, but that they *should* always do so. Without this leap from the "is" category to the "ought" category, this allegedly "purely economic" evaluation could not be made in any clear-cut fashion. Otherwise one cannot speak of the interests of producers and consumers as if they were the interests of persons who live on indefinitely. The individual's taking into account of the interests of his heirs is, however, not a purely *economic* datum. For concrete human beings are substituted impersonal interests who use "capital" in "plants" and who exist for the sake of these plants. This is a fiction which is useful for theoretical purposes, but even as a fiction it does not apply to the position of the worker, especially the childless worker. Secondly, it ignores the fact of "class position" which, under competitive market conditions, can interfere with the provision of certain strata of consumers with goods, not only in spite of, but indeed in consequence of the "optimally" profitable distribution of capital and labor in the various branches of production. That "optimally" profitable distribution which conditions the constancy of capital investment, is for its part, dependent on the distribution of power between the different classes, the consequences of which in concrete cases, can (but need not necessarily) weaken the position of those strata on the market. Thirdly, it ignores the possibility of persistently irreconcilable conflicts of interest between members of various political groups and takes an *a priori* position in favor of the "free trade argument." The latter is thus transformed from a very useful heuristic instrument into a by no means self-evident evaluation as soon as one begins to derive value-judgments from it. When, however, the attempt to avoid this conflict is made by assuming the political unity of the world economic system — as is theoretically allowable — the destruction of those consumable goods in the interest of the producer's and consumer's optimum return requires that the forcus of the criticism be shifted. The criticism should then be directed against the whole principle as such of market provision by means of such indicators as are given by the optimal returns, expressive in money, to the economic units participating in exchange. An organization of the provision of goods which is not based on the competitive market will have no occasion to take account of the constellation of interests as found in the competitive market. It will not, therefore, be required to withdraw consumable goods from consumption once they have been produced.

Only when the following conditions exist — (1) persistent interests in profit on the part of unchanging persons guided by fixed wants, (2) the unqualified prevalence of private capitalist methods of satisfying wants through exchange in an entirely free market, and (3) a disinterested state which serves only as a guarantor of the law — is Professor Liefmann's proposition correct and then it is, of course, self-evident. For the evaluation is then concerned with the rational means for the optimal solution of a technical problem of distribution. The constructs of pure economics which are useful for analytical purposes cannot, however, be made the sources of practical value-judgments. Economic theory can tell us absolutely nothing more than that for the attainment of the given technical end x, y is the sole appropriate means or is such together with y^1 and y^2; that in the last analysis these and these differences in consequences and in rationality are associated with y, y^1 and y^2 respectively; and that their application and thus the attainment of the end x requires that the "subsidiary consequences," z, z^1 and z^2 be taken into account. These are all merely reformulations of causal propositions, and to the extent that "evaluations" can be imputed to them, they are exclusively of the type which is concerned with the degree of rationality of a prospective action. The evaluations are unambiguous *only* when the economic end and the social context are definitely given and all that remains is to choose between several economic means, when these differ only with respect to their certainty, rapidity, and quantitative productiveness, and are completely identical in every other value-relevant aspect. It is only when these conditions have been met that we evaluate a given means as "technically most correct," and it is only then that the evaluation is unambiguous. In every other case, i.e., in every case which is not purely a matter of technique, the evaluation ceases to be unambiguous and evaluations enter which are not determinable exclusively by economic analysis.

But the unambiguousness of the final "evaluation" is naturally not attained by the establishment of the unambiguousness of a *technical* evaluation within the strictly economic sphere. Once we pass from the sphere of technical standards, we are face to face with the endless multiplicity of possible evaluations which can be reduced to manageability only by reducing them to their ultimate axioms. For — to mention only one — behind the particular "action" stands the human being. An increase in the subjective rationality and in the objective-technical "correctness" of an individual's conduct can, beyond a certain limit — or even quite generally from a certain standpoint — threaten goods of the greatest (ethical or religious) importance in his value-system. Scarcely any of us will share the Buddhist ethic in its maximum demands which rejects all purposeful conduct just because it is purposeful and distracts one from salvation. But to "refute" it in the way one refutes an incorrect solution in arithmetic or an erroneous medical diagnosis is absolutely impossible. Even without drawing on such an extreme example, it is easy to see that as far as an evaluation of them is concerned even indisputably "technically correct" economic actions are not validated through this quality *alone*. This is true without exception for all rationalized actions, including even such apparently technical fields as banking. Those who oppose such types of rationalization are by no means necessarily fools. Rather, whenever one desires to state a value-judgment, it is necessary to take into account the subjective and objective social influence of technical rationalization. The use of the term "progress" is legitimate in our disciplines when it refers to "technical" problems, i.e., to the "means" of attaining an unambiguously given end. It can never elevate itself into the sphere of "ultimate" evaluations.

After all has been said, I still regard the use of the term "progress," even in the limited sphere of its empirically unobjectionable application, as very unfortunate. But the use of words is not subject to censorship; one can, in the end, avoid the possible misunderstandings.

Another group of problems concerning the place of the rational in the empirical disciplines still remains to be discussed.

When the normatively valid is the object of empirical investigation, its normative validity is disregarded. Its "existence" and not its "validity" is what concerns the investigator. When, for example, a statistical analysis is made of the number of "arithmetical errors" in a certain group of calculations — which can indeed have a scientific meaning, — the basic propositions of the multiplication table are valid for the investigator in two quite different senses. In the first sense, its normative validity is naturally presupposed in his own calculations. In the second, however, in which the degree of "correctness" of the application of the multiplication table enters as the object of the investigation, the situation is, logically, quite different. Here the application of the multiplication table, by the persons whose calculations are the subject-matter of the statistical analysis, is treated as a maxim of conduct which they have acquired through education. The investigator examines the frequency with which this maxim is applied, just as another statistical investigation might examine the frequency of certain types of perceptual error. The normative "validity," i.e., the "correctness" of the multiplication table is logically irrelevant when its application is being investigated. The statistician, in studying the calculations of the person investigated, must naturally accept the convention of calculating according to the multiplication table. But he would indeed also have to apply methods of calculation which are "incorrect" when viewed normatively, if such methods happened to be regarded as correct in some social group and he had to investigate statistically the frequency of its "correct" application (i.e., "correct" from the standpoint of the group). For the purposes of empirical, sociological or historical analysis, our multiplication table, as the object of such an analysis, is a maxim of practical conduct which is valid according to the conventions of a given culture and which is adhered to more or less closely. It is nothing more than this. Every exposition of the Pythagorean theory of music must accept the calculation which is, to our knowledge, "false," namely, that twelve fifths equal seven octaves. Every history of logic must likewise accept the historical existence of logical statements which, for us, are contradictory. Although it is empathically understandable, it is outside the realm of science to respond to such "absurdities" with explosions of rage as a particularly eminent historian of medieval logic once did.

This transformation of normatively valid truths into conventionally valid opinions, to which all intellectual activities, including even logic or mathematics, are subject whenever they become the objects of empirical analysis[7] is completely independent of the fact that the normative validity of logical and mathematical propositions is at the same time that *a priori* basis of all empirical science. Their logical structure is less simple in the case of their function in the empirical investigation of cultural phenomena. This "function" must be carefully differentiated from (*a*) their function as the object of the investigation and (*b*) their function as the *a priori* basis of the investigation. Every science of psychological and social phenomena is a science of *human conduct* (which includes all thought and attitudes). These sciences seek to "understand" this conduct and by means of this understanding to "explain" it "interpretatively." We cannot deal here with the complex phenomenon of "understanding." All that we are interested in here is one particular type: namely "rational" interpretation. We obviously "understand" without further question a person's solution of a certain problem in a manner which we ourselves regard as normatively correct. The same is true of calculation which is "correct" in the sense that means, which are "correct" from our viewpoint, are applied to attain a desired goal. Our understanding of these events is particularly evident (i.e., plausible) because it is concerned with the realization of the objectively "valid." And nevertheless one must guard one's self against the belief that in this case what is normatively correct has, from the point of view of logic, the same function as it has in its general position as the *a priori* of all scientific investigation. Rather its function as a means of "understanding" is exactly the same as it is in the case of purely psychological "empathy" with logically

---

[7]The empirical analysis referred to above does not attempt to determine their normative correctness.

irrational feeling and affect-complexes, where it is a matter of obtaining an "understanding" knowledge of them. The means employed by the method of "understanding explanation" are not *normative* correctness, but rather, on the one hand, the conventional habits of the investigator and teacher in thinking in a particular way, and on the other, as the situation requires, his capacity to "feel himself" empathically into a mode of thought which deviates from his own and which is normatively "false" according to his own habits of thought. The fact that "error" is, in principle, just as accessible to the understanding as "correct" thinking proves that we are concerned here with the normatively "correct" type of validity, not *as such* but only as an especially easily understandable *conventional* type. This leads now to a final statement about the role of "normative correctness" in social science.

In order to be able to "understand" an "incorrect" calculation or an "incorrect" logical assertion and to analyze its consequences, one must not only test it in using methods of correct calculation or logical thought but must indeed indicate by reference to the "correct" calculation or "correct" logic, those points at which the calculation or the logical assertion in question *deviates* from the one which the analyst regards as normatively "correct." This is not merely necessary for pedagogical purposes, which Windelband, for example, emphasized in the Introduction to his *History of Philosophy* ("warning signs" against "wrong roads"), and which is in itself only a desirable by-product of historical study. Nor is it necessitated by the fact that every historical inquiry, among the objects of which are included all sorts of logical, mathematical, or other scientific knowledge, rests *only* on the foundation of "truth-value" which we accept and which is the only possible ultimate value criterion which determines its selection and progress. Even if this were actually the case, it would still be necessary to consider Windelband's often-made point: i.e., that progress in the sense of an increase in correct propositions, instead of taking the direct path, has — speaking in terms of economics — frequently followed the "most productive round-about path" in passing through "errors," i.e., problem-confusions. This procedure is called for because and only to the extent of the *importance* of those aspects in which the knowledge investigated deviate from those which the investigator himself regards as "correct." By *importance* we mean that the specifically "characteristic" aspects in question are from the investigator's point of view either directly value-relevant or are causally connected with other value-relevant phenomena. This will, ordinarily, be the case, to the degree that the truth-value of ideas is the guiding value in the writing of intellectual history, e.g., in a history of a particular branch of knowledge like philosophy or economic theory.

But it is by no means necessarily restricted to such cases. A somewhat similar situation arises whenever one investigates a subjectively rational action, in which errors in thinking or calculation can constitute *causal* factors of the course of the action. In order, for example, to understand how a war is conducted, it is necessary to imagine an ideal commander-in-chief for each side — even though not explicitly or in detailed form. Each of these commanders must know the total fighting resources of each side and all the possibilities arising therefrom of attaining the concretely unambiguous goal, namely, the destruction of the enemy's military power. On the basis of this knowledge, they must act entirely without error and in a logically "perfect" way. For only then can the consequences of the fact that the real commanders neither had the knowledge nor were they free from error, and that they were not purely rational thinking machines, be unambiguously established. The rational construction is useful here as a means of correct causal imputation. The "ideal" constructions of rigorous and errorless rational conduct which we find in pure economic theory have exactly the same significance.

For purposes of the causal *imputation* of empirical events, we need the rational, empirical-technical and logical constructions, which help us to answer the question as to what a behavior pattern or thought pattern (e.g., a philosophical system) would be like if it possessed completely rational, empirical and logical "correctness" and "consistency." From the logical viewpoint, the construction of such a rationally "correct" "utopia" or "ideal" is, however, only one of the various possible forms of the "ideal-type" — as I have called such logical constructs. For not only are there cases in which an *incorrect* inference or a *self-defeating* action would be more serviceable as ideal-types, but there are whole spheres of action (the sphere of the "irrational") where the simplicity offered by isolating abstraction is more convenient than an ideal-type of optimal logical rationality. It is true that, in practice, the investigator frequently uses normatively "correctly" constructed "ideal-types." From the logical point of view, however, the normative "correctness" of these types is not essential. For the purpose of characterizing a specific type of attitude, the investigator may construct either an ideal-type which is identical with his own personal ethical norms, and in this sense objectively "correct," or one which ethically is thoroughly in conflict with his own normative attitudes; and he may then compare the behavior of the people being investigated with it. Or else he may construct an ideal-typical attitude of which he has neither positive nor negative evaluations. Normative "correctness" has no monopoly for such purposes. Whatever the content of the ideal-type, be it an ethical, a legal, an æsthetic, or a religious norm, or a technical, an economic, or a cultural maxim or any other type of valuation in the most rational form possible, it has only one function in an empirical investigation. Its function is the comparison with empirical reality in order to establish its divergences or similarities, to describe them with the *most unambiguously intelligible concepts,* and to understand and explain them causally. Rational juridicial concepts supply this need for the empirical history of law, and the theory of the rational calculation of costs and revenue supplies the same service for the analysis of the actual behavior of individual economic units in a profit-economy. Both of these disciplines, in addition to this heuristic function, have as "practical arts" distinctly normative-practical aims. In this respect, these disciplines are no more empirical in the sense used here than are, for instance, mathematics, logic, normative ethics, and æsthetics, from which they differ in other respects as much as the latter differ among themselves.

Economic theory is an axiomatic discipline in a way which is logically very different from that of the systematic science of law. Its relationship to economic reality is very different from the relationship of jurisprudence to the phenomena treated by the history and sociology of law. The concepts of jurisprudence may and should be used as ideal-types in empirical legal studies. Pure economic theory, in its analysis of past and present society, utilizes ideal-tye concepts exclusively. Economic theory makes certain assumptions which scarcely ever correspond completely with reality but which approximate it in various degrees and asks: how would men act under these assumed conditions, if their actions were entirely rational? It assumes the dominance of pure economic interests and precludes the operation of political or other non-economic considerations.

Its fate, however, has been typical of "problem-confusions." Pure economics is a theory which is "apolitical," which asserts "no moral evaluations," and which is "individualistic" in its orientation in the senses specified above. It is and will always be indispensable for analytical purposes. The extreme free-traders, however, conceived of it as an adequate picture of "natural" reality, i.e., reality not distorted by human stupidity, and they proceeded to set it up as a moral imperative — as a valid normative ideal — whereas it is only a convenient ideal type to be used in empirical analysis. When in consequence of changes in economic and social policy, the high estimation of the state was reflected in the evaluative sphere, pure economic theory was rejected not only as an ideal — in which role it could never claim validity — but as a methodological device for the investigation of empirical facts. "Philosophical" considerations of the most varied sort were to supplant rational procedure. The identification of the "psychologically" existent with the ethically valid obstructed the precise distinction of value-judgments from assertions of fact.

The extraordinary accomplishments of the representatives of this scientific tendency in the fields of history, sociology, and social policy are generally acknowledged. But the unbiased observer also perceives that theoretical and rigorously scientific analysis in economics has been in a state of decay for decades as a natural consequence of that confusion of problems. The first of the two main theses which the opponents of pure economics set forth is that its rational constructions are "pure fictions" which tell us nothing about reality. If rightly interpreted, this contention is correct. Theoretical constructions never do more than assist in the attainment of a knowledge of reality which they alone cannot provide, and which, as a result of the operation of other factors and complexes of motives which are not contained in their assumptions, even in the most extreme cases, only approximate to the hypothesized course of events. This, of course, does not diminish the utility and necessity of pure theory. The second thesis of the opponents of economic theory is that there cannot be a non-evaluative theory of economic policy as a science. This is fundamentally false; non-evaluativeness, in the sense presented above, is on the contrary presupposed by *every* purely scientific analysis of politics, particularly of social and economic policy. It would be superfluous to repeat that it is obviously possible and scientifically useful and necessary to establish propositions of the following type: in order to attain the end x (in economic policy), y is the only means, or under conditions b_1, b_2, and b_3, y_1, y_2, and y_3 are the only or the most effective means. It should be emphatically recalled that the possibility of the exact definition of the end sought for is a prerequisite to the formulation of the problem. Hence it is simply a question of inverting causal propositions; in other words, it is a purely "technical" problem. It is indeed on this account that science is not compelled to formulate these technical teleological propositions in any form other than that of simple causal propositions, e.g., x is produced by y, or x, under conditions b_1, b_2, and b_3 is produced by y_1, y_2, and y_3. For these say exactly the same thing, and the "man of action" can derive his "prescriptions" from them quite easily. In addition to the formulation of pure ideal-typical formulæ and the establishment of such causal economic propositions — for such are without exception involved when x is sufficiently unambiguous —, scientific economics has other problems. These problems include the causal influence of economic events on the whole range of social phenomena (by means of the hypotheses offered by the economic interpretation of history). Likewise included among the problems of economics is the analysis of the various ways in which non-economic social events influence economic events (economic sociology and economic history). Political actions and structures, especially the state and the state-guaranteed legal system are of primary importance among these non-economic social events. But obviously, political events are not the only ones — all those structures which influence *economic* actions to the extent that they become relevant to scientific interest must also be included. The phrase "theory of economic *policy*" is naturally not very suitable for the totality of these problems. The fact that it is nevertheless used for this purpose is due to the character of the universities as training schools for state officials and to the great power of the state to influence the economic system in very far-reaching ways. The inversion of "cause and effect" propositions into "means-ends" propositions is possible whenever the effect in question can be stated precisely. Naturally, this does not at all affect the logical relationship between value-judgments and judgments of fact. In conclusion, we should like to make one more comment on this point.

The developments of the past few decades, and especially the unprecedented events to which we are now witness, have heightened the prestige of the state tremendously. Of all the various associations, it alone is accorded "legitimate" power over life, death, and liberty. Its agencies use these powers against external enemies in wartime, and against internal resistance in both war and peace. In peacetime, it is the greatest entrepreneur in economic life and the most powerful collector of tributes from the citizenry; and in time of war, it disposes of unlimited power over all available economic goods. Its modern rationalized form of organization has made achievements possible in many spheres which could not have been approximated by any other sort of social organization. It is almost inevitable that people should conclude that it represents the "ultimate" value — especially in the political sphere — and that all social actions should be evaluated in terms of their relations to its interests. This is an inadmissible deduction of a value-judgment from a statement of fact, even if we disregard, for the time being, the ambiguity of the conclusions drawn from that value-judgment. The ambiguity would of course become immediately apparent once we begin to discuss the means (of maintaining or "advancing" the state). In the face of the great prestige of the state, it is worthwhile pointing out that there are certain things which the state cannot do. This is the case even in the sphere of military activity, which might be regarded as its most proper domain. The observation of many phenomena which the present war has brought about in the armies of nationally heterogeneous states leads us to conclude that the voluntary devotion of the individual to the tasks which his state calls for but which it cannot compel, is not irrelevant in the determination of military success.

And in the economic sphere, it should be pointed out that the transformation of wartime forms and measures into permanent features of the peacetime economy can have rapid results which will spoil the ideal of an expansive state for those who hold it. Nonetheless, we will not concern ourselves further with this point. In the sphere of value-judgments, however, it is possible to defend quite meaningfully the view that the power of the state should be increased in order to strengthen its power to eliminate obstacles, while maintaining that the state itself has no *intrinsic* value, that it is a purely technical instrument for the realization of other values from which alone it derives its value, and that it can retain this value only as long as it does not seek to transcend this merely auxiliary status.

We will not expound or defend either this or any other possible evaluative standpoint here. We shall only state that if the professional thinker has an immediate obligation at all, it is to keep a cool head in the face of the ideals prevailing at the time, even those which are associated with the throne, and if necessary, "to swim against the stream." The "German ideas of 1914" were produced by dilettantes. The "socialism of the future" is a phrase for the rationalization of economic life by combining further bureaucratization and interest-group adminstration. Today fanatical office-holding patriots are invoking the spirit not only of German philosophy, but of religion as well, to justify these purely technical measures instead of soberly discussing their feasibility, which is quite prosaically conditioned by financial factors. This kind of activity is nothing but a highly objectionable form of poor taste manifested by dilettantish litterateurs who take themselves over-seriously. But what the real "German ideas of 1918," on the formation of which the returning soldiers will have to be heard, can or should be like, no one today can say in advance. This will depend on the future.

"Objectivity" in Social Science and Social Policy

Wherever assertions are explicitly made in the name of the editor or when tasks are set for the Archiv *in the course of Section I of the foregoing essay, the personal views of the author are not involved. Each of the points in question has the express agreement of the co-editors. The author alone bears the responsibility for the form and content of Section II.*

The fact that the points of view, not only of the contributors but of the editors as well, are not identical even on methodological issues, stands as a guarantee that the Archiv *will not fall prey to any sectarian outlook. On the other hand, agreement as to certain fundamental issues is a presupposition of the joint assumption of editorial responsibility. This agreement refers particularly to the value of* theoretical *knowledge from "one-sided" points of view, the* construction *of precisely defined concepts and the insistence on the* rigorous *distinction between empirical knowledge and value-judgments as here understood. Naturally we do not claim to present anything new therewith.*

The extensiveness of the discussion (Section II) and the frequent repetition of the same thought are intended only to maximize the general understanding of our argument in wider circles. *For the sake of this intention, much — let us hope not too much — precision in expression has been sacrificed. For the same reason, we have omitted the presentation of a* systematic *analysis in favor of the present listing of a few methodological viewpoints. A systematic inquiry would have required the treatment of a large number of epistemological questions which are far deeper than those raised here. We are not interested here in the furtherance of logical analysis* per se. *We are attempting only to apply the well-known results of modern logic to our own problems. Nor are we solving problems here; we are trying only to make their significance apparent to non-specialists. Those who know the work of the modern logicians — I cite only Windelband, Simmel, and for our purposes particularly Heinrich Rickert — will immediately notice that everything of importance in this essay is bound up with their work.*

W HEN A SOCIAL SCIENCE journal which also at times concerns itself with a social policy, appears for the first time or passes into the hands of a new editorial board, it is customary to ask about its "line." We, too, must seek to answer this question and following up the remarks in our "Introductory Note" we will enter into the question in a more fundamental theoretical way. Even though or perhaps because, we are concerned with "self-evident truths," this occasion provides the opportunity to cast some light on the nature of the "social sciences" as we understand them, in such a manner that it can be useful, if not to the specialist, then to the reader who is more remote from actual scientific work.

In addition to the extension of our knowledge of the "social conditions of all countries," i.e., the facts of social life, the express purpose of the *Archiv* ever since its establishment has been the education of judgment about practical social problems — and in the very modest way in which such a goal can be furthered by private scholars — the criticism of practical social policy, extending even as far as legislation. In spite of this, the *Archiv* has firmly adhered, from the very beginning, to its intention to be an exclusively scientific journal and to proceed only with the methods of scientific research. Hence arises the question of whether the purpose stated above is compatible in principle with self-confinement to the latter method. What has been the meaning of the value-judgments found in the pages of the *Archiv* regarding legislative and administrative measures, or practical recommendations for such measures? What are the standards governing these judgments? What is the validity of the value-judgments which are uttered by the critic, for instance, or on which a writer recommending a policy founds his arguments for that policy? In what sense, if the criterion of scientific knowledge is to be found in the "objective" validity of its results, has he remained within the sphere of *scientific* discussion? We will first present our own attitude on this question in order later to deal with the broader one: in what sense are there in general "objectively valid truths" in those disciplines concerned with social and cultural phenomena? This question, in view of the continuous changes and bitter conflict about the apparently most elementary problems of our discipline, its methods, the formulation and validity of its concepts, cannot be avoided. We do not attempt to offer solutions but rather to disclose problems — problems of the type to which our journal, if it is to meet its past and future responsibilities, must turn its attention.

I

We all know that our science, as is the case with every science treating the institutions and events of human culture, (with the possible exception of political history) first arose in connection with *practical* considerations. Its most immediate and often sole purpose was the attainment of value-judgments concerning measures of State economic policy. It was a "technique" in the same sense as, for instance, the clinical disciplines in the medical sciences are. It has now become known how this situation was gradually modified. This modification was not, however, accompanied by a formulation of the logical (*prinzipielle*) distinction between "existential knowledge," i.e., knowledge of what "is," and "normative knowledge," i.e., knowledge of what "should be." The formulation of this distinction was hampered, first, by the view that immutably invariant natural laws, — later, by the view that an unambiguous evolutionary principle — governed economic life and that accordingly, *what was normatively right* was identical — in the former case — with the immutably *existent* — and in the latter —

---

[1]This essay was published when the editorship of the *Archiv fur Sozialwissenschaft und Socialpolitik* was transferred to Edgar Jaffé, Werner Sombart and Max Weber. Its form was influenced by the occasion for which it was written and the content should be considered in this light. (Marianne Weber.)

with the inevitably *emergent*.   With the awakening of the historical
sense, a combination of ethical evolutionism and historical relativism
became the predominant attitude in our science.   This attitude
sought to deprive ethical norms of their formal character and through
the incorporation of the totality of cultural values into the "ethical"
(*Sittlichen*) sphere tried to give a *substantive content* to ethical
norms.   It was hoped thereby to raise economics to the status of an
"ethical science" with empirical foundations.   To the extent that
an "ethical" label was given to all possible cultural ideals, the particular autonomy of the ethical imperative was obliterated, without however increasing the "objective" validity of those ideals.   Nonetheless
we can and must forego a discussion of the principles at issue.   We
merely point out that even today the confused opinion that economics
does and should derive value-judgments from a specifically "economic
point of view" has not disappeared but is especially current, quite
understandably, among men of practical affairs.

Our journal as the representative of an empirical specialized discipline must, as we wish to show shortly, reject this view in principle.
It must do so because, in our opinion, it can never be the task of
an empirical science to provide binding norms and ideals from which
directives for immediate practical activity can be derived.

What is the implication of this proposition?   It is certainly not
that value-judgments are to be withdrawn from scientific discussion
in general simply because in the last analysis they rest on certain
ideals and are therefore "subjective" in origin.   Practical action and
the aims of our journal would always reject such a proposition.
Criticism is not to be suspended in the presence of value-judgments.
The problem is rather: what is the meaning and purpose of the
scientific criticism of ideals and value-judgments?   This requires a
somewhat more detailed analysis.

All serious reflection about the ultimate elements of meaningful
human conduct is oriented primarily in terms of the categories "end"
and "means."   We desire something concretely either "for its own
sake" or as a means of achieving something else which is more highly
desired.   The question of the appropriateness of the means for achieving a given end is undoubtedly accessible to scientific analysis.   Inasmuch as we are able to determine (within the present limits of our

knowledge) which means for the achievement of a proposed end are appropriate or inappropriate, we can in this way estimate the chances of attaining a certain end by certain available means. In this way we can indirectly criticize the setting of the end itself as practically meaningful (on the basis of the existing historical situation) or as meaningless with reference to existing conditions. Furthermore, when the possibility of attaining a proposed end appears to exist, we can determine (naturally within the limits of our existing knowledge) the consequences which the application of the means to be used will produce in addition to the eventual attainment of the proposed end, as a result of the interdependence of all events. We can then provide the acting person with the ability to weigh and compare the undesirable as over against the desirable consequences of his action. Thus, we can answer the question: what will the attainment of a desired end "cost" in terms of the predictable loss of other values? Since, in the vast majority of cases, every goal that is striven for does "cost" or can "cost" something in this sense, the weighing of the goal in terms of the incidental consequences of the action which realizes it cannot be omitted from the deliberation of persons who act with a sense of responsibility. One of the most important functions of the *technical criticism* which we have been discussing thus far is to make this sort of analysis possible. To apply the results of this analysis in the making of a decision, however, is not a task which science can undertake; it is rather the task of the acting, willing person: he weighs and chooses from among the values involved according to his own conscience and his personal view of the world. Science can make him realize that all action and naturally, according to the circumstances, inaction imply in their consequences the espousal of certain values — and herewith — what is today so willingly overlooked — the rejection of certain others. The act of choice itself is his own responsibility.

We can also offer the person, who makes a choice, insight into the significance of the desired object. We can teach him to think in terms of the context and the meaning of the ends he desires, and among which he chooses. We do this through making explicit and developing in a logically consistent manner the "ideas" which actually do or which can underlie the concrete end. It is self-evident that one of the most important tasks of every science of cultural life is to arrive at a rational understanding of these "ideas" for which men either really or allegedly struggle. This does not overstep the boundaries of a science which strives for an "analytical ordering of empirical reality," although the methods which are used in this interpretation of cultural (*geistiger*) values are not "inductions" in the usual sense. At any rate, this task falls at least partly beyond the limits of economics as defined according to the conventional division of labor. It belongs among the tasks of social philosophy. However, the historical influence of ideas in the development of social life has been and still is so great that our journal cannot renounce this task. It shall rather regard the investigation of this phenomenon as one of its most important obligations.

But the scientific treatment of value-judgments may not only understand and empathically analyze (*nacherleben*) the desired ends and the ideals which underlie them; it can also "judge" them critically. This criticism can of course have only a dialetical character, i.e., it can be no more than a formal logical judgment of historically given value-judgments and ideas, a testing of the ideals according to the postulate of the internal *consistency* of the desired end. It can, insofar is it sets itself this goal, aid the acting willing person in attaining self-clarification concerning the final axioms from which his desired ends are derived. It can assist him in becoming aware of the ultimate standards of value which he does not make explicit to himself or, which he must presuppose in order to be logical. The elevation of these ultimate standards, which are manifested in concrete value-judgments, to the level of explicitness is the utmost that the scientific treatment of value-judgments can do without entering into the realm of speculation. As to whether the person expressing these value-judgments *should* adhere to these ultimate standards is his personal affair; it involves will and conscience, not empirical knowledge.

An empirical science cannot tell anyone what he *should* do — but rather what he *can* do — and under certain circumstances — what he wishes to do. It is true that in our sciences, personal value-judgments have tended to influence scientific arguments without being explicitly admitted. They have brought about continual confusion and have caused various interpretations to be placed on scientific arguments even in the sphere of the determination of simple casual interconnections among facts according to whether the results increased or decreased the chances of realizing one's personal ideals, i.e., the possibility of desiring a certain thing. Even the editors and the collaborators of our journal will regard "nothing human as alien" to them in this respect. But it is a long way from this acknowledgement of human frailty to the belief in an "ethical" science of economics, which would derive ideals from its subject matter and produce concrete norms by applying general ethical imperatives. It is true that we regard as *objectively* valuable those innermost elements of the "personality," those highest and most ultimate value-judgments which determine our conduct and give meaning and significance to our life. We can indeed espouse these values only when they appear to us as valid, as derived from our highest values and when they are developed in the struggle against the difficulties which life presents. Certainly, the dignity of the "personality" lies in the fact that for it there exist values about which it organizes its life; — even if these values are in certain cases concentrated exclusively within the sphere of the person's "individuality," then "self-realization" in *those* interests for which it claims *validity* as *values,* is the idea with respect to which its whole existence is oriented. Only on the assumption of belief in the validity of values is the attempt to espouse value-judgments meaningful. However, to *judge* the *validity* of such values is a matter of *faith.* It may perhaps be a task for the speculative interpretation of life and the universe in quest of their meaning. But it certainly does not fall within the province of an empirical science in the sense in which it is to be practised here. The empirically demonstrable fact that these ultimate ends undergo historical changes and are debatable does not affect this distinction between empirical science and value-judgments, contrary to what is often thought. For even the knowledge of the most certain proposition of our theoretical sciences — e.g., the exact natural sciences or mathematics, is, like the cultivation and refinement of the conscience, a product of culture. However, when we call to mind the practical problems of economic and social policy (in the usual sense), we see that there are many, indeed countless, practical questions in the discussion of which there seems to be general agreement about the self-evident character of

certain goals. Among these we may mention emergency credit, the
concrete problems of social hygiene, poor relief, factory inspection,
industrial courts, employment exchanges, large sections of protective
labor legislation — in short, all those issues in which, at least in appearance, only the *means* for the attainment of the goal are at issue.
But even if we were to mistake the illusion of self-evidence for truth
— which science can never do without damaging itself — and wished
to view the conflicts immediately arising from attempts at practical
realization as purely technical questions of expediency — which would
very often be incorrect — even in this case we would have to recognize that this illusion of the self-evidence of normative standards of
value is dissipated as soon as we pass from the concrete problems of
philanthropic and protective social and economic services to problems of economic and social policy.   The distinctive characteristic
of a problem of social *policy* is indeed the fact that it cannot be
resolved merely on the basis of purely technical considerations which
assume already settled ends.   Normative standards of value can and
must be the objects of *dispute* in a discussion of a problem of social
policy because the problem lies in the domain of general *cultural*
values.   And the conflict occurs not merely, as we are too easily
inclined to believe today, between "class interests" but between general views on life and the universe as well.   This latter point, however, does not lessen the truth that the particular ultimate value-
judgment which the individual espouses is decided among other factors and certainly to a quite significant degree by the degree of affinity
between it and his class interests — accepting for the time being this
only superficially unambiguous term.   One thing is certain under all
circumstances, namely, the more "general" the problem involved, i.e.,
in this case, the broader its cultural *significance,* the less subject it is
to a single unambiguous answer on the basis of the data of empirical
sciences and the greater the role played by value-ideas (*Wertideen*)
and the ultimate and highest personal axioms of belief.   It is simply
naive to believe, although there are many specialists who even now
occasionally do, that it is possible to establish and to demonstrate as
scientifically valid "a principle" for practical social science from
which the norms for the solution of practical problems can be unambiguously derived.   However much the social sciences need the dis-

cussion of practical problems in terms of fundamental principles, i.e., the reduction of unreflective value-judgments to the premises from which they are logically derived and however much our journal intends to devote itself specially to them — certainly the creation of a lowest common denominator for our problems in the form of generally valid ultimate value-judgments cannot be its task or in general the task of any empirical science. Such a thing would not only be impracticable; it would be entirely meaningless as well. Whatever the interpretation of the basis and the nature of the validity of the ethical imperatives, it is certain that from them, as from the norms for the concretely conditioned conduct of the *individual, cultural values* cannot be unambiguously derived as being normatively desirable; it can do so the less, the more inclusive are the values concerned. Only positive religions — or more precisely expressed: dogmatically bound *sects* — are able to confer on the content of *cultural values* the status of unconditionally valid *ethical* imperatives. Outside these sects, cultural ideals which the individual wishes to realize and ethical obligations which he *should* fulfil do not, in principle, share the same status. The fate of an epoch which has eaten of the tree of knowledge is that it must know that we cannot learn the *meaning* of the world from the results of its analysis, be it ever so perfect; it must rather be in a position to create this meaning itself. It must recognize that general views of life and the universe can never be the products of increasing empirical knowledge, and that the highest ideals, which move us most forcefully, are always formed only in the struggle with other ideals which are just as sacred to others as ours are to us.

Only an optimistic syncretism, such as is, at times, the product of evolutionary-historical relativism, can theoretically delude itself about the profound seriousness of this situation or practically shirk its consequences. It can, to be sure, be just as obligatory subjectively for the practical politician, in the individual case, to mediate between antagonistic points of view as to take sides with one of them. But this has nothing whatsoever to do with scientific "objectivity." *Scientifically the "middle course" is not truer even by a hair's breadth,* than the most extreme party ideals of the right or left. Nowhere are the interests of science more poorly served in the long run than in those situations where one refuses to see uncomfortable facts and the realities of life in all their starkness. The *Archiv* will struggle relentlessly against the severe self-deception which asserts that through the synthesis of several party points of view, or by following a line between them, practical norms of *scientific validity* can be arrived at. It is necessary to do this because, since this piece of self-deception tries to mask its own standards of value in relativistic terms, it is more dangerous to the freedom of research than the former naive faith of parties in the scientific "demonstrability" of their dogmas. The capacity to distinguish between empirical knowledge and value-judgments, and the fulfillment of the scientific duty to see the factual truth as well as the practical duty to stand up for our own ideals constitute the program to which we wish to adhere with ever increasing firmness.

There is and always will be — and this is the reason that it concerns us — an unbridgeable distinction among (1) those arguments which appeal to our capacity to become enthusiastic about and our feeling for concrete practical aims, or cultural forms and values, (2) those arguments in which, once it is a question of the validity of ethical norms, the appeal is directed to our conscience, and finally (3) those arguments which appeal to our capacity and need for *analytically ordering* empirical reality in a manner which lays claim to *validity* as empirical truth. This proposition remains correct, despite, as we shall see, the fact that those highest "values" underlying the practical interest are and always will be decisively significant in determining the focus of attention of analytical activity (*ordnende Tätigkeit des Denkens*) in the sphere of the cultural sciences. It has been and remains true that a systematically correct scientific proof in the social sciences, if it is to achieve its purpose, must be acknowledged as correct even by a Chinese — or — more precisely stated — it must constantly *strive* to attain this goal, which perhaps may not be completely attainable due to faulty data. Furthermore, the successful *logical* analysis of the content of an ideal and its ultimate axioms and the discovery of the consequences which arise from pursuing it, logically and practically, must also be valid for the Chinese. At the same time, our Chinese can lack a "sense" for our ethical imperative and he can and certainly often will deny the ideal itself and the concrete value-judgments derived from it. Neither of these two latter attitudes can affect the scientific value of the analysis in any way. Quite certainly our journal will not ignore the ever and inevitably recurrent attempts to give an unambiguous interpretation to culture. On the contrary, these attempts themselves rank with the most important products of this cultural life and, under certain circumstances, among its dynamic forces. We will therefore constantly strive to follow with care the course of these discussions of "social philosophy" (as here understood). We are furthermore completely free of the prejudice which asserts that reflections on culture which go beyond the analysis of empirical data in order to interpret the world metaphysically can, because of their metaphysical character fulfil no useful cognitive tasks. Just what these cognitive tasks are is primarily an epistemological question, the answer to which we must and can, in view of our purpose, disregard at this point. There is one tenet to which we adhere most firmly in our work, namely, that a social science journal, in our sense, to the extent that it is *scientific* should be a place where those truths are sought, which — to remain with our illustration — can claim, even for a Chinese, the validity appropriate to an analysis of empirical reality.

Of course, the editors cannot once and for all deny to themselves or their contributors the possibility of expressing in value-judgments the ideals which motivate them. However two important duties arise in connection with this. First, to keep the readers and themselves sharply aware at every moment of the standards by which they judge reality and from which the value-judgment is derived, instead of, as happens too often, deceiving themselves in the conflict of ideals by a value mélange of values of the most different orders and types, and seeking to offer something to everybody. If this obligation is rigorously heeded, the practical evaluative attitude can be not only harmless to scientific interests but even directly useful, and indeed mandatory. In the scientific criticism of legislative and other practical recommendations, the motives of the legislator and the ideals of the critic in all their scope often can not be clarified and analyzed in a tangible and intelligible form in any other way than through the confrontation of the standards of value underlying the ideas criticized with others, preferably the critic's own. Every meaningful *value-judgment* about someone else's *aspirations* must be a criticism from the standpoint of one's own *Weltanschauung;* it must be a struggle against *another's* ideals from the standpoint of one's *own.* If in a particular concrete case, the ultimate value-axioms which underlie practical activity are not only to be designated and scientifically analyzed but are also to be shown in their relationship to *other* value-axioms, "positive" criticism by means of a systematic exposition of the latter is unavoidable.

In the pages of this journal, especially in the discussion of legislation, there will inevitably be found social *policy,* i.e., the statement of ideals, in addition to social *science,* i.e., the analysis of facts. But we do not by any means intend to present such discussions as "science" and we will guard as best we can against allowing these two to be confused with each other. In such discussions, *science* no longer has the floor. For that reason, the second fundamental imperative of scientific freedom is that in such cases it should be constantly made clear to the readers (and — again we say it — above all to one's self!) exactly at which point the scientific investigator becomes silent and the evaluating and acting person begins to speak. In other words, it should be made explicit just where the arguments are addressed to the analytical understanding and where to the sentiments. The constant confusion of the scientific discussion of facts and their evaluation is still one of the most widespread and also one of the most damaging traits of work in our field. The foregoing arguments are directed against this confusion, and not against the clear-cut introduction of one's own ideals into the discussion. An *attitude of moral indifference* has no connection with *scientific* "objectivity." The *Archiv,* at least in its intentions, has never been and should never be a place where polemics against certain currents in politics or social policy are carried on, nor should it be a place where struggles are waged for or against ideals in politics or social-policy. There are other journals for these purposes. The peculiar characteristic of the journal has rather been from the very beginning and, insofar as it is in the power of the editors, shall continue to be that political antagonists can meet in it to carry on scientific work. It has not been a "socialist" organ hitherto and in the future it shall not be "bourgeois."

It excludes no one from its circle of contributors who is willing to place himself within the framework of scientific discussion. It cannot be an arena for "objections," replies and rebuttals, but in its pages no one will be protected, neither its contributors nor its editors, from being subjected to the sharpest factual, scientific criticism. Whoever cannot bear this or who takes the viewpoint that he does not wish to work, in the service of scientific knowledge, with persons whose other ideals are different from his own, is free not to participate.

However, we should not deceive ourselves about it — this last sentence means much more in practice than it seems to do at first glance. In the first place, there are psychological limits everywhere and especially in Germany to the possibility of coming together freely with one's political opponents in a neutral forum, be it social or intellectual. This obstacle which should be relentlessly combatted as a sign of narrow-minded party fanaticism and backward political culture, is reenforced for a journal like ours through the fact that in social sciences the stimulus to the posing of scientific problems is in actuality always given by *practical* "questions." Hence the very recognition of the existence of a scientific problem coincides, personally, with the possession of specifically oriented motives and values. A journal which has come into existence under the influence of a general interest in a concrete problem, will always include among its contributors persons who are personally interested in these problems because certain concrete situations seem to be incompatible with, or seem to threaten, the realization of certain ideal values in which they believe. A bond of similar ideals will hold this circle of contributors together and it will be the basis of a further recruitment. This in turn will tend to give the journal, at least in its treatment of questions of practical social *policy,* a certain *"character"* which of course inevitably accompanies every collaboration of vigorously sensitive persons whose evaluative standpoint regarding the problems cannot be entirely expressed even in purely theoretical analysis; in the criticism of *practical* recommendations and measures it quite legitimately finds expression — under the particular conditions above discussed. The *Archiv* first appeared at a time in which certain practical aspects of the "labor problem" (as traditionally understood) stood in the forefront of social science discussions. Those persons for whom the problems which the *Archiv* wished to treat were bound up with ultimate and decisive value-judgments and who on that account became its most regular contributors also espoused at the same time the view of culture which was strongly influenced by these value-judgments. We all know that though this journal, through its explicit self-restriction to "scientific" discussions and through the express invitation to the "adherents of all political standpoints," denied that it would pursue a certain "tendency," it nonetheless possessed a "character" in the above sense. This "character" was created by the group of its regular contributors. In general they were men who, whatever may have been other divergences in their points of view, set as their goal the protection of the physical well-being of the laboring masses and the increase of the latters' share of the material and intellectual values of our culture. As a means, they employed the combination of state intervention into the arena of material interests with the freer shaping of the existing political and legal order. Whatever may have been their opinion as to the form of the social order in the more remote future — for the present, they accepted the emergent trends of the capitalist system, not because they seemed better than the older forms of social organization but because they seemed to be practically inevitable and because the attempt to wage a fundamental struggle against it appeared to hinder and not aid the cultural rise of the working class. In the situation which exists in Germany today — we need not be more specific at this point — this was not and is not to be avoided. Indeed, it bore direct fruit in the successful many-sidedness of the participation in the scientific discussion and it constituted a source of strength for the journal; under the given circumstances it was perhaps even one of its claims to the justification for its existence.

There can be no doubt that the development of a "character," in this sense, in a scientific journal can constitute a threat to the freedom of scientific analysis; it really does amount to that when the selection of contributors is purposely one-sided. In this case the cultivation of a "character" in a journal is practically equivalent to the existence of a "tendency." The editors are aware of the responsibility which this situation imposes upon them. They propose neither the deliberate transformation of the character of the *Archiv* nor its artificial preservation by means of a careful restriction of the contributors to scholars of certain definite party loyalties. They accept it as given and await its further "development." The form which it takes in the future and the modifications which it may undergo as a result of the inevitable broadening of its circle of contributors will depend primarily on the character of those persons who, seeking to serve the cause of science, enter the circle and become or remain frequent contributors. It will be further affected by the broadening of the *problems*, the advancement of which is a goal of the journal.

With these remarks we come to the question on which we have not yet touched, namely, the factual delimitation of our field of operations. No answer can, however, be given without raising the question as to the goal of social science knowledge in general. When we distinguished in principle between "value-judgments" and "empirical knowledge," we presupposed the existence of an unconditionally valid type of knowledge in the social sciences, i.e., the analytical ordering of empirical social reality. This presupposition now becomes our problem in the sense that we must discuss the meaning of objectively "valid" truth in the social sciences. The genuineness of the problem is apparent to anyone who is aware of the conflict about methods, "fundamental concepts" and presuppositions, the incessant shift of "viewpoints," and the continuous redefinition of "concepts" and who sees that the theoretical and historical modes of analysis are still separated by an apparently unbridgeable gap. It consitutes, as a despairing Viennese examinee once sorrowfully complained, "*two* sciences of economics." What is the meaning of "objectivity" in this context? The following discussion will be devoted to this question.

III

This journal has from the beginning treated social-economic data as its subject-matter. Although there is little point in entering here into the definition of terms and the delineation of the proper boundaries of the various sciences, we must nonetheless state briefly what we mean by this.

Most roughly expressed, the basic element in all those phenomena which we call, in the widest sense, "social-economic" is constituted by the fact that our physical existence and the satisfaction of our most ideal needs are everywhere confronted with the quantitative limits and the qualitative inadequacy of the necessary external means, so that their satisfaction requires planful provision and work, struggle with nature and the association of human beings. The quality of an event as a "social-economic" event is not something which it possesses "objectively." It is rather conditioned by the orientation of our cognitive interest, as it arises from the specific cultural significance which we attribute to the particular event in a given case. Wherever those aspects of a cultural event which constitute its specific significance for us are connected with a social-economic event either directly or most indirectly, they involve, or at least to the extent that this connection exists, can involve a problem for the social sciences. By a social science problem, we mean a task for a discipline the object of which is to throw light on the ramifications of that fundamental social-economic phenomenon: the scarcity of means.

Within the total range of social-economic problems, we are now able to distinguish events and constellations of norms, institutions, etc., the economic aspect of which constitutes their primary cultural significance for us. Such are, for example, the phenomena of the stock exchange and the banking world, which, in the main, interest us only in *this* respect. This will be the case regularly (but not exclusively) when institutions are involved which were *deliberately* created or used for economic ends. Such objects of our knowledge we may call "economic" events (or institutions, as the case may be). There are other phenomena, for instance, religious ones, which do not interest us, or at least do not primarily interest us with respect to their economic significance but which, however, under certain circumstances do acquire significance in this regard because they have consequences which are of interest from the economic point of view. These we shall call "economically relevant" phenomena. Finally there are phenomena which are *not* "economic" in our sense and the economic effects of which are of no, or at best slight, interest to us (e.g., the developments of the artistic taste of a period) but which in individual instances are in their turn more or less strongly influenced in certain important aspects by economic factors such as, for instance, the social stratification of the artistically interested public. We shall call these "economically *conditioned* phenomena." The constellation of human relationships, norms, and normatively determined conduct which we call the "state" is for example in its fiscal aspects, an "economic" phenomenon; insofar as it influences economic life through legislation or otherwise (and even where other than economic considerations deliberately guide its behavior), it is "economically relevant." To the extent that its behavior in non-"economic" affairs is partly influenced by economic motives, it is "economically conditioned." After what has been said, it is self-evident that: firstly), the boundary lines of "economic" phenomena are vague and not easily defined; secondly), the "economic" aspect of a phenomenon is by no means *only* "economically conditioned" or *only* "economically relevant"; thirdly), a phenomenon is "economic" only insofar as and *only* as long as our *interest* is exclusively focused on its constitutive significance in the material struggle for existence.

Like the science of social-economics since Marx and Roscher, our journal is concerned not only with economic phenomena but also with those which are "economically relevant" and "economically conditioned." The domain of such subjects extends naturally — and varyingly in accordance with the focus of our interest at the moment — through the totality of cultural life. Specifically economic motives — i.e., motives which, in their aspect most significant to us, are rooted in the above-mentioned fundamental fact — operate wherever the satisfaction of even the most immaterial need or desire is bound up with the application of *scarce* material means. Their force has everywhere on that account conditioned and transformed not only the mode in which cultural wants or preferences are satisfied, but their content as well, even in their most subjective aspects. The indirect influence of social relations, institutions and groups governed by "material interests" extends (often unconsciously) into all spheres of culture without exception, even into the finest nuances of æsthetic and religious feeling. The events of everyday life no less than the "historical" events of the higher reaches of political life, collective and mass phenomena as well as the "individuated" conduct of statesmen and individual literary and artistic achievements are influenced by it. They are "economically conditioned." On the other hand, all the activities and situations constituting an historically given culture affect the formation of the material wants, the mode of their satisfaction, the integration of interest-groups and the types of power which they exercise. They thereby affect the course of "economic development" and are accordingly "economically relevant." To the extent that our science imputes particular causes — be they economic or non-economic — to *economic* cultural phenomena, it seeks "historical" knowledge. Insofar as it traces a specific element of cultural life (the economic element in its cultural significance) through the most diverse cultural contexts, it is making an historical interpretation from a specific point of view, and offering a partial picture, a *preliminary* contribution to a more complete historical knowledge of culture.

Social economic *problems* do not exist everywhere that an economic event plays a role as cause or effect — since problems arise only where the significance of those factors is *problematical* and can be precisely determined only through the application of the methods of social-economics. But despite this, the range of social-economics is almost overwhelming.

After due consideration our journal has generally excluded hitherto the treatment of a whole series of highly important special fields in our discipline, such as descriptive economics, economic history in the narrower sense, and statistics. It has likewise left to other journals, the discussion of technical fiscal questions and the technical-economic problems of prices and markets in the modern exchange economy. Its sphere of operations has been the present significance and the historical development of certain conflicts and constellations of interests which have arisen through the dominant role of investment-seeking capital in modern societies. It has not thereby restricted itself to those practical and historical problems which are designated by the term "the social question" in its narrower sense, i.e., the place of the modern working class in the present social order. Of course, the scientific elaboration of the interest in this special question which became widespread in Germany in the '80's, has had to be one of its main tasks. The more the practical treatment of labor conditions became a permanent object of legislation and public discussion in Germany, the more the accent of scientific work had to be shifted to the analysis of the more universal dimensions of the problem. It had thereby to culminate in the analysis of all the cultural problems which have arisen from the peculiar nature of the economic bases of our culture and which are, in that sense, specifically modern. The journal soon began to deal historically, statistically and theoretically with the most diverse, partly "economically relevant," and partly "economically conditioned" conditions of the other great social classes of modern states and their interrelations. We are only drawing the conclusions of this policy when we state that the scientific investigation of the *general cultural significance of the social-economic structure of the human community* and its historical forms of organization is the central aim of our journal. This is what we mean when we call our journal the *Archiv fur Sozialwissenschaft*. The title is intended to indicate the historical and theoretical treatment of the same problems, the practical solution of which constitutes "social *policy*" in the widest sense of this word. We thereby utilize the right to apply the word "social" in the meaning which concrete present-day problems give to it. If one wishes to call those disciplines which treat the events of human life with respect to their cultural significance "cultural sciences," then social science in our sense belongs in that category. We shall soon see what are the logical implications of this.

Undoubtedly the selection of the *social-economic* aspect of cultural life signifies a very definite delimitation of our theme. It will be said that the economic, or as it has been inaccurately called, the "materialistic" point of view, from which culture is here being considered, is "one-sided." This is true and the one-sidedness is intentional. The belief that it is the task of scientific work to cure the "one-sidedness" of the economic approach by broadening it into a *general* social science suffers primarily from the weakness that the "social" criterion (i.e., the relationships among persons) acquires the specificity necessary for the delimitation of scientific problems only when it is accompanied by some substantive predicate. Otherwise, as the subject matter of a science, it would naturally comprehend philology, for example, as well as church history and particularly all those disciplines which concern themselves with the state which is the most important form of the normative regulation of cultural

life. The fact that social-economics concerns itself with "social" relations is no more justification for regarding it as the necessary precursor
of a "general social science" than its concern with vital phenomena
makes it a part of biology, or its preoccupation with events on one
of the planets makes it a part of an extended and improved astronomy
of the future. It is not the "actual" interconnections of "things"
but the *conceptual* interconnections of *problems* which define the
scope of the various sciences. A new "science" emerges where new
problems are pursued by new methods and truths are thereby discovered which open up significant new points of view.

It is now no accident that the term: "social" which seems to have
a quite general meaning, turns out to have, as soon as one carefully
examines its application, a particular specifically colored though often
indefinite meaning. Its "generality" rests on nothing but its ambiguity. It provides, when taken in its "general" meaning, no specific
point of view, from which the *significance* of given elements of culture can be analyzed.

Liberated as we are from the antiquated notion that all cultural
phenomena can be *deduced* as a product or function of the constellation of "material" interests, we believe nevertheless that the analysis
of social and cultural phenomena with special reference to their economic conditioning and ramifications was a scientific principle of
creative fruitfulness and with careful application and freedom from
dogmatic restrictions, will remain such for a very long time to come.
The so-called "materialistic conception of history" as a *Weltanschauung* or as a formula for the casual explanation of historical reality is
to be rejected most emphatically. The advancement of the economic
interpretation of history is one of the most important aims of our
journal. This requires further explanation.

The so-called "materialistic conception of history" with the crude
elements of genius of the early form which appeared, for instance,
in the *Communist Manifesto* still prevails only in the minds of laymen and dilettantes. In these circles one still finds the peculiar condition that their need for a casual explanation of an historical event
is never satisfied until somewhere or somehow economic causes are
shown (or seem) to be operative. Where this however, is the case,
they content themselves with the most threadbare hypotheses and

the most general phrases since they have then satisfied their dogmatic need to believe that the economic "factor" is the "real"· one, the only "true" one, and the one which "in the last instance is everywhere decisive." This phenomenon is by no means unique. Almost all the sciences, from philology to biology have occasionally claimed to be the sources not only of specialized scientific knowledge but of *"Weltanschauungen"* as well. Under the impression of the profound cultural significance of *modern* economic transformations and especially of the far-reaching ramifications of the "labor question," the inevitable monistic tendency of every type of thought which is not self-critical naturally follows this path.

The same tendency is now appearing in anthropology where the political and commercial struggles of nations for world dominance are being fought with increasing acuteness. There is a widespread belief that "in the last analysis" all historical events are results of the interplay of innate "racial qualities." In place of uncritical descriptions of "national characters," there emerges the even more uncritical concoction of "social theories" based on the "natural sciences." We shall carefully follow the development of anthropological research in our journal insofar as it is significant from our point of view. It is to be hoped that the situation in which the casual explanation of cultural events by the invocation of "racial characteristics" testifies to our ignorance — just as the reference to the "milieu" or, earlier, to the "conditions of the age" — will be gradually overcome by research which is the fruit of systematic training. If there is anything that has hindered this type of research, it is the fact that eager dilettantes have thought that they could contribute something different and better to our knowledge of culture than the broadening of the possibility of the sure imputation of individual concrete cultural events occurring in historical reality to *concrete, historically* given causes through the study of precise empirical data which have been selected from specific points of view. Only to the extent that they are able to do this, are their results of interest to us ʼand only then does "racial biology" become something more than a product of the modern passion for founding new sciences.

The problem of the significance of the economic interpretation of history is the same. If, following a period of boundless over-estimation, the danger now exists that its scientific value will be underestimated, this is the result of the unexampled naiveté with which the economic interpretation of reality was applied as a "universal" canon which explained all cultural phenomena — i.e., all those which are meaningful to us — as, in the last analysis, economically conditioned. Its present logical form is not entirely unambiguous. Wherever the strictly economic explanation encounters difficulties, various devices are available for maintaining its general validity as the decisive casual factor. Sometimes every historical event which is *not* explicable by the invocation of economic motives is regarded *for that very reason* as a scientifically insignificant "accident." At others, the definition of "economic" is stretched beyond recognition so that all human interests which are related in any way whatsoever to the use of material means are included in the definition. If it is historically undeniable that different responses occur in two situations which are economically identical — due to political, religious, climatic and countless other non-economic determinants — then in order to maintain the primacy of the economic all these factors are reduced to historically accidental "conditions" upon which the economic factor operates as a "cause." It is obvious however that all those factors which are "accidental" according to the economic interpretation of history follow their own laws in the same sense as the economic factor. From a point of view which traces the specific meaning of these non-economic factors, the existing *economic* "conditions" are "historically accidental" in quite the same sense. A favorite attempt to preserve the supreme significance of the economic factor despite this consists in the interpretation of the constant interaction of the individual elements of cultural life as a casual or functional dependence of one on the other, or rather of all the others on one, namely, the economic element. When a certain *non*-economic institution has functioned for the benefit of certain economic class interests, as, for example, where certain religious institutions allowed themselves to be and actually were used as "black police," the whole institution is conceived either as having been created for this function or — quite metaphysically — as being impelled by a "developmental tendency" emanating from the economic factor.

It is unnecessary nowadays to go into detail to prove to the specialist that this interpretation of the purpose of the economic analysis of culture is in part the expression of a certain historical constellation which turned its scientific interest towards certain economically conditioned cultural problems, and in part the rabid chauvinism of a specialized department of science. It is clear that today it is antiquated at best. The explanation of everything by economic causes *alone* is never exhaustive in any sense whatsoever in *any* sphere of cultural phenomena, not even in the "economic" sphere itself. In principle, a banking history of a nation which adduces only economic motives for explanatory purposes is naturally just as unacceptable as an explanation of the Sistine Madonna as a consequence of the social-economic basis of the culture of the epoch in which it was created. It is no way more complete than, for instance, the explanation of capitalism by reference to certain shifts in the content of the religious ideas which played a role in the genesis of the capitalistic attitude; nor is it more exhaustive than the explanation of a political structure from its geographical background. In *all* of these cases, the degree of significance which we are to attribute to economic factors is decided by the class of causes to which we are to impute those specific elements of the phenomenon in question to which we attach significance in given cases and in which we are interested. The justification of the *one-sided* analysis of cultural reality from specific "points of view" — in our case with respect to its economic conditioning — emerges purely as a technical expedient from the fact that training in the observation of the effects of qualitatively similar categories of causes and the repeated utilization of the same scheme of concepts and hypotheses (*begrifflich-methodischen Apparates*) offers all the advantages of the division of labor. It is free from the charge of arbitrariness to the extent that it is successful in producing insights into interconnections which have been shown to be valuable for the casual explanation of concrete historical events. However — the *"one-sidedness"* and the unreality of the purely economic interpretation of history is in general only a special case of a principle which is generally valid for the scientific knowledge of cultural reality. The main task of the discussion to follow is to make explicit the logical foundations and the general methodological implications of this principle.

There is no absolutely "objective" scientific analysis of culture — or put perhaps more narrowly but certainly not essentially differently for our purposes — of "social phenomena" independent of special and "one-sided" viewpoints according to which — expressly or tacitly, consciously or unconsciously — they are selected, analyzed and organized for expository purposes. The reasons for this lie in the character of the cognitive goal of all research in social science which seeks to transcend the purely *formal* treatment of the legal or conventional norms regulating social life.

The type of social science in which we are interested is an *empirical science* of concrete *reality* (*Wirklichkeitswissenschaft*). Our aim is the understanding of the characteristic uniqueness of the reality in which we move. We wish to understand on the one hand the relationships and the cultural significance of individual events in their contemporary manifestations and on the other the causes of their being historically *so* and not *otherwise*. Now, as soon as we attempt to reflect about the way in which life confronts us in immediate concrete situations, it presents an infinite multiplicity of successively and coexistently emerging and disappearing events, both "within" and "outside" ourselves. The absolute infinitude of this multiplicity is seen to remain undiminished even when our attention is focused on a single "object," for instance, a concrete act of exchange, as soon as we seriously attempt an exhaustive description of *all* the individual components of this "individual phenomena," to say nothing of explaining it casually. All the analysis of infinite reality which the finite human mind can conduct rests on the tacit assumption that only a finite portion of this reality constitutes the object of scientific investigation, and that only it is "important" in the sense of being "worthy of being known." But what are the criteria by which this segment is selected? It has often been thought that the decisive criterion in the cultural sciences, too, was in the last analysis, the "regular" recurrence of certain casual relationships. The "laws" which we are able to perceive in the infinitely manifold stream of events must — according to this conception — contain the scientifically "essential" aspect of reality. As soon as we have shown some causal reltaionship to be a "law," i.e., if we have shown it to be universally valid by means of comprehensive historical induction or have made it immediately and tangibly plausible according to our subjective experience, a great number of similar cases order themselves under the formula thus attained. Those elements in each individual event which are left unaccounted for by the selection of their elements subsumable under the "law" are considered as scientifically unintegrated residues which will be taken care of in the further perfection of the system of "laws." Alternatively they will be viewed as "accidental" and therefore scientifically unimportant *because* they do not fit into the structure of the "law"; in other words, they are not typical of the event and hence can only be the objects of "idle curiosity." Accordingly, even among the followers of the Historical School we continually find the attitude which declares that the ideal which all the sciences, including the cultural sciences, serve and towards which they should strive even in the remote future is a system of propositions from which reality can be "deduced." As is well known, a leading natural scientist believed that he could designate the (factually unattainable) ideal goal of such a treatment of cultural reality as a sort of *"astronomical"* knowledge.

Let us not, for our part, spare ourselves the trouble of examining these matters more closely — however often they have already been discussed. The first thing that impresses one is that the "astronomical" knowledge which was referred to is not a system of laws at all. On the contrary, the laws which it presupposes have been taken from other disciplines like mechanics. But it too concerns itself with the question of the *individual* consequence which the working of these laws in an unique *configuration* produces, since it is these individual configurations which are *significant* for us. Every individual constellation which it "explains" or predicts is causally explicable only as the consequence of another equally individual constellation which has preceded it. As far back as we may go into the grey mist of the far-off past, the reality to which the laws apply always remains equally *individual*, equally *undeducible* from laws. A cosmic "primeval state" which had no individual character or less individual character than the cosmic reality of the present would naturally be a meaningless notion. But is there not some trace of similar ideas in our field in those propositions sometimes derived from natural law and sometimes verified by the observation of "primitives," concerning an economic-social "primeval state" free from historical "accidents," and characterized by phenomena such as "primitive agrarian communism," sexual "promiscuity," etc., from which individual historical development emerges by a sort of fall from grace into concreteness?

The social-scientific interest has its point of departure, of course, in the *real,* i.e., concrete, individually-structured configuration of our cultural life in its universal relationships which are themselves no less individually-structured, and in its development out of other social cultural conditions, which themselves are obviously likewise individually structured. It is clear here that the situation which we illustrated by reference to astronomy as a limiting case (which is regularly drawn on by logicians for the same purpose) appears in a more accentuated form. Whereas in astronomy, the heavenly bodies are of interest to us only in their *quantitative* and exact aspects, the *qualitative* aspect of phenomena concerns us in the social sciences. To this should be added that in the social sciences we are concerned with psychological and intellectual (*geistig*) phenomena the empathic understanding of which is naturally a problem of a specifically different type from those which the schemes of the exact natural sciences in general can or seek to solve. Despite that, this distinction in itself is not a distinction in principle, as it seems at first glance. Aside from pure mechanics, even the exact natural sciences do not proceed without qualitative categories. Furthermore, in our own field we encounter the idea (which is obviously distorted) that at least the phenomena characteristic of a money-economy — which are basic to our culture — are quantifiable and on that account subject to formulation as "laws." Finally it depends on the breadth or narrowness of one's definition of "law" as to whether one will also include regularities which because they are not quantifiable are not subject to numerical analysis. Especially insofar as the influence of psychological and intellectual (*gestige*) factors is concerned, it does not in any case exclude the establishment of *rules* governing rational conduct. Above all, the point of view still persists which claims that the task of psychology is to play a role comparable to mathematics for the *Geisteswissenschaften* in the sense that it analyzes the complicated phenomena of social life into their psychic conditions and effects, reduces them to their most elementary possible psychic factors and then analyzes their functional interdependences. Thereby, a sort of "chemistry" if not "mechanics" of the psychic foundations of social life would be created. Whether such investigations can produce valuable and—what is something else—useful results for the cultural sciences, we cannot decide here. But this would be irrelevant to the question as to whether the aim of social-economic knowledge in our sense, i.e., knowledge of *reality* with respect to its cultural *significance* and its casual relationships can be attained through the quest for recurrent sequences. Let us assume that we have succeeded by means of psychology or otherwise in analyzing all the observed and imaginable relationships of social phenomena into some ultimate elementary "factors," that we have made an exhaustive analysis and classification of them and then formulated rigorously exact laws covering their behavior.—What would be the significance of these results for our knowledge of the *historically* given culture or any individual phase thereof, such as capitalism, in its development and cultural significance? As an,analytical tool, it would be as useful as a textbook of organic chemical combinations would be for our knowledge of the biogenetic aspect of the animal and plant world. In each case, certainly an important and useful preliminary step would have been taken. In neither case can concrete reality be deduced from "laws" and "factors." This is not because some higher mysterious powers reside in living phenomena (such as "dominants," "entelechies," or whatever they might be called). This, however, a problem in its own right. The real reason is that the analysis of reality is concerned with the *configuration* into which those (hypothetical!) "factors" are arranged to form a cultural phenomenon which is historicaliy significant to us. Furthermore, if we wish to "explain" this individual configuration "causally" we must invoke other equally individual configurations on the basis of which we will explain it with the aid of those (hypothetical!) "laws."

The determination of those (hypothetical) "laws" and "factors" would in any case only be the first of the many operations which would lead us to the desired type of knowledge. The analysis of the historically given individual configuration of those "factors" and their *significant* concrete interaction, conditioned by their historical context and especially the *rendering intelligible* of the basis and type of this significance would be the next task to be achieved. This task must be achieved, it is true, by the utilization of the preliminary analysis but it is nonetheless an entirely new and *distinct* task. The tracing as far into the past as possible of the individual features of these historically evolved configurations which are *contemporaneously* significant, and their historical explanation by antecedent and equally individual configurations would be the third task. Finally the prediction of possible future constellations would be a conceivable fourth task.

For all these purposes, clear concepts and the knowledge of those (hypothetical) "laws" are obviously of great value as heuristic means — but only as such. Indeed they are quite indispensable for this purpose. But even in this function their limitations become evident at a decisive point. In stating this, we arrive at the decisive feature of the method of the cultural sciences. We have designated as "cultural sciences" those disciplines which analyze the phenomena of life in terms of their cultural significance. The *significance* of a configuration of cultural phenomena and the basis of this significance cannot however be derived and rendered intelligible by a system of analytical laws (*Gesetzesbegriffen*), however perfect it may be, since the significance of cultural events presupposes a *value-orientation* towards these events. The concept of culture is a *value-concept*. Empirical reality becomes "culture" to us because and insofar as we relate it to value ideas. It includes those segments and only those segments of reality which have become significant to us because of this value-relevance. Only a small portion of existing concrete reality is colored by our value-conditioned interest and it alone is significant to us. It is significant because it reveals relationships which are important to us due to their connection with our values. Only because and to the extent that this is the case is it worthwhile for us to know it in its individual features. We cannot discover, however, what is meaningful to us by means of a "presuppositionless" investigation of empirical data. Rather perception of its meaningfulness to us is the presupposition of its becoming an *object* of investigation. Meaningfulness naturally does not coincide with laws as such, and the more general the law the less the coincidence. For the specific meaning which a phenomenon has for us is naturally *not* to be found in those relationships which it shares with many other phenomena.

The focus of attention on reality under the guidance of values which lend it significance and the selection and ordering of the phenomena which are thus affected in the light of their cultural significance is entirely different from the analysis of reality in terms of laws and general concepts. Neither of these two types of the analysis of reality has any necessary logical relationship with the other. They can coincide in individual instances but it would be most disastrous if their occasional coincidence caused us to think that they were not distinct *in principle*. The *cultural significance* of a phenomenon, e.g., the significance of exchange in a money economy, can be the fact that it exists on a mass scale as a fundamental component of modern culture. But the historical fact that it plays this role must be causally explained in order to render its cultural significance understandable. The analysis of the *general* aspects of exchange and the technique of the market is a — highly important and indispensable — *preliminary task*. For not only does this type of analysis leave unanswered the question as to how exchange historically acquired its fundamental significance in the modern world; but above all else, the fact with which we are primarily concerned, namely, the *cultural significance* of the money-economy, for the sake of which we are interested in the description of exchange technique and for the sake of which alone a science exists which deals with that technique — is not derivable from any "law." The *generic features* of exchange, purchase, etc., interest the jurist —but we are concerned with the analysis of the *cultural significance* of the concrete *historical* fact that today exchange exists on a mass scale. When we require an explanation, when we wish to understand what distinguishes the social-economic aspects of our culture for instance from that of antiquity in which exchange showed precisely the same generic traits as it does today and when we raise the question as to where the significance of "money economy" lies, logical principles of quite heterogeneous derivation enter into the investigation. We will apply those concepts with which we are provided by the investigation of the general features of economic mass phenomena — indeed, insofar as they are relevant to the meaningful aspects of our culture, we shall use them as *means* of exposition. The *goal* of our investigation is not reached through the exposition of those laws and concepts, precise as it may be. The question as to what should be the object of universal conceptualization cannot be decided "presuppositionlessly" but only with reference to the *significance* which certain segments of that infinite multiplicity which we call "commerce" have for culture. We seek knowledge of an historical phenomenon, meaning by historical: significant in its individuality (*Eigenart*). And the decisive element in this is that only through the presupposition that a finite part alone of the infinite variety of phenomena is significant, does the knowledge of an individual phenomenon become logically meaningful. Even with the widest imaginable knowledge of "laws," we are helpless in the face of the question: how is the *causal explanation* of an *individual* fact possible — since a *description* of even the smallest slice of reality can never be exhaustive? The number and type of causes which have influenced any given event are always infinite and there is nothing in the things themselves to set some of them apart as alone meriting attention. A chaos of "existential judgments" about countless individual events would be the only result of a serious attempt to analyze reality "without presuppositions." And even this result is only seemingly possible, since every single perception discloses on closer examination an infinite number of constituent perceptions which can never be exhaustively expressed in a judgement. Order is brought into this chaos only on the condition that in every case only a *part* of concrete reality is interesting and *significant* to us, because only it is related to the *cultural values* with which we approach reality. Only certain sides of the infinitely complex concrete phenomenon, namely those to which we attribute a general *cultural significance* — are therefore worthwhile knowing. They alone are objects of causal explanation. And even this causal explanation evinces the same character; an *exhaustive* causal investigation of any concrete phenomena in its full reality is not only practically impossible — it is simply nonsense. We select only those causes to which are to be imputed in the invidiual case, the "essential" feature of an event. Where the *individuality* of a phenomenon is concerned, the question of causality is not a question of *laws* but of concrete causal *relationships;* it is not a question of the subsumption of the event under some general rubric as a representative case but of its imputation as a consequence of some constellation. It is in brief a *question of imputation*. Wherever the causal explanation of a "cultural phenomenon — an "historical individual"[2] is under consideration, the knowledge of causal *laws* is not the *end* of the investigation but only a *means*. It facilitates and renders possible the causal imputation to their concrete causes of those components of a phenomenon the individuality of which is culturally significant. So far and only so far as it achieves this, is it valuable for our knowledge of concrete relationships. And the more "general," i.e., the more abstract the laws, the less they can contribute to the causal imputation of *individual* phenomena and, more indirectly, to the understanding of the significance of cultural events .

What is the consequence of all this?

Naturally, it does not imply that the knowledge of *universal* propositions, the construction of abstract concepts, the knowledge of regularities and the attempt to formulate *"laws"* have no scientific justification in the cultural sciences. Quite the contrary, if the causal knowledge of the historians consists of the imputation of concrete effects to concrete causes, a *valid* imputation of any individual effect without the application of *"nomological"* knowledge — i.e., the knowledge of recurrent causal sequences — would in general be impossible. Whether a single individual component of a relationship is, in a concrete case, to be assigned causal responsibility for an effect, the causal explanation of which is at issue, can in doubtful cases be determined only by estimating the effects which we *generally* expect from it and from the other components of the same complex which are relevant to the explanation. In other words, the *"adequate"* effects of the causal elements involved must be considered in arriving at any such conclusion. The extent to which the historian (in the widest sense of the word) can perform this imputation in a reasonably certain manner with his imagination sharpened by personal experience and trained in analytic methods and the extent to which he must have recourse to the aid of special disciplines which make it possible, varies

---

[2] We will use the term which is already occasionally used in the methodology of our discipline and which is now becoming widespread in a more precise forumlation in logic.

with the individual case. Everywhere, however, and hence also in the sphere of complicated economic processes, the more certain and the more comprehensive our general knowledge the greater is the *certainty* of imputation. This proposition is not in the least affected by the fact that even in the case of all so-called "economic laws" without exception, we are concerned here not with "laws" in the narrower exact natural science sense, but with *adequate* causal relationships expressed in rules and with the application of the category of "objective possibility." The establishment of such regularities is not the *end* but rather the *means* of knowledge. It is entirely a question of expediency, to be settled separately for each individual case, whether a regularly recurrent causal relationship of everyday experience should be formulated into a "law." Laws are important and valuable in the exact natural sciences, in the measure that those sciences are *universally valid*. For the knowledge of historical phenomena in their concreteness, the most general laws, because they are most devoid of content are also the least valuable. The more comprehensive the validity, — or scope — of a term, the more it leads us away from the richness of reality since in order to include the common elements of the largest possible number of phenomena, it must necessarily be as abstract as possible and hence *devoid* of content. In the cultural sciences, the knowledge of the universal or general is never valuable in itself.

The conclusion which follows from the above is that an "objective" analysis of cultural events, which proceeds according to the thesis that the ideal of science is the reduction of empirical reality of "laws," is meaningless. It is not meaningless, as is often maintained, because cultural or psychic events for instance are "objectively" less governed by laws. It is meaningless for a number of other reasons. Firstly, because the knowledge of social laws is not knowledge of social reality but is rather one of the various aids used by our minds for attaining this end; secondly, because knowledge of *cultural* events is inconceivable except on a basis of the *significance* which the concrete constellations of reality have for us in certain *individual* concrete situations. In *which* sense and in *which* situations this is the case is not revealed to us by any law; it is decided according to the *value-ideas* in the light of which we view "culture" in each individual case. "Culture" is a finite segment of the meaningless in-finity of the world process, a segment on which *human beings* confer meaning and significance. This is true even for the human being who views a *particular* culture as a mortal enemy and who seeks to "return to nature." He can attain this point of view only after view-ing the culture in which he lives from the standpoint of his values, and finding it "too soft." This is the purely logical-formal fact which is involved when we speak of the logically necessary rootedness of all historical entities (*historische Individuen*) in "evaluative ideas." The transcendental presupposition of every *cultural science* lies not in our finding a certain culture or any "culture" in general to be *valuable* but rather in the fact that we are *cultural beings,* en-dowed with the capacity and the will to take a deliberate attitude towards the world and to lend it *significance*. Whatever this signifi-cance may be, it will lead us to judge certain phenomena of human existence in its light and to respond to them as being (positively or negatively) meaningful. Whatever may be the content of this attitude — these phenomena have cultural significance for us and on this significance alone rests its scientific interest. Thus when we speak here of the conditioning of cultural knowledge through *evaluative* ideas (*Wertideen*) (following the terminology of modern logic), it is done in the hope that we will not be subject to crude misunderstandings such as the opinion that cultural significance should be attributed only to *valuable* phenomena. Prostitution is a *cultural* phenomenon just as much as religion or money. All three are cultural phenomena *only* because and *only* insofar as their exist-ence and the form which they historically assume touch directly or indirectly on our cultural *interests* and arouse our striving for knowl-edge concerning problems brought into focus by the evaluative ideas which give *significance* to the fragment of reality analyzed by those concepts.

All knowledge of cultural reality, as may be seen, is always knowl-edge from *particular points of view*. When we require from the his-torian and social research worker as an elementary presupposition that they distinguish the important from the trivial and that he should have the necessary "point of view" for this distinction, we mean that they must understand how to relate the events of the real world consciously or unconsciously to universal "cultural values" and to select out those relationships which are significant for us. If the notion that those standpoints can be derived from the "facts themselves" continually recurs, it is due to the naive self-deception of the specialist who is unaware that it is due to the evaluative ideas with which he unconsciously approaches his subject matter, that he has selected from an absolute infinity a tiny portion with the study of which he *concerns* himself. In connection with this selection of individual special "aspects" of the event which always and everywhere occurs, consciously or unconsciously, there also occurs that element of cultural-scientific work which is referred to by the often-heard assertion that the "personal" element of a scientific work is what is really valuable in it, and that personality must be expressed in every work if it existence is to be justified. To be sure, without the investigator's evaluative ideas, there would be no principle of selection of subject-matter and no meaningful knowledge of the concrete reality. Just as without the investigator's conviction regarding the significance of particular cultural facts, every attempt to analyze concrete reality is absolutely meaningless, so the direction of his personal belief, the refraction of values in the prism of his mind, gives direction to his work. And the values to which the scientific genius relates the object of his inquiry may determine, i.e., decide the "conception" of a whole epoch, not only concerning what is regarded as "valuable" but also concerning what is significant or insignificant, "important" or "unimportant" in the phenomena.

Accordingly, cultural science in our sense involves "subjective" presuppositions insofar as it concerns itself only with those components of reality which have some relationship, however indirect, to events to which we attach cultural *significance*. Nonetheless, it is entirely *causal* knowledge exactly in the same sense as the knowledge of significant concrete (*individueller*) natural events which have a qualitative character. Among the many confusions which the overreaching tendency of a formal-juristic outlook has brought about in the cultural sciences, there has recently appeared the attempt to "refute" the "materialistic conception of history" by a series of clever but fallacious arguments which state that since all economic life must take place in legally or conventionally *regulated forms,* all economic "development" must take the form of striving for the creation of new *legal* forms. Hence, it is said to be intelligible only through ethical maxims and is on this account essentially different from every type of "natural" development. Accordingly the knowledge of economic development is said to be "teleological" in character. Without wishing to discuss the meaning of the ambiguous term "development," or the logically no less ambiguous term "teleology" in the social sciences, it should be stated that such knowledge need not be "teleological" in the sense assumed by this point of view. The cultural significance of normatively regulated legal *relations* and even norms themselves can undergo fundamental revolutionary changes even under conditions of the formal identity of the prevailing legal norms. Indeed, if one wishes to lose one's self for a moment in phantasies about the future, one might theoretically imagine, let us say, the "socialization of the means of production" unaccompanied by any conscious "striving" towards this result, and without even the disappearance or addition of a single paragraph of our legal code; the statistical frequency of certain legally regulated relationships might be changed fundamentally, and in many cases, even disappear entirely; a great number of legal norms might become *practically* meaningless and their whole cultural significance changed beyond identification. *De lege ferenda* discussions may be justifiably disregarded by the "materialistic conception of history" since its central proposition is the indeed inevitable change in the *significance* of legal institutions. Those who view the painstaking labor of causally understanding historical reality as of secondary importance can disregard it, but it is impossible to supplant it by any type of "teleology." From our viewpoint, "purpose" is the conception of an *effect* which becomes a *cause* of an action. Since we take into account every cause which produces or can produce a significant effect, we also consider this one. Its specific significance consists only in the fact that we not only *observe* human conduct but can and desire to understand it.

Undoubtedly, all evaluative ideas are "subjective." Between the "historical" interest in a family chronicle and that in the development of the greatest conceivable cultural phenomena which were and are common to a nation or to mankind over long epochs, there exists an infinite gradation of "significance" arranged into an order which differs for each of us. And they are, naturally, historically variable in accordance with the character of the culture and the ideas which rule men's minds. But it obviously does not follow from this that research in the cultural sciences can only have results which are "subjective" in the sense that they are *valid* for one person and not for others. Only the degree to which they interest different persons varies. In other words, the choice of the object of investigation and the extent or depth to which this investigation attempts to penetrate into the infinite causal web, are determined by the evaluative ideas which dominate the investigator and his age. In the *method* of investigation, the guiding "point of view" is of great importance for the *construction* of the conceptual scheme which will be used in the investigation. In the mode of their *use,* however, the investigator is obviously bound by the norms of our thought just as much here as elsewhere. For scientific truth is precisely what is *valid* for all who *seek* the truth.

However, there emerges from this the meaninglessness of the idea which prevails occasionally even among historians, namely, that the goal of the cultural sciences, however far it may be from realization, is to construct a closed system of concepts, in which reality is synthesized in some sort of *permanently* and *universally* valid classification and from which it can again be deduced. The stream of immeasurable events flows unendingly towards eternity. The cultural problems which move men form themselves ever anew and in different colors, and the boundaries of that area in the infinite stream of concrete events which acquires meaning and significance for us, i.e., which becomes an "historical individual," are constantly subject to change. The intellectual contexts from which it is viewed and scientifically analyzed shift. The points of departure of the cultural sciences remain changeable throughout the limitless future as long as a Chinese ossification of intellectual life does not render mankind incapable of setting new questions to the eternally inexhaustible flow of life. A systematic science of culture, even only in the sense of a definitive, objectively valid, systematic fixation of the problems which it should treat, would be senseless in itself. Such an attempt could only produce a collection of numerous, specifically particularized, heterogeneous and disparate viewpoints in the light of which reality becomes "culture" through being significant in its unique character.

Having now completed this lengthy discussion, we can finally turn to the question which is *methodologically* relevant in the consideration of the "objectivity" of cultural knowledge. The question is: what is the logical function and structure of the *concepts* which our science, like all others, uses? Restated with special reference to the decisive problem, the question is: what is the significance of *theory* and theoretical conceptualization (*theoretische Begriffsbildung*) for our knowledge of cultural reality?

Economics was originally — as we have already seen — a "technique," at least in the central focus of its attention. By this we mean that it viewed reality from an at least ostensibly unambiguous and stable practical evaluative standpoint: namely, the increase of the "wealth" of the population. It was on the other hand, from the very beginning, more than a "technique" since it was integrated into the great scheme of the natural law and rationalistic *Weltanschauung* of the eighteenth century. The nature of that *Weltanschauung* with its optimistic faith in the theoretical and practical rationalizability of reality had an important consequence insofar as it *obstructed* the discovery of the *problematic* character of that standpoint which had been assumed as self-evident. As the rational analysis of society arose in close connection with the modern development of natural science, so it remained related to it in its whole method of approach. In the natural sciences, the practical evaluative attitude toward what was immediately and technically useful was closely associated from the very first with the hope, taken over as a heritage of antiquity and further elaborated, of attaining a purely "objective" (i.e., independent of all individual contingencies) monistic knowledge of the totality of reality in a *conceptual* system of metaphysical *validity* and mathematical *form*. It was thought that this hope could be realized by the method of generalizing abstraction and the formulation of laws based on empirical analysis. The natural sciences which were bound to evaluative standpoints, such as clinical medicine and even more what is conventionally called "technology" became purely practical "arts." The values for which they strove, e.g., the health of the patient, the technical perfection of a concrete productive process, etc., were fixed for the time being for all of them. The methods which they used could only consist in the application of the laws formulated by the theoretical disciplines. Every theoretical advance in the construction of these laws was or could also be an advance for the practical disciplines. With the end given, the progressive reduction of concrete practical questions (e.g., a case of illness, a technical problem, etc.) to special cases of generally valid laws, meant that extension of theoretical knowledge was closely associated and identical with the extension of technical-practical possibilities.

When modern biology subsumed those aspects of reality which interest us *historically*, i.e., in all their concreteness, under a universally valid evolutionary principle, which at least had the appearance — but not the actuality — of embracing everything essential about the subject ·in a scheme of universally valid laws, this seemed to be the final twilight of all evaluative standpoints in all the sciences. For since the so-called historical event was a segment of the totality of reality, since the principle of causality which was the presupposition of all scientific work, seemed to require the analysis of all events into generally valid "laws," and in view of the overwhelming success of the natural sciences which took this idea seriously, it appeared as if there was in general no conceivable meaning of scientific work other than the discovery of the *laws* of events. Only those aspects of phenomena which were involved in the "laws" could be essential from the scientific point of view, and concrete "individual" events could be considered only as "types," i.e., as representative illustrations of laws. An interest in such events in themselves did not seem to be a "scientific" interest.

It is impossible to trace here the important repercussions of this will-to-believe of naturalistic monism in economics. When socialist criticism and the work of the historians were beginning to transform the original evaluative standpoints, the vigorous development of zoological research on one hand and the influence of Hegelian panlogism on the other prevented economics from attaining a clear and full understanding of the relationship between concept and reality. The result, to the extent that we are interested in it, is that despite the powerful resistance to the infiltration of naturalistic dogma due to

German idealism since Fichte and the achievement of the German Historical School in law and economics and partly because of the very work of the Historical School, the naturalistic viewpoint in certain decisive problems has not yet been overcome. Among these problems we find the relationship between "theory" and "history," which is still problematic in our discipline.

The "abstract"-theoretical method even today shows unmediated and ostensibly irreconcilable cleavage from empirical-historical research. The proponents of this method recognize in a thoroughly correct way the methodological impossibility of supplanting the historical knowledge of reality by the formulation of laws or, vice versa, of constructing "laws" in the rigorous sense through the mere juxtaposition of historical observations. Now in order to arrive at these laws — for they are certain that science should be directed towards these as its highest goal — they take it to be a fact that we always have a direct awareness of the structure of human actions in all their reality. Hence — so they think — science can make human behavior directly intelligible with axiomatic evidentness and accordingly reveal its laws. The only exact form of knowledge — the formulation of immediately and intuitively *evident* laws — is however at the same time the only one which offers access to events which have not been directly observed. Hence, at least as regards the fundamental phenomena of economic life, the construction of a system of abstract and therefore purely formal propositions analogous to those of the exact natural sciences, is the only means of analyzing and intellectually mastering the complexity of social life. In spite of the fundamental methodological distinction between historical knowledge and the knowledge of "laws" which the creator of the theory drew as the *first* and *only* one, he now claims empirical *validity*, in the sense of the *deducibility* of reality from "laws," for the propositions of abstract theory. It is true that this is not meant in the sense of empirical validity of the abstract economic laws as such, but in the sense that when equally "exact" theories have been constructed for all the other relevant factors, all these abstract theories together must contain the true reality of the object — i.e., whatever is worthwhile knowing about it. Exact economic theory deals with the operation of *one* psychic motive, the other theories have as their task the formulation of the behavior of all the other motives into similar sorts of propositions enjoying hypothetical validity. Accordingly, the fantastic claim has occasionally been made for economic theories — e.g., the abstract theories of price, interest, rent, etc., — that they can, by ostensibly following the analogy of physical science propositions, be validly applied to the derivation of quantitatively stated conclusions from given real premises, since given the ends, economic behavior with respect to means is unambiguously "determined." This claim fails to observe that in order to be able to reach this result even in the simplest case, the totality of the existing historical reality including every one of its causal relationships must be assumed as "given" and presupposed as known. But if *this* type of knowledge were accessible to the finite mind of man, abstract theory would have no cognitive value whatsoever. The naturalistic prejudice that every concept in the cultural sciences should be similar to those in the exact natural sciences has led in consequence to the misunderstanding of the meaning of this theoretical construction (*theoretische Gedankengebilde*). It has been believed that is is a matter of the psychological isolation of a specific "impulse," the acquisitive impulse, or of the isolated study of a specific maxim of human conduct, the so-called economic principle. Abstract theory purported to be based on psychological *axioms* and as a result historians have called for an *empirical* psychology in order to show the invalidity of those axioms and to derive the course of economic events from psychological principles. We do not wish at this point to enter into a detailed criticism of the belief in the significance of a —still to be created — systematic science of "social psychology" as the future foundation of the cultural sciences, and particularly of social economics. Indeed, the partly brilliant attempts which have been made hitherto to interpret economic phenomena psychologically, show in any case that the procedure does not begin with the analysis of psychological qualities, moving then to the analysis of social institutions, but that, on the contrary, insight into the psychological preconditions and consequences of institutions presupposes a precise knowledge of the latter and the scientific analysis of their structure. In concrete cases, psychological analysis can contribute then an extremely valuable deepening of the knowledge of the historical cultural *conditioning* and cultural *significance* of institutions. The interesting aspect of the psychic attitude of a person in a social situation is specifically particularized in each case, according to the special cultural significance of the situation in question. It is a question of an extremely heterogeneous and highly concrete structure of psychic motives and influences. Social-psychological research involves the study of various very disparate *individual* types of cultural elements with reference to their interpretability by our empathic understanding. Through social-psychological research, with the knowledge of individual institutions as a point of departure, we will learn increasingly how to understand institutions in a psychological way. We will not however deduce the institutions from psychological laws or explain them by elementary psychological phenomena.

Thus, the far-flung polemic, which centered on the question of the psychological justification of abstract theoretical propositions, on the scope of the "acquisitive impulse" and the "economic principle," etc., turns out to have been fruitless.

In the establishment of the propositions of abstract theory, it is only apparently a matter of "deductions" from fundamental psychological motives. Actually, the former are a special case of a kind of concept-construction which is peculiar and to a certain extent, indispensable, to the cultural sciences. It is worthwhile at this point to describe it in further detail since we can thereby approach more closely the fundamental question of the significance of theory in the social sciences. Therewith we leave undiscussed, once and for all, whether *the* particular analytical concepts which we cite or to which we allude as illustrations, correspond to the purposes they are to serve, i.e., whether in fact they are well-adapted. The question as to how far, for example, contemporary "abstract theory" should be further elaborated, is ultimately also a question of the strategy of science, which must, however concern itself with other problems as well. Even the "theory of marginal utility" is subsumable under a "law of marginal utility."

We have in abstract economic theory an illustration of those synthetic constructs which have been designated as *"ideas"* of historical phenomena. It offers us an ideal picture of events on the commodity-market under conditions of a society organized on the principles of an exchange economy, free competition and rigorously rational conduct. This conceptual pattern brings together certain relationships and events of historical life into a complex, which is conceived as an internally consistent system. Substantively, this construct in itself is like a *utopia* which has been arrived at by the analytical accentuation of certain elements of reality. Its relationship to the empirical data consists solely in the fact that where market-conditioned relationships of the type referred to by the abstract construct are discovered or suspected to exist in reality to some extent, we can make the *characteristic* features of this relationship pragmatically *clear* and *understandable* by reference to an *ideal-type*. This procedure can be indispensable for heuristic as well as expository purposes. The ideal typical concept will help to develop our skill in imputation in *research*: it *is* no "hypothesis" but it offers guidance to the construction of hypotheses. It is not a *description* of reality but it aims to give unambiguous means of expression to such a description. It is thus the "idea" of the *historically* given modern society, based on an exchange economy, which is developed for us by quite the same logical principles as are used in constructing the idea of the medieval "city economy" as a "genetic" concept. When we do this, we construct the concept "city economy" not as an average of the economic structures actually existing in all the cities observed but as an *ideal-type*. An ideal type is formed by the one-sided *accentuation* of one or more points of view and by the synthesis of a great many diffuse, discrete, more or less present and occasionally absent *concrete individual* phenomena, which are arranged according to those one-sidedly emphasized viewpoints into a unified *analytical* construct (*Gedankenbild*). In its conceptual purity, this mental construct (*Gedankenbild*) cannot be found empirically anywhere in reality. It is a *utopia*. Historical research faces the task of determining in each individual case, the extent to which this ideal-construct approximates to or diverges from reality, to what extent for example, the economic structure of a certain city is to be classified as a "city-economy." When carefully applied, those concepts are particularly useful in research and exposition. In very much the same way one can work the "idea" of "handicraft" into a utopia by arranging certain traits, actually found in an unclear, confused state in the industrial enterprises of the most diverse epochs and countries, into a consistent ideal-construct by an accentuation of their essential tendencies. This ideal-type is then related to the idea (*Gedankenausdruck*) which one finds expressed there. One can further delineate a society in which all branches of economic and even intellectual activity are governed by maxims which appear to be applications of the same principle which charactrizes the ideal-typical "handicraft" system. Furthermore, one can juxtapose alongside the ideal typical "handicraft" system the antithesis of a correspondingly ideal-typical capitalistic productive system, which has been abstracted out of certain features of modern large scale industry. On the basis of this, one can delineate the utopia of a "capitalistic" culture, i.e., one in which the governing principle is the investment of private capital. This procedure would accentuate certain individual concretely diverse traits of modern material and intellectual culture in its unique aspects into an ideal construct which from our point of view would be completely self-consistent. This would then be the delineation of an *"idea"* of *capitalistic culture*. We must disregard for the moment whether and how this procedure could be carried out. It is possible, or rather, it must be accepted as certain that numerous, indeed a very great many, utopias of this sort can be worked out, of which *none* is like another, and *none* of which can be observed in empirical reality as an actually existing economic system, but *each* of which however claims that it is a representation of the "idea" of capitalistic culture. *Each* of these can claim to be a representation of the "idea" of capitalistic culture to the extent that it has really taken certain traits, meaningful in their essential features, from the empirical reality of our culture and brought them together into a unified ideal-construct. For those phenomena which interest us as cultural phenomena are interesting to us with respect to very different kinds of evaluative ideas to which we relate them. Inasmuch as the "points of view" from which they can become significant for us are very diverse, the most varied criteria can be applied to the selection of the traits which are to enter into the construction of an ideal-typical view of a particular culture.

What is the significance of such ideal-typical constructs for an *empirical* science, as we wish to constitute it? Before going any further, we should emphasize that the idea of an ethical *imperative*, of a "model" of what "ought" to exist is to be carefully distinguished from the analytical construct, which is "ideal" in the strictly logical sense of the term. It is a matter here of constructing relationships which our imagination accepts as plausibly motivated and hence as "objectively possible" and which appear as *adequate* from the nomological standpoint.

Whoever accepts the proposition that the knowledge of historical reality can or should be a "presuppositionless" copy of "objective" facts, will deny the value of the ideal-type. Even those who recognize that there is no "presuppositionlessness" in the logical sense and that even the simplest excerpt from a statute or from a documentary source can have scientific meaning only with reference to "significance" and ultimately to evaluative ideas, will more or less regard the construction of any such historical "utopias" as an expository device which endangers the autonomy of historical research and which is, in any case, a vain sport. And, in fact, *whether* we are dealing simply with a conceptual game or with a scientifically fruitful method of conceptualization and *theory*-construction can never be decided a *priori*. Here, too, there is only one criterion, namely, that of success in revealing concrete cultural phenomena in their interdependence, their causal conditions and their *significance*. The construction of abstract ideal-types recommends itself not as an end but as a *means*. Every conscientious examination of the conceptual elements of historical exposition shows however that the historian as soon as he attempts to go beyond the bare establishment of concrete relationships and to determine the *cultural* significance of even the simplest individual event in order to "characterize" it, *must* use concepts which are precisely and unambiguously definable only in the form of ideal types. Or are concepts such as "individualism," "imperialism," "feudalism," "mercantilism," "conventional," etc., and innumerable concepts of like character by means of which we seek analytically and empathically to understand reality constructed substantively by the "presuppositionless" *description* of some concrete phenomenon or through the abstract synthesis of those traits which are *common* to numerous concrete phenomena? Hundreds of words in the historian's vocabulary are ambiguous constructs created to meet the unconsciously felt need for adequate expression and the meaning of which is only concretely felt but not clearly thought out. In a great many cases, particularly in the field of descriptive political history, their ambiguity has not been prejudicial to the clarity of the presentation. It is sufficient that in each case the reader should *feel* what the historian had in mind; or, one can content one's self with the idea that the author used a *particular* meaning of the concept with special reference to the concrete case at hand. The greater the need however for a sharp appreciation of the significance of a cultural phenomenon, the more imperative is the need to operate with unambiguous concepts which are not only particularly but also systematically defined. A "definition" of such synthetic historical terms according to the scheme of *genus proximum* and *differentia specifica* is naturally nonsense. But let us consider it. Such a form of the establishment of the meanings of words is to be found only in axiomatic disciplines which use syllogisms. A simple "descriptive analysis" of these concepts into their components either does not exist or else exists only illusorily, for the question arises, as to *which* of these components should be regarded as essential. When a genetic definition of the content of the concept is sought, there remains only the ideal-type in the sense explained above. It is a conceptual construct (*Gedankenbild*) which is neither historical reality nor even the "true" reality. It is even less fitted to serve as a schema under which a real situation or action is to be subsumed as one *instance*. It has the significance of a purely ideal *limiting* concept with which the real situation or action is *compared* and surveyed for the explication of certain of its significant components. Such concepts are constructs in terms of which we formulate relationships by the application of the category of objective possibility. By means of this category, the adequacy of our imagination, oriented and disciplined by reality, is *judged*.

In this function especially, the ideal-type is an attempt to analyze historically unique configurations or their individual components by means of genetic concepts. Let us take for instance the concepts "church" and "sect." They may be broken down purely classificatorily into complexes of characteristics whereby not only the distinction between them but also the content of the concept must constantly remain fluid. If however I wish to formulate the concept of "sect" genetically, e.g., with reference to certain important cultural significances which the "sectarian spirit" has had for modern culture, certain characteristics of both become *essential* because they stand in an adequate causal relationship to those influences. However, the concepts thereupon become ideal-typical in the sense that they appear in full conceptual *integrity* either not at all or only in individual instances. Here as elsewhere every concept which is not purely classificatory diverges from reality. But the discursive nature of our knowledge, i.e., the fact that we comprehend reality only through a chain of intellectual modifications postulates such a conceptual shorthand. Our imagination can often dispense with explicit conceptual formulations as a means of *investigation*. But as regards exposition, to the extent that it wishes to be unambiguous, the use of precise formulations in the sphere of cultural analysis is in many cases absolutely necessary. Whoever disregards it entirely must confine himself to the formal aspect of cultural phenomena, e.g., to legal history. The universe of legal norms is naturally clearly definable and is valid (in the *legal* sense!) for historical reality. But social science in our sense is concerned with practical *significance*. This significance however can very often be brought unambiguously to mind only by relating the empirical data to an ideal limiting case. If the historian (in the widest sense of the word) rejects an attempt to construct such ideal types as a "theoretical construction," i.e., as useless or dispensable for his concrete heuristic purposes, the inevitable consequence is either that he consciously or unconsciously uses other similar concepts without formulating them verbally and elaborating them logically or that he remains stuck in the realm of the vaguely "felt."

Nothing, however, is more dangerous than the *confusion* of theory and history stemming from naturalistic prejudices. This confusion expresses itself firstly in the belief that the "true" content and the essence of historical reality is portrayed in such theoretical constructs or secondly, in the use of these constructs as a procrustean bed into which history is to be forced or thirdly, in the hypostatization of such "ideas" as real "forces" and as a "true" reality which operates behind the passage of events and which works itself out in history.

This latter danger is especially great since we are also, indeed primarily, accustomed to understand by the "ideas" of an epoch the thoughts or ideals which dominated the mass or at least an historically decisive number of the persons living in that epoch itself, and who were therefore significant as components of its culture. Now there are two aspects to this: in the first place, there are certain relationships between the "idea" in the sense of a tendency of practical or theoretical thought and the "idea" in the sense of the ideal-*typical* portrayal of an epoch constructed as a heuristic device. An ideal type of certain situations, which can be abstracted from certain characteristic social phenomena of an epoch, might — and this is indeed quite often the case — have also been present in the minds of the persons living in that epoch as an ideal to be striven for in practical life or as a maxim for the regulation of certain social relationships. This is true of the "idea" of "provision" (*Nahrungsschutz*) and many other Canonist doctrines, especially those of Thomas Aquinas, in relationship to the modern ideal type of medieval "city economy" which we discussed above. The same is also true of the much talked of "basic concept" of economics: economic "value." From Scholasticism to Marxism, the idea of an objectively "valid" value, i.e., of an *ethical imperative* was amalgamated with an abstraction drawn from the empirical process of price formation. The notion that the "value" of commodities should be regulated by certain principles of natural law, has had and still has immeasurable significance for the development of culture — and not merely the culture of the Middle Ages. It has also influenced actual price formation very markedly. But what was meant and what can be meant by that *theoretical* concept can be made unambiguously clear *only* through precise, ideal-typical constructs. Those who are so contemptuous of the "Robinsonades" of classical theory should restrain themselves if they are unable to replace them with better concepts, which in this context means clearer concepts.

Thus the causal relationship between the historically determinable idea which governs the conduct of men and those components of historical reality from which their corresponding ideal-*type* may be abstracted, can naturally take on a considerable number of different forms. The main point to be observed is that in *principle* they are both fundamentally different things. There is still another aspect: those "ideas" which govern the behavior of the population of a certain epoch i.e., which are concretely influential in determining their conduct, can, if a somewhat complicated construct is involved, be formulated precisely only in the form of an ideal type, since empirically it exists in the minds of an indefinite and constantly changing mass of individuals and assumes in their minds the most multifarious nuances of form and content, clarity and meaning. Those elements of the spiritual life of the individuals living in a certain epoch of the Middle Ages, for example, which we may designate as the "Christianity" of those individuals, would, if they could be completely portrayed, naturally constitute a chaos of infinitely differentiated and highly contradictory complexes of ideas and feelings. This is true despite the fact that the medieval church was certainly able to bring about a unity of belief and conduct to a particularly high degree. If we raise the question as to what in this chaos was the "Christianity" of the Middle Ages (which we must nonetheless use as a stable concept) and wherein lay those "Christian" elements which we find in the institutions of the Middle Ages, we see that here too in every individual case, we are applying a purely analytical construct created by ourselves. It is a combination of articles of faith, norms from church law and custom, maxims of conduct, and countless concrete interrelationships which we have fused into an "idea." It is a synthesis which we could not succeed in attaining with consistency without the application of ideal-type concepts.

The relationship between the logical structure of the conceptual system in which we present such "ideas" and what is immediately given in empirical reality naturally varies considerably. It is relatively simple in cases in which one or a few easily formulated theoretical main principles as for instance Calvin's doctrine of predestination or clearly definable ethical postulates govern human conduct and produce historical effects, so that we can analyze the "idea" into a hierarchy of ideas which can be logically derived from those theses. It is of course easily overlooked that however important the significance even of the purely logically persuasive force of ideas — Marxism is an outstanding example of this type of force — nonetheless empirical-historical events occurring in men's minds must be understood as primarily *psychologically* and not logically conditioned. The ideal-typical character of such syntheses of historically effective ideas is revealed still more clearly when those fundamental main principles and postulates no longer survive in the minds of those individuals who are still dominated by ideas which were logically or associatively derived from them because the "idea" which was historically and originally fundamental has either died out or has in general achieved wide diffusion only for its broadest implications. The basic fact that the synthesis is an "idea" which *we* have created emerges even more markedly when those fundamental main principles have either only very imperfectly or not at all been raised to the level of explicit consciousness or at least have not taken the form of explicitly elaborated complexes of ideas. When we adopt this procedure, as it very often happens and must happen, we are concerned in these ideas, e.g., the "liberalism" of a certain period or "Methodism" or some intellectually unelaborated variety of "socialism," with a *pure* ideal type of much the same character as the synthetic "principles" of economic epochs in which we had our point of departure. The more inclusive the relationships to be presented, and the more many-sided their cultural *significance* has been, the *more* their comprehensive systematic exposition in a conceptual system approximates the character of an ideal type, and the less is it possible to operate with *one* such concept. In such situations the frequently repeated attempts to discover ever *new* aspects of significance by the construction of new ideal-typical concepts is all the more natural and unavoidable. All expositions for example of the "essence" of Christianity are ideal types enjoying only a necessarily very relative and problematic validity when they are intended to be regarded as the historical portrayal of empirically existing facts. On the other hand, such presentations are of great value for research and of high systematic value for expository purposes when they are used as conceptual instruments for *comparison* with and the *measurement* of reality. They are indispensable for this purpose.

There is still another even more complicated significance implicit in such ideal-typical presentations. They regularly seek to be, or are unconsciously, ideal-types not only in the *logical* sense but also in the *practical* sense, i.e., they are *model types* which — in our illustration — contain what, from the point of view of the expositor, *should* be and what *to him* is "essential" in Christianity *because it is enduringly valuable.* If this is consciously or — as it is more frequently — unconsciously the case, they contain ideals *to* which the expositor *evaluatively* relates Christianity. These ideals are tasks and ends towards which he orients his "idea" of Christianity and which naturally can and indeed doubtless always will differ greatly from the values which other persons, for instance, the early Christians, connected with Christianity. In this sense, however, the "ideas" are naturally no longer purely *logical* auxiliary devices, no longer concepts with which reality is compared, but ideals by which it is evaluatively *judged.* Here it is no longer a matter of the purely theoretical procedure of treating empirical reality with respect to values but of *value-judgments* which are integrated into the concept of *"Christianity."* Because the ideal type claims empirical *validity* here, it penetrates into the realm of the evaluative *interpretation* of Christianity. The sphere of empirical science has been left behind and we are confronted with a profession of faith, not an ideal-typical construct. As fundamental as this distinction is in principle, the confusion of these two basically different meanings of the term "idea" appears with extraordinary frequency in historical writings. It is always close at hand whenever the descriptive historian begins to develop his "conception" of a personality or an epoch. In contrast with the fixed ethical standards which Schlosser applied in the spirit of rationalism, the modern relativistically educated historian who on the one hand seeks to "understand" the epoch of which he speaks "in its own terms," and on the other still seeks to "judge" it, feels the need to derive the standards for his judgment from the subject-matter itself, i.e., to allow the "idea" in the sense of the *ideal* to emerge from the "idea" in the sense of the "ideal-type." The esthetic satisfaction produced by such a procedure constantly tempts him to disregard the line where these two ideal types diverge — an error which on the one hand hampers the value-judgment and on the other, strives to free itself from the responsibility for its own judgment. In contrast with this, the *elementary duty of scientific self-control* and the only way to avoid serious and foolish blunders requires a sharp, precise distinction between the logically *comparative* analysis of reality by ideal-*types* in the logical sense and the *value-judgment* of reality *on the basis of ideals.* An "ideal type" in our sense, to repeat once more, has no connection at all with *value-judgments,* and it has nothing to do with any type of perfection other than a purely *logical* one. There are ideal types of brothels as well as of religions; there are also ideal types of those kinds of brothels which are technically "expedient" from the point of view of police ethics as well as those of which the exact opposite is the case.

It is necessary for us to forego here a detailed discussion of the case which is by far the most complicated and most interesting, namely, the problem of the logical structure of the *concept of the state*. The following however should be noted: when we inquire as to what corresponds to the idea of the "state" in empirical reality, we find an infinity of diffuse and discrete human actions, both active and passive, factually and legally regulated relationships, partly unique and partly recurrent in character, all bound together by an idea, namely, the belief in the actual or normative validity of rules and of the authority-relationships of some human beings towards others. This belief is in par consciously, in part dimly felt, and in part passively accepted by persons who, should they think about the "idea" in a really clearly defined manner, would not first need a "general theory of the state" which aims to articulate the idea. The scientific conception of the state, however it is formulated, is naturally always a synthesis which we construct for certain heuristic purposes. But on the other hand, it is also abstracted from the unclear syntheses which are found in the minds of human beings. The concrete content, however, which the historical "state" assumes in those syntheses in the minds of those who make up the state, can in its turn only be made explicit through the use of ideal-typical concepts. Nor, furthermore, can there be the least doubt that the manner in which those syntheses are made (always in a logically imperfect form) by the members of a state, or in other words, the "ideas" which *they* construct for themselves about the state — as for example, the German "organic" metaphysics of the state in contrast with the American "business" conception, is of great practical significance. In other words, here too the *practical idea* which should be *valid* or *is believed to be valid* and the heuristically intended, theoretically ideal type approach each other very closely and constantly tend to merge with each other.

We have purposely considered the ideal type essentially — if not exclusively — as a mental construct for the scrutiny and systematic characterization of individual concrete patterns which are significant in their uniqueness, such as Christianity, capitalism, etc. We did this in order to avoid the common notion that in the sphere of cultural phenomena, the abstract *type* is identical with the abstract *kind* (*Gattungsmässigen*). This is not the case. Without being able to make here a full logical analysis of the widely discussed concept of the "typical" which has been discredited through misuse, we can state on the basis of our previous discussion that the construction of type-concepts in the sense of the exclusion of the "accidental" also has a place in the analysis of historically individual phenomena. Naturaly, however, those *generic* concepts which we constantly encounted as elements of historical analysis and of concrete historical concepts, can also be formed as ideal-types by abstracting and accentuating certain conceptually essential elements. Practically, this is indeed a particularly frequent and important instance of the application of ideal-typical concepts. Every *individual* ideal type comprises both *generic* and ideal-typically constructed conceptual *elements*. In this case too, we see the specifically logical function of ideal-typical concepts. The concept of "exchange" is for instance a simple class concept (*Gattungsbegriff*) in the sense of a complex of traits which are common to many phenomena, as long as we disregard the *meaning* of the component parts of the concept, and simply analyze the term in its everyday usage. If however we relate this concept to the concept of "marginal utility" for instance, and construct the concept of "economic exchange" as an economically rational event, this then contains as every concept of "economic exchange" does which is fully elaborated logically, a judgment concerning the "typical" *conditions* of exchange. It assumes a *genetic* character and becomes therewith ideal-typical in the logical sense, i.e., it removes itself from empirical reality which can only be compared or related to it. The same is true of all the so-called "fundamental concepts" of economics: they can be developed in genetic form only as ideal types. The distinction between simple class or generic concepts (*Gattungsbegriffe*) which merely summarize the common features of certain empirical phenomena and the quasi-generic (*Gattungsmässigen*) *ideal type* — as for instance and ideal-typical concept of the "nature" of "handicraft" — varies naturally with each concrete case. But no class or generic concept as such has a "typical" character and there is no purely generic "average" type. Wherever we speak of typical magnitudes — as for example, in statistics — we speak of something more than a mere average. The more it is a matter of the simple classification of events which appear in reality as mass phenomena, the more it is a matter of class concepts. On the other hand, the greater the event to which we conceptualize complicated historical patterns with respect to those components in which their specific *cultural significance* is contained, the greater the extent to which the concept — or system of concepts — will be ideal-typical in character. The goal of ideal-typical concept-construction is always to make clearly explicit not the class or average character but rather the unique individual character of cultural phenomena.

The fact that ideal types, even classificatory ones, can be and are applied, first acquires methodological significance in connection with another fact.

Thus far we have been dealing with ideal-types only as abstract concepts of relationships which are conceived by us as stable in the flux of events, as historically individual complexes in which developments are realized. There emerges however a complication, which reintroduces with the aid of the concept of "type" the naturalistic prejudice that the goal of the social sciences must be the reduction of reality to "laws." *Developmental* sequences too can be constructed into ideal types and these constructs can have quite considerable heuristic value. But this quite particularly gives rise to the danger that the ideal type and reality will be confused with one another. One can, for example, arrive at the theoretical conclusion that in a society which is organized on *strict* "handicraft" principles, the only source of capital accumulation can be ground rent. From this perhaps, one can — for the correctness of the construct is not in question here — construct a pure ideal picture of the shift, conditioned by certain specific factors — e.g., limited land, increasing population, influx of precious metals, rationalisation of the conduct of life — from a handicraft to a capitalistic economic organization. Whether the empirical-historical course of development was actually identical with the constructed one, can be investigated only by using this construct as a heuristic device for the comparison of the ideal type and the "facts." If the ideal type were "correctly" constructed and the actual course of events did *not* correspond to that predicted by the ideal type, the hypothesis that medieval society was *not* in certain respects a *strictly* "handicraft" type of society would be proved. And if the ideal type were constructed in a heuristically *"ideal"* way — whether and in what way this could occur in our example will be entirely disregarded here — it will guide the investigation into a path leading to a more precise understanding of the non-handicraft components of medieval society in their peculiar characteristics and their historical significance. *If* it leads to this result, it fulfils its logical purpose, even though, in doing so, it demonstrates its divergence from reality. It was — in this case — the test of an hypothesis. This procedure gives rise to no methodological doubts so long as we clearly keep in mind that ideal-typical developmental *constructs* and *history* are to be sharply distinguished from each other, and that the construct here is no more than the means for explicitly and validly imputing an historical event to its real causes while eliminating those which on the basis of our present knowledge seem possible.

The maintenance of this distinction in all its rigor often becomes uncommonly difficult in practice due to a certain circumstance. In the interest of the concrete demonstration of an ideal type or of an ideal-typical developmental sequence, one seeks to *make it clear* by the use of concrete illustrative material drawn from empirical-historical reality. The danger of this procedure which in itself is entirely legitimate lies in the fact that historical knowledge here appears as a *servant* of theory instead of the opposite role. It is a great temptation for the theorist to regard this relationship either as the normal one or, far worse, to mix theory with history and indeed to confuse them with each other. This occurs in an extreme way when an ideal construct of a developmental sequence and a conceptual classification of the ideal-types of certain cultural structures (e.g., the forms of industrial production deriving from the "closed domestic economy" or the religious concepts beginning with the "gods of the moment") are integrated into a *genetic* classification. The series of types which results from the selected conceptual criteria appears then as an historical sequence unrolling with the necessity of a law. The logical classification of analytical concepts on the one hand and the empirical arrangements of the events thus conceptualized in space, time, and causal relationship, on the other, appear to be so bound up together that there is an almost irresistible temptation to do violence to reality in order to prove the real validity of the construct.

We have intentionally avoided a demonstration with respect to that ideal-typical construct which is the most important one from our point of view; namely, the Marxian theory. This was done in order not to complicate the exposition any further through the introduction of an interpretation of Marx and in order not to anticipate the discussions in our journal which will make a regular practice of presenting critical analyses of the literature concerning and following the great thinker. We will only point out here that naturally all specifically Marxian "laws" and developmental constructs — insofar as they are theoretically sound — are ideal types. The eminent, indeed unique, *heuristic* significance of these ideal types when they are used for the *assessment* of reality is known to everyone who has ever employed Marxian concepts and hypotheses. Similarly, their perniciousness, as soon as they are thought of as empirically valid or as real (*i.e.*, truly metaphysical) "effective forces," "tendencies," etc. is likewise known to those who have used them.

Class or generic concepts (*Gattungsbegriffe*) — ideal types|— ideal-typical generic concepts — ideas in the sense of thought-patterns which actually exist in the minds of human beings — ideal types of such ideas — ideals which govern human beings — ideal types of such ideals — ideals with which the historian approaches historical facts — *theoretical* constructs using empirical data illustratively — *historical* investigations which utilize theoretical concepts as ideal limiting cases — the various possible combinations of these which could only be hinted at here; they are pure mental constructs, the relationships of which to the empirical reality of the immediately given is problematical in every individual case. This list of possibilities only reveals the infinite ramifications of the conceptual-methodological problems which face us in the sphere of the cultural sciences. We must renounce the serious discussion of the practical methodological issues the problems of which were only to be exhibited, as well as the detailed treatment of the relationships of ideal types to "laws," of ideal-typical concepts to collective concepts, etc. . .

The historian will still insist, even after all these discussions, that the prevalence of ideal-typical concepts and constructs are characteristic symptoms of the adolescence of a discipline. And in a certain sense this must be conceded, but with other conclusions than he could draw from it. Let us take a few illustrations from other disciplines. It is certainly true that the harried fourth-form boy as well as the primitive philologist first conceives of a language "organically," i.e., as a meta-empirical totality regulated by norms, but the task of linguistic science is to establish which grammatical rules should be valid. The logical elaborations of the written language, i.e., the reduction of its content to rules, as was done for instance by the *Accademia della Crusca,* is normally the first task which "philology" sets itself. When, in contrast with this, a leading philologist today declares that the subject-matter of philology is the "speech of *every individual,"* even the formulation of such a program is possible only after there is a relatively clear ideal type of the written language, which the otherwise entirely orientationless and unbounded investigation of the infinite variety of *speech* can utilize (at least tacitly). The constructs of the natural law and the organic theories of the state have exactly the same function and, to recall an ideal type in *our* sense, so does Benjamin Constant's theory of the ancient state. It serves as a harbor until one has learned to navigate safely in the vast sea of empirical facts. The coming of age of science in fact always implies the transcendance of the ideal-type, insofar as it was thought of as possessing empirical validity or as a class *concept (Gattungsbegriff)*. However, it is still legitimate today to use the brilliant Constant hypothesis to demonstrate certain aspects and historically unique features of ancient political life, as long as one carefully bears in mind its ideal-typical character. Moreover, there are sciences to which eternal youth is granted, and the historical disciplines are among them — all those to which the eternally onward flowing stream of culture perpetually brings new problems. At the very heart of their task lies not only the transciency of *all* ideal types *but* also at the same time the inevitability of *new* ones.

The attempts to determine the "real" and the "true" meaning of historical concepts always reappear and never succeed in reaching their goal. Accordingly the synthetic concepts used by historians are either imperfectly defined or, as soon as the elimination of ambiguity is sought for, the concept becomes an abstract ideal type and reveals itself therewith as a theoretical and hence "one-sided" viewpoint which illuminates the aspect of reality with which it can be related. But these concepts are shown to be obviously inappropriate as schema into which reality could be completely *integrated*. For none of those systems of ideas, which are absolutely indispensable in the understanding of those segments of reality which are meaningful at a particular moment, can exhaust its infinite richness. They are all attempts, on the basis of the present state of our knowledge and the available conceptual patterns, to bring order into the chaos of those facts which we have drawn into the field circumscribed by our *interest*. The intellectual apparatus which the past has developed through the analysis, or more truthfully, the analytical rearrangement of the immediately given reality, and through the latter's integration by concepts which correspond to the state of its knowledge and the focus of its interest, is in constant tension with the new knowledge which we can and *desire* to wrest from reality. The progress of cultural science occurs through this conflict. Its result is the perpetual reconstruction of those concepts through which we seek to comprehend reality. The history of the social sciences is and remains a continuous process passing from the attempt to order reality analytically through the construction of concepts — the dissolution of the analytical constructs so constructed through the expansion and shift of the scientific horizon — and the reformulation anew of concepts on the foundations thus transformed. It is not the error of the attempt to construct conceptual systems *in general* which is shown by this process — every science, even simple descriptive history, operates with the conceptual stock-in-trade of its time. Rather, this process shows that in the cultural sciences concept-construction depends on the setting of the problem, and the latter varies with the content of culture itself. The relationship between concept and reality in the cultural sciences involves the transitoriness of all such syntheses. The great attempts at theory-eonstruction in our science were always useful for revealing the limits of the significance of those points of view which provided their foundations. The greatest advances in the sphere of the social sciences are substantively tied up with the shift in practical cultural problems and take the guise of a critique of concept-construction. Adherence to the purpose of this critique and therewith the investigation of the *principles of syntheses* in the social sciences shall be among the primary tasks of our journal.

In the conclusions which are to be drawn from what has been said, we come to a point where perhaps our views diverge here and there from those of many, and even the most outstanding, representatives of the Historical School, among whose offspring we too are to be numbered. The latter still hold in many ways, expressly or tacitly, to the opinion that it is the end and the goal of every science to order its data into a system of concepts, the content of which is to be acquired and slowly perfected through the observation of empirical regularities, the construction of hypotheses, and their verification, until finally a "completed" and *hence* deductive science emerges. For this goal, the historical-inductive work of the present-day is a preliminary task necessitated by the imperfections of our discipline. Nothing can be more suspect, from this point of view, that the construction and application of clear-cut concepts since this seems to be an over-hasty anticipation of the remote future.

This conception was, in principle, impregnable within the framework of the classical-scholastic epistemology which was still fundamentally assumed by the majority of the research-workers identified with the Historical School. The function of concepts was assumed to be the *reproduction* of "objective" reality in the analyst's imagination. Hence the recurrent references to the *unreality* of all clear-cut concepts. If one perceives the implications of the fundamental ideas of modern epistemology which ultimately derives from Kant; namely, that concepts are primarily analytical instruments for the intellectual mastery of empirical data and can be only that, the fact that precise genetic concepts are necessarily ideal types will not cause him to desist from constructing them. The relationship between concept and historical research is reversed for those who appreciate this; the goal of the Historical School then appears as logically impossible, the concepts are not ends but are means to the end of understanding phenomena which are significant from concrete individual viewpoints.

Indeed, it is just *because* the content of historical concepts is necessarily subject to change that they must be formulated precisely and
clearly on all occasions. In their application, their character as ideal
analytical constructs should be carefully kept in mind, and the ideal-
type and historical reality should not be confused with each other. It
should be understood that since really definitive historical concepts
are not in general to be thought of as an ultimate end in view of the
inevitable shift of the guiding value-ideas, the construction of sharp
and unambiguous concepts relevant to the concrete *individual* viewpoint which directs our interest at any given time, affords the possibility of clearly realizing the *limits* of their validity.

It will be pointed out and we ourselves have already admitted, that
in a particular instance the course of a concrete historical event can
be made vividly clear without its being analyzed in terms of explicitly defined concepts. And it will accordingly be claimed for the
historians in our field, that they may, as has been said of the political
historians, speak the "language of life itself." Certainly! But it should
be added that in this procedure, the attainment of a level of explicit
awareness of the viewpoint from which the events in question get
their significance remains highly accidental. We are in general not in
the favorable position of the political historian for whom the cultural
views to which he orients his presentation are usually unambiguous —
or seem to be so. Every type of purely direct concrete description
bears the mark of *artistic* portrayal. "Each sees what is in his own
heart." Valid *judgments* always presuppose the *logical* analysis of
what is concretely and immediately perceived, i.e. the use of *concepts*.
It is indeed possible and often aesthetically satisfying to keep these
in petto but it always endangers the security of the reader's orientation, and often that of the author himself concerning the content and
scope of his judgments.

The neglect of clear-cut concept-construction in practical discussions of practical, economic and social policy can, however, become
particularly dangerous. It is really unbelievable to an outsider what
confusion has been fostered, for instance, by the use of the term
"value" — that unfortunate child of misery of our science, which can
be given an unambiguous meaning *only* as an ideal type — or terms
like "productive," "from an economic viewpoint," etcetera, which in

general will not stand up under a conceptually precise analysis. *Collective* concepts taken from the language of everyday life have particularly unwholesome effects. In order to have an illustration easy for the layman to understand, let us take the concept of "agriculture" especially as it appears in the term "the interests of agriculture." If we begin with "the interests of agriculture" as the empirically determinable, more or less clear *subjective* ideas of concrete economically active individuals about their own interests and disregard entirely the countless conflicts of interest taking place among the cattle breeders, the cattle growers, grain growers, corn consumers, corn-using, whiskey-distilling farmers, perhaps not all laymen, but certainly every specialist will know the great whirlpool of antagonistic and contradictory forms of value-relationship (*Wertbeziehung*) which are vaguely thought of under that heading. We will enumerate only a few of them here: the interests of farmers, who wish to sell their property and who are therefore interested in a rapid rise of the price of land; the diametrically opposed interest of those who wish to buy, rent or lease; the interest of those who wish to retain a certain property to the social advantage of their descendants and who are therefore interested in the stability of *landed* property; the antagonistic interests of those who, in their own or their childrens' interests, wish to see the land go to the most enterprising farmer — or what is not exactly the same — to the purchaser with the most capital; the purely economic interest in economic freedom of movement of the most "competent farmer" in the business sense; the antagonistic interests of certain dominating classes in the maintenance of the traditional social and political position of their own "class" and thereby of their descendants; the interest of the socially subordinated strata of farmers in the decline of the strata which are above them and which oppress them; in occasional contradition to this the interest of this stratum in having the leadership of those above them to protect their economic interests. This list could be tremendously increased, without coming to an end although we have been as summary and imprecise as possible.

We will pass over the fact that most diverse purely ideal values are mixed and associated with, hinder and divert the more "egoistic" interests in order to remind ourselves, above all, that when we speak of the "interests of agriculture" we think not *only* of those material and ideal values to which the farmers themselves at a given time relate their interests, but rather those partly quite heterogeneous value-ideas which *we* can relate with agriculture. As instances of these value-ideas related to agriculture we may cite the *interests in production* derived from the interests in cheap and qualitatively good food, which two interests are themselves not always congruous and in connection with which many clashes between the interests of city and country can be found, and in which the interests of the present generation need not by any means always be identical with the interests of coming generations; *interests in a numerous population,* particularly in a large rural population, derived either from the foreign or domestic interests of the "State," or from other ideal interests of the most diverse sort, e.g., the expected influence of a large rural population on the character of the nation's culture. These "population-interests" can clash with the most diverse economic interests of all sections of the rural population, and indeed with all the present interests of the mass of rural inhabitants. Another instance is the interest in a certain type of social stratification of the rural population, because of the type of political or cultural influence which will be produced therefrom; this interest can, depending on its orientation, conflict with every conceivable (even the most urgent present and future) interests of the individual farmers as well as those "of the State." To this is added a further complication: the "state," to the "interests" of which we tend to relate such and numerous other similar individual interests, is often only a blanket term for an extremely intricate tangle of evaluative-ideas, to which it in its turn is related in individual cases, e.g., purely military security from external dangers; security of the dominant position of a dynasty or a certain class at home; interest in the maintenance and expansion of the formal-juridicial unity of the nation for its own sake or in the interest of maintaining certain objective cultural values which in their turn again are very differentiated and which we as a politically unified people believe we represent; the reconstruction of the social aspects of the state according to certain once more diverse cultural ideas. It would lead us too far even merely to mention what is contained under the general label "state-interests" to which we can relate "agriculture." The illustrations which we have chosen and our even briefer analyses are crude and simplified. The non-specialist may now analyze similarly (and more thoroughly) for instance "the class interests of the worker" in order to see what contradictory elements, composed partly of the workers' interests and ideals, and partly of the ideals with which *we* view the workers, enter into this concept. It is impossible to overcome the slogans of the conflict of interests through a purely empirical emphasis on their "relative" character. The clear-cut, sharply defined analysis of the various possible standpoints is the only path which will lead us out of verbal confusion. The "free trade argument" as a *Weltanschauung* or as a valid *norm* is ridiculous but — and this is equally true whichever ideals of commercial policy the individual accepts — our underestimation of the heuristic value of the wisdom of the world's greatest merchants as expressed in such ideal-typical formulæ has caused serious damage to our discussions of commercial policy. Only through ideal-typical concept-construction do the viewpoints with which we are concerned in individual cases become explicit. Their peculiar character is brought out by the *confrontation* of empirical reality with the ideal-type. The use of the undifferentiated collective concepts of everyday speech is always a cloak for confusion of thought and action. It is, indeed, very often an instrument of specious and fraudulent procedures. It is, in brief, always a means of obstructing the proper formulation of the problem.

We are now at the end of this discussion, the only purpose of which was to trace the course of the hair-line which separates science from faith and to make explicit the *meaning* of the quest for social and economic knowledge. The *objective* validity of all empirical knowledge rests exclusively upon the ordering of the given reality according to categories which are *subjective* in a specific sense, namely, in that they present the *presuppositions* of our knowledge and are based on the presupposition of the *value* of those *truths* which empirical knowledge alone is able to give us. The means available to our science offer nothing to those persons to whom this truth is of no value. It should be remembered that the belief in the value of scientific truth is the product of certain cultures and is not a product of man's original nature. Those for whom scientific truth is of no value will seek in vain for some other truth to take the place of science in just those respects in which it is unique, namely, in the provision of concepts and judgments which are neither empirical reality nor reproductions of it but which facilitate its analytical ordering in a valid manner. In the empirical social sciences, as we have seen, the possibility of meaningful knowledge of what is essential for us in the infinite richness of events is bound up with the unremitting application of viewpoints of a specifically particularized character, which, in the last analysis, are oriented on the basis of evaluative ideas. These evaluative ideas are for their part empirically discoverable and analyzable as elements of meaningful human conduct, but their validity can *not* be deduced from empirical data as such. The "objectivity" of the social sciences depends rather on the fact that the empirical data are always related to those evaluative ideas which alone make them worth knowing and the significance of the empirical data is derived from these evaluative ideas. But these data can never become the foundation for the empirically impossible proof of the validity of the evaluative ideas. The belief which we all have in some form or other, in the meta-empirical validity of ultimate and final values, in which the meaning of our existence is rooted, is not incompatible with the incessant changefulness of the concrete viewpoints, from which empirical reality gets its significance. Both these views are, on the contrary, in harmony with each other. Life with its irrational reality and its store of possible meanings is inexhaustible. The *concrete* form in which value-relevance occurs remains perpetually in flux, ever subject to change in the dimly seen future of human culture. The light which emanates from those highest evaluative ideas always falls on an ever changing finite segment of the vast chaotic stream of events, which flows away through time.

Now all this should not be misunderstood to mean that the proper task of the social sciences should be the continual chase for new viewpoints and new analytical constructs. *On the contrary*: nothing should be more sharply emphasized than the proposition that the knowledge of the *cultural significance* of *concrete historical events and patterns* is exclusively and solely the final end which, among other means, concept-construction and the criticism of constructs also seek to serve.

There are, to use the words of F. Th. Vischer, "subject matter specialists" and "interpretative specialists." The fact-greedy gullet of the former can be filled only with legal documents, statistical worksheets and questionnaires, but he is insensitive to the refinement of a new idea. The gourmandise of the latter dulls his taste for facts by ever new intellectual subtilities. That genuine artistry which, among the historians, Ranke possessed in such a grand measure, manifests itself through its ability to produce new knowledge by interpreting already *known* facts according to known viewpoints.

All research in the cultural sciences in an age of specialization, once it is oriented towards a given subject matter through particular settings of problems and has established its methodological principles, will consider the analysis of the data as an end in itself. It will discontinue assessing the value of the individual facts in terms of their relationships to ultimate value-ideas. Indeed, it will lose its awareness of its ultimate rootedness in the value-ideas in general. And it is well that should be so. But there comes a moment when the atmosphere changes. The significance of the unreflectively utilized viewpoints becomes uncertain and the road is lost in the twilight. The light of the great cultural problems moves on. Then science too prepares to change its standpoint and its analytical apparatus and to view the streams of events from the heights of thought. It follows those stars which alone are able to give meaning and direction to its labors:

> "....... der neue Trieb erwacht,
> Ich eile fort, ihr ewiges Licht zu trinken,
> Vor mir den Tag und unter mir die Nacht,
> Den Himmel über mir und unter mir die Wellen."[3]

---

[3]*Faust*: Act I, Scene II. (Translated by Bayard-Taylor)
  "The newborn impulse fires my mind,
  I hasten on, his beams eternal drinking,
  The Day before me and the Night behind,
  Above me Heaven unfurled, the floor of waves beneath me."

Critical Studies in the Logic
of the Cultural Sciences

A CRITIQUE OF EDUARD MEYER'S
METHODOLOGICAL VIEWS

I

W HEN ONE OF OUR most eminent historians feels impelled
to give an account to himself and his colleagues of the aims and
methods of his scholarly work, this must necessarily arouse an
interest far beyond the limits of his special discipline because in doing so he passes beyond the boundaries of his special discipline and
enters into the area of methodological analysis.   This has to begin
with certain unfavorable consequences.   The categories of logic,
which in its present state of development is a specialized discipline
like any other, require, if they are to be utilized with assurance, the
same daily familiarity as those of any other discipline.   Obviously,
Eduard Meyer, whose *Zur Theorie und Methodik der Geschitchte*
(Hadle, 1900)) we are discussing here, does not and cannot claim
such constant contact with logic anymore thàn the author of the following pages.   The methodological details of that work are, so to
speak, a diagnosis not by the physician but by the patient himself,
and they are intended to be evaluated and understood as such.   The
professional methodologist will take umbrage at many of Meyer's
formulations and he will not learn much that is really new for his

purposes from the work itself. But this does not diminish its significance for the neighboring special disciplines.[1]

Indeed, the most significant achievements of specialist methodology use "ideal-typically" constructed conceptions of the objectives and methods of the special disciplines, and are therefore so far risen over the heads of the latter that it is often difficult for the special disciplines to recognize themselves with the naked eye in these discussions. For this reason methodological discussions rooted within their own subject matter may be more useful for the self-clarification of special disciplines in spite of, and in a sense even because of, their methodologically imperfect formulation. Indeed, the easy intelligibility of Meyer's exposition offers the specialist in the neighboring disciplines the opportunity to focus attention on a whole series of points for the purpose of resolving certain logical problems which he shares in common with "historians" in the narrower sense of the word.

Such is the aim of the following discussions which, in connection with Meyer's book, will attempt to elucidate concretely a whole series, in sequence, of specific logical problems, and will then critically review a number of further newer works on the logic of the cultural sciences from the standpoint arrived at in the course of our discussion of Meyer. We are intentionally taking our point of departure in purely *historical* problems and will enter only in the later stage of our discussions on those disciplines concerned with social life which seek to arrive at "rules" or "laws"; we do this especially because hitherto the attempt has usually been made to define the nature of the social sciences by distinguishing them from the "natural sciences." In this procedure there is always the tacit assumption that history is a discipline which devotes itself exclusively to the collection of materials, or if not that, is a purely descriptive discipline which in fortunate cases drags in "facts" which serve as the

---

(1) It is to be hoped that the reader will not attribute the following criticism, which purposely searches out the weaknesses in Meyer's formulations, to the need to appear clever. The errors which an outstanding author makes are more instructive than the correct statements of a scientific nonentity. It is not our intention to assess the achievement of Eduard Meyer but rather the contrary: to learn from his inadequacies in such a way that we can understand how he attempted, with very different degrees of success, to cope with certain important problems of historical methodology.

building materials for the intellectual work which "really" begins only after the historical work has been done. And what is more, even the professional historians, unfortunately, have contributed not a little to the strengthening of the prejudice that "historical work" is something qualitatively different from "scientific work" because "concepts" and "rules" are of "no concern" to history; they have done this by the way in which they have sought to define the specific character of "history" in the specialist's sense of the word. Since social science is itself usually given an "historical" foundation because of the persisting influence of the "historical school," and since for this reason the relationship of our discipline to theory has remained problematic even as it was twenty-five years ago, it appears to be correct procedure to ask, first, what is to be understood logically by "historical" research, and to decide this question in the domain of what is indubitably and generally acknowledged to be historiography, with which the book we are now criticizing is primarily concerned.

Eduard Meyer begins with a warning against the over-estimation of the significance of methodological studies for the *practice* of history: the most comprehensive methodological knowledge will not make anyone into an historian, and incorrect methodological viewpoints do not necessarily entail erroneous scientific practice; they show, rather, only that the historian can formulate or interpret incorrectly his own correct maxims of procedure. The following proposition recommends itself as essentially true: methodology can only bring us reflective understanding of the means which have *demonstrated* their value in practice by raising them to the level of explicit consciousness; it is no more the precondition of fruitful intellectual work than the knowledge of anatomy is the precondition for "correct" walking. Indeed, just as the person who attempted to govern his mode of walking continuously by anatomical knowledge would be in danger of stumbling so the professional scholar who attempted to determine the aims of his own research extrinsically on the basis of methodological reflections would be in danger of falling into the same difficulties.[2] If methodological work — and this is naturally its

---

[2] This would, as we shall show, also happen in the case of Eduard Meyer if he began taking many of his own assertions with literal seriousness.

intention — can at some point serve the practice of the historian directly, it is indeed, by enabling him once and for all to escape from the danger of being imposed on by a philosophically embellished dilettantism. Only by laying bare and solving *substantive problems* can sciences be established and their methods developed. On the other hand, purely epistemological and methodological reflections have never played the crucial role in such developments. Such discussions can become important for the enterprise of science only when, as a result of considerable shifts of the "viewpoint" from which a datum becomes the object of analysis, the idea emerges that the new "viewpoint" also requires a revision of the logical forms in which the "enterprise" has heretofore operated, and when, accordingly, uncertainty about the "nature" of one's own work arises. This situation is unambiguously the case at present as regards history, and Eduard Meyer's view about the insignificance in principle of methodology for "practice" has rightly not prevented him from now busying himself with methology.

He begins, first, with an exposition of those theories which recently, from the methodological standpoint, have sought to transform historical studies, and he formulates the standpoint which he will wish to criticize in particular (page 3), as asserting that:

1. the following are insignificant for history and are thus not to be looked upon as properly belonging to a scientific exposition:
    a. the "accidental";
    b. the "freely" willed decision of concrete personalities;
    c. the influence of "ideas" on the actions of human beings;
— as asserting on the contrary,

2. that the proper objects of scientific knowledge are:
    a. "mass phenomena" in contrast to individual actions;
    b. the "typical" in contrast with the "particular";
    c. the development of "communities," especially social "classes" or "nations," in contrast with the political actions of individuals;
and as asserting finally that

3. historical development, because it is scientifically intelligible only in a causal manner is to be conceived as a process

following "laws." Consequently, the discovery of the necessary "typical" sequence of "developmental stages" of human communities and the integration of the rich variety of historical data into this sequence are the proper aims of historical research.

In the following discussion, all of those points in Meyer's analysis which deal particularly with the criticism of Lamprecht will, for the time being, be left entirely to one side, and I allow myself the liberty of rearranging Meyer's arguments, singling out certain of them for particular discussion in the following sections in accordance with the requirements of the following studies, which do not have as their goal the mere criticism of Eduard Meyer's book.

In order to oppose the point of view which he is combatting, Meyer first refers to the very great role which "free will" and "chance"— both of which are in his view perfectly "definite and clear concepts" — have played in history and in life in general.

As regards the discussion of "chance" (p. 17 ff.), Eduard Meyer obviously does not interpret this concept as objective "causelessness" ("absolute" chance in the metaphysical sense), nor does he interpret it as the absolute subjective impossibility of knowledge of the causal conditions which necessarily recurs in regard to each individual instance of the class of events (as, for example, in the toss of dice) ("absolute" chance in the epistemological sense).[3] He understands by "chance," rather, "relative" chance in the sense of a logical relationship between groups of causes conceived as distinct complexes and understands it, in the main, in the way, although naturally not always "correctly" formulated, that this concept is accepted by professional logicians, who despite many advances in detail still base their theory in this regard on Windelband's earliest writing. In the main, he makes a correct distinction between two concepts of chance: (1) the *causal* concept of "chance" ("relative chance" so-called) : —the "chance" effect here stands in contrast with such an effect as would

---

[3] This sort of "chance" lies, for example, at the basis of the so-called games of "chance" such as dice and lotteries. The *absolute* unknowability of the influence of certain parts of the concrete determining conditions of the specific effect on the outcome of the event is constitutive for the possibility of "probability calculation" in the strict sense of the term.

be "expected" from the event's causal components which we have synthesized into a conceptual unity — that is a matter of "chance" which is not usually *derivable* in accordance with general rules of change from those determinants which alone have been taken into account in the unification of causal components into causes but which has been caused by the operation of some conditions lying "outside" them (pp. 17-19). From this causal conception of "chance," he distinguishes (2) the rather different teleological concept of "chance," the opposite of which is the "essential" reality; here either it is a question of the construction of a concept for heuristic purposes through the exclusion of those elements or components of reality which are "unessential" ("chance" or "individual") for the knowledge, or it is a question of assessment of certain real or conceptualized objects as "means" to an "end," in which case, then, certain characteristics alone are practically relevant as "means" while the others are treated in practice as "indifferent" (pp. 20-21).[4] Of course, the formulation (especially on page 20 et seq., where the contrast is conceived as one between "events" and "things") leaves much to be desired, and it will become quite clear by our further discussion of Meyer's attitude toward the concept of development (in Section II) that the problem has not been fully thought out in its logical implications. However, what he says is adequate for the needs of historical practice. What interests us here, however, is the way in which at a subsequent passage (p. 28) he recurs to the concept of "chance." "Natural science can ... assert," Meyer says, "that when dynamite is set on fire an explosion will take place. But to predict whether and when in a specific instance this explosion will take place, and whether in such a situation a particular person will be wounded, killed, or saved, that is impossible for natural science because that depends on chance and on the *free will of which science knows nothing but with which history deals.*" Here we see the very close union of "chance" with "free will." It

---

[4] These concepts of "chance" are not to be excluded from a discipline which is only relatively historical (for example, biology). L. M. Hartmann (*Die geschichtliche Entwicklung*, pp. 15 and 25) speaks only of this and the "pragmatic" concept of "chance"—obviously following Meyer; he does not, however, in any case, in spite of his false formulation, do as Eulenburg claims, that is, transform "the causeless into the casual" (*Deutsche Literaturzeitung* 1905, No. 24).

appears even more prominently when Meyer cites as a second example the possibility of "calculating" with "certainty" the possibility of a constellation by use of the devices of astronomy, meaning by "certainty" the assumption of the non-occurrence of "disturbances" such as, for example, the intrusion of strange or foreign planets into the solar system. In contrast with this, he declares it to be impossible to predict with certainty that the constellation will be "observed." In the first place, that intrusion of the foreign planet, according to Meyer's assumption, would be "incalculable" — in that sense astronomy, and not only history, has to take "chance" into account. Secondly, it is normally very easily "calculable" that some astronomer will also attempt to "observe" the calculated constellation, and when no "chance" disturbances intrude, will actually succeed in observing it. One obtains the impression that Meyer, although interpreting "chance" in a thoroughly deterministic fashion, has in mind, without, however, clearly expressing it, a particularly close affinity between "chance" and "free will" which determines a characteristic irrationality in historical events. Let us examine this more closely.

What Meyer designates as "free will" does not involve, according to him, in any way (p. 14) a contradiction of the "axiomatic" "principle of sufficient reason" which is, in his view, unconditionally valid even for human conduct. Rather, the distinction between "freedom" and "necessity" in conduct is resolved into a simple distinction of points of view. In one case, we are contemplating what *has happened,* and this appears to us as "necessary," including the decision that was once actually made. In the case of freedom, however, we look on the event as "becoming," that is, as not yet having occurred, and thus as not "necessary"; it is, in this form, only one of infinitely numerous "possibilities." From the point of view of a development in process, we can, however, never assert that a human decision could not have been made differently than it actually was made later. In the discussion of human action, "we can never transcend the 'I will'."

The question now arises: is it Meyer's view that this distinction between two viewpoints (i.e. (1) "development in process" which is for that reason conceived as "free" and (2) "events" which have "occurred" and for that reason conceived as "necessary") is to be applied only in the sphere of human motivation and not in the sphere of "dead" nature? Since he remarks on page 15 that the person who "knows the personality and the circumstances" can predict the result, that is, the decision which is "evolving" "perhaps with a very high probability," he does not appear to accept such a distinction. But a really exact prediction of an individual event from given conditions is also dependent, in the sphere of "dead" nature, on these two presuppositions: (1) that there are involved "calculable," that is, quantitatively exprèssible components of the event, and (2) that all of the conditions which are relevant for the occurrence can really be known and measured exactly. Otherwise, and this is always the rule wherever it is a question of the concrete individuality of an event, such as the exact character of the weather on a particular day in the future, we cannot transcend probability judgments of various degrees of certainty. "Free" will, then, would not have any special status, and "I will" would only be the same as the formal "fiat" of consciousness discussed by James, which is, for example, accepted by the determinist criminologists without any damage to their theories of legal responsibility.[5] "Free will" signifies, then, only that causal significance has been attributed to the "decision" which has arisen from causes which are, perhaps, never fully to be discovered, but which are in any case "sufficient"; and this will not be seriously contested even by a strict determinist. If there were nothing more involved in this, then we would be unable to see why the concept of irrationality of historical events, which is occasionally mentioned in discussions of "chance," would not be acceptable.

But for such an interpretation of Meyer's point of view, it is disturbing to note that he finds it necessary in this context to emphasize freedom of the will, as a fact of inner experience, as indispensable if the individual is to be responsible for his own voluntary acts. This would be justified only if Meyer were intending to assign to history the task of judging its heroes. It is therefore a question to what extent Meyer actually holds this position. He remarks (p. 16): "We attempt to uncover the motives which have led them" — for example, Bismarck in 1866 — "to their decisions and to judge the correctness of these decisions and the value (*nota bene!*) of their personality."

---

[5] See, for example, Liepmann's *Einleitung in das Strafrecht*.

In view of this formulation, one may well believe that Meyer regards it as the highest task of history to obtain *value judgments* concerning the "historically acting" personality. Not only his attitude toward "biography," which is still to be mentioned, but also the highly pertinent remarks regarding the non-equivalence of the "intrinsic value" of historical personalities and their causal significance (pp. 50-51) make it certain that by "value" of personality in the foregoing sentence he means only, or can consistently only mean, the *causal* significance of certain actions or certain qualities of those concrete persons which may be positive, or also, as in the case of Friedrich Wilhelm IV, negative, for some *value judgment*. But what is meant by the "judgment" of the "correctness" of those decisions may be understood again in a variety of ways: as either (1) a judgment of the "value" of the goal which lay at the basis of the decision — for example, the goal of driving Austria out of Germany from the standpoint of the German patriot — or as (2) an analysis of those decisions with reference to the question whether, or, rather, since history has answered this question affirmatively, — why the decision to go to war was at that moment the appropriate means to achieve the goal of the unification of Germany. We may pass over the question whether Meyer has, in actuality, clearly distinguished in his own mind these two ways of putting the question. In an argument regarding historical causality, obviously only the second one is relevant; for this judgment of the historical situation, "teleological" in form, and expressed in terms of the categories of "means and ends," is obviously meaningful in a presentation which takes the form, not of a book of instructions for diplomats, but of "history," as rendering possible a judgment of the *causal* historical significance of events. Such a judgment asserts that at that moment an "opportunity" to make a decision was not "passed over" because the "maker" of the decision, as Meyer says, possessed the "strength of soul and mind" to maintain it in the face of all obstacles; in this way is determined what is to be attributed causally to that decision and its characterological and other preconditions; in other words, the extent to which, and the sense in which, for example, the presence of those "character qualities" constituted a "factor" of historical "importance." Such problems causally relating a certain historical event to the actions of concrete persons are, however, obviously to be sharply distinguished from the question of the meaning and significance of *ethical* "responsibility."

We may interpret this last expression in Eduard Meyer's writing in the purely "objective" meaning of the causal ascription of certain effects to the given "characterological" qualities and to the "motives" of the acting personalities which are to be explained by these characterological qualities and the numerous "environmental" circumstances and by the concrete situation. But then it becomes strikingly noteworthy that Meyer, in a subsequent passage in his treatise (pp. 44-45), indicates that the "investigation of motives" is "secondary" for history. The reason which is alleged, namely, that inquiry into motives passes beyond what is secure knowledge, that it often indeed results in a "genetic formulation" of an action which cannot be satisfactorily explained in the light of the available data and which action is, therefore, to be simply accepted as a "datum," cannot, however correct it may be in individual instances, be adhered to as a logical criterion in view of the often equally problematic "explanations" of concrete external natural or physical events. However that may be, Meyer's point of view regarding inquiry into motives, in association with his strong emphasis on the significance of the essential factor of the "willed decision" for history and the quoted remark concerning "responsibility" leads in any case to the suspicion that as far as Meyer is concerned, the ethical and the causal modes of analyzing human action — "evaluation" and "explanation" — reveal a certain tendency to fuse with one another.[6] For quite apart from the question as to whether one regards as adequate Windelband's formulation that the idea of responsibility has a meaning which does not involve that of causality and constitutes a positive basis for the normative dignity of ethical consciousness,— in any case this formulation adequately indicates how the world of "norms" and "values" as envisaged from the empirical, scientific, causal point of view is delimitable from such a standpoint.[7]

---

[6] What is to be included under "investigation into motives" is not clearly stated here, but quite obviously it is understood that we regard the "decision" of a "concrete personality" as the absolutely "ultimate" fact only when it appears to us to be, in a "pragmatic" view, accidental, that is neither accessible nor worthy of a meaningful interpretation; thus, for example, the wild decrees of

Naturally, in judging a certain mathematical proposition to be "correct," the question as to how the knowledge of it came about "psychologically" and whether "mathematical imagination," for instance, is possible to the highest degree only as an accompaniment of certain anatomical abnormalities of the "mathematical brain," does not arise at all. The consideration that one's own ethically judged "motive" is, according to the theory of empirical science, causally determined does not carry any weight before the forum of conscience; nor does the consideration that an instance of artistic bungling must be regarded as being as much determined in its genesis as the Sistine Chapel carry any weight in aesthetic judgment. Causal analysis provides absolutely no value judgment[8] and a value judgment is absolutely not a causal explanation. And for this very reason the evaluation of an event — such as, for instance, the "beauty" of a natural phenomenon — occurs in a sphere quite different from its causal explanation; for this reason concern on the part of history to judge of historical actions as responsible before the conscience of history or before the judgment seat of any god or man and all other modes of introducing the philosophical problem of "freedom" into the procedures of history would suspend its character as an empirical science (*Erfahrungwissenschaft*) just as much as the insertion of miracles into its causal sequences. Following Ranke, the latter is natur-

Czar Paul, which were impelled by madness. However, one of the most certain tasks of history has always consisted in understanding empirically given "external actions" and their results in the light of historically given "conditions," "goals," and "means" of action. Nor does Meyer himself proceed in any other fashion. The "investigation of motives" that is, the analysis of what was really "sought" and the basis of this desire — is on the one hand the means of avoiding the petering out of the analysis into an unhistorical body of pragmatic rules, while on the other it is one of the major points of departure of the "historical interest": we wish, indeed, among other things, to see "how the desires" of human beings are transformed in their "significance" by the concatenation of historical "destinies."

[7] Windelband, (*Uber Willensfreiheit,* last chapter), selects this formulation in particular in order to exclude the question of "freedom of the will" from criminological discussions. However, it is a question whether it is adequate for the criminologist since the type of casual interconnection is never entirely irrelevant for the applicability of the norms of criminal law.

[8] But we do not mean by this that the "psychological' faciliation of the "understanding" of the value-significance of an object (e.g., a work of art) does not gain something very essential from the causal analysis of its genesis. We shall come back to this later.

ally rejected by Eduard Meyer (p. 20) in the name of the "sharp distinction between historical knowledge and religious Weltanschauung" and it would have been better, in my opinion, if he had not allowed himself to be misled by Stammler's arguments which he cites (p. 26; fn. 2) and which blur the equally sharp distinction between historical knowledge and ethics. Just how disastrous this mixing up of different standpoints can be from the methodological point of view is demonstrated immediately when Meyer (p. 20) claims that by means of the empirically given ideas of freedom and responsibility a "purely *individual* factor" is present in historical development, which is "never capable of being reduced to a formula" without "annihilating its true nature" and when he then seeks to illustrate this proposition by the high historical (causal) significance of the individually willed decision of particular personalities. This old error[9] is so dangerous precisely from the point of view of preserving the specific character of history because it introduces problems from quite distinct fields into history and produces the illusion that a certain (anti-deterministic) conviction is a presupposition of the validity of the historical method. The error in the assumption that any freedom of the will — however it is understood — is identical with the "irrationality" of action, or that the latter is conditioned by the former, is quite obvious. The characteristic of "incalculability," equally great but not greater than that of "blind forces of nature," is the privilege of — the insane.[10] On the other hand, we associate the highest measure of an empirical "feeling of freedom" with those actions which we are conscious of performing rationally — i.e., *in the absence of physical and psychic "coercion," emotional "affects" and "accidental"*

---

[9] I have criticized this error in detail in my essay "Roscher und Knies und die logischen Probleme der historischen Nationalökonomie."

[10] The actions of Czar Paul of Russia in the last stages of his mad reign are treated by us as not meaningful interpretable and therefore as "incalculable," like the storm which broke up the Spanish Armada. In the case of the one as well as the other we forbear from the "investigation of motives," obviously not because we interpret these events as "free" and also not because their concrete causation must remain hidden from us—in the case of Czar Paul pathology could perhaps supply the answer—but because they are not sufficiently interesting to us historically. We shall deal with this more closely later.

disturbances of the clarity of judgment, in which we pursue a clearly perceived end by "means" which are the most adequate in accordance with the extent of our knowledge, i.e., in accordance with empirical *rules.* If history had only to deal with such rational actions which are "free" in this sense, its task would be immeasurably lightened: the goal, the "motive," the "maxims" of the actor would be unambiguously derivable from the means applied and all the irrationalities which constitute the "personal" element in *conduct* would be excluded. Since all strictly teleologically (purposefully) occurring actions involve applications of empirical rules, which tell what the appropriate "means" to ends are, history would be nothing but the applications of those rules.[11] The impossibility of purely pragmatic history is determined by the fact that the action of men is *not* interpretable in such purely rational terms, that not only irrational "prejudices," errors in thinking and factual errors but also "temperament," "moods" and "affects" disturb his freedom — in brief, that his action too — to very different degrees — partakes of the empirical "meaninglessness" of "natural change." Action *shares* this kind of "irrationality" with every natural event, and when the historian in the interpretation of historical interconnections speaks of the "irrationality" of human action as a disturbing factor, he is comparing historical-empirical action not with the phenomena of nature but with the ideal of a purely rational, i.e., absolutely purposeful, action which is also absolutely oriented towards the adequate means.

Eduard Meyer's exposition of the categories of "chance" and "free will" which are characteristic of historical analysis, reveals a somewhat unclear disposition to introduce heterogeneous problems into

---

[11] Cf. in this connection, the considerations present in "Roscher und Knies"— strictly rational action—one could also put it thus—would be the simple and complete "adaptation" to the given "situation." Menger's theoretical schemata, for example, presuppose the strictly rational "adaptation" to the "market situation" and exhibit the consequences there of in "ideal-typical" purity. History would in fact be nothing more than a body of practical patterns (pragmatics) of "adaptation"—which is what L. M. Hartmann would like to make it—if it were solely an analysis of the emergence and interconnections of the particular "free," i.e., teleologically absolutely rational, actions of single individuals. If one excludes this teleological-rational meaning from the conception of "adaptation," as Hartmann does, it becomes, as we shall have further occasion to show, an absolutely indifferent idea for historical studies.

historical methodolgy; it is further to be observed that his conception of historical causality contains striking contradictions. He emphasizes very strongly on page 40 that historical research always seeks out causal sequences by proceeding from effect to cause. Even this — in Eduard Meyer's formulation[12]— can be disputed: is is from the nature of the case quite possible to formulate in the form of an hypethesis the effects which could have been produced by a given historical event or by a newly ascertained historical occurrence and to verify this hypothesis by testing it with the "facts." What is really meant, as we shall see, is something quite different — that which has recently been called the principle of "teleological dependence" and which dominates history's interests in causes. Furthermore, it is of course also unsatisfactory when the aforementioned ascent from effect to cause is claimed to be peculiar to history. The causal "explanattion" of a concrete "natural event" proceeds exactly in this way and in no other. And while the view is put forward on page 14—as we have seen—that what has already "occurred" is for us tantamount to the absolutely "necessary" and only what is conceived as "becoming" is to be interpreted by us as mere "possibility," on page 40 he emphasizes the contrary proposition, stressing the particularly problematic element in the inference of the cause from the effect, in such a way that Eduard Meyer himself feels called upon to avoid the term "cause" in historical studies and, as we have seen, the "investigation of motives" becomes discredited in his eyes.

One could try, taking Eduard Meyer's point of view, to resolve this last contradiction by a formulation in which the problematic element in the inference from effect to cause was seen to be grounded in the fundamental limitations of our capacities for knowledge, while determinism remained an ideal postulate. But he decisively rejects this procedure too (p. 23) and follows it (p. 24) with a discussion which once more raises serious doubts. At one time Eduard Meyer identified, in the introduction to *Die Geschichte des Altertums,* the relation between the "general" and the "particular" with that between "freedom" and "necessity" and both of these with the relationship

---

[12] He says rather unfortunately: "historical research proceeds in its inferences from effect to cause."

between the "individual" and the "collectivity"; in consequence of this (cf. above), the "individual" was dominant in "detail" (in the particular instance), while the "major trends" of historical events were governed by "law" or "rule." This view, which prevails among many "modern" historians and which in this formulation is entirely and basically confused is expressly withdrawn by him on page 25, partly on the authority of Rickert, partly on the authority of von Below. The latter had taken particularly objection to the notion of a "development governed by law"; against Eduard Meyer's example — that the development of Germany to a unified nation appears to us as an "historical necessity," while the time and form of the unification into a federal state with twenty-five members depends, on the contrary, on the "individuality of the historically operating factors," von Below complained: "Could it not have happened otherwise?" Meyer is unquestionably open to this criticism. But it appears to me to be quite easy to see — however one judges the Meyerian formulation which is attacked by von Below — that this criticism in any case proves too much and therefore proves nothing. For the same objection is appropriate when we, along with von Below and Eduard Meyer, apply the concept of "law-governed development" without any qualms. The fact that a human being has developed or will develop from a human foetus appears to us as a *law*-governed development — and still it could undoubtedly "have a different outcome" as a result of external "accidents" or "pathological" inheritance. In the polemic against the theorists of "development" it is obviously only a question of correctly perceiving and logically delimiting the meaning of the concept of "development" — the concept obviously can not simply be eliminated by such arguments as the foregoing. Eduard Meyer himself is the best instance of this contention. For it is the case that only two pages later (p. 27) he again proceeds in a footnote which designates the concept of "middle ages" as "a clearly defined concept," in accordance with a schema set forth in the "Introduction" which he had repudiated: and in the text, he says that the word "necessity" in history signifies only that the "probability" of an historical consequence following from given conditions, attains a very high level, that the *whole development so to speak, presses on to a single outcome.* He did not wish, more-ever, to say more than that by his remark about the unification of Germany. And when he emphasizes in this connection that there was, despite everything, a possibility of the event's non-occurrence, we wish to recall that he had stressed in connection with astronomical calculations that they could possibly be "disturbed" by wandering heavenly bodies. There is indeed in this respect no distinction from particular natural events, and even in explanations in the sphere of nature,[13] whenever it is a question of concrete events, the judgment of necessity is by no means the only or even merely the major form in which the category of causality can appear. One will not go wrong with the hypothesis that Eduard Meyer arrived at his distrust of the concept of "development" through his discussions with J. Wellhausen in which it was essentially (but not only) a matter of the following contrast: whether to interpret the "development" of Judaism as one which had occurred essentially "from the inside outwards" ("evolutionalistically") or as one that had been conditioned by certain concrete historical forces entering from the "outside," in particular, the imposition of "laws" by the Persian kings out of considerations deriving from Persian politics and which are not related to the intrinsic characteristics of the Jews ("epigenetically"). However that may be, it is in no case no improvement on the formulation used in the Introduction when (p. 46) "the general" appears as "the essentially (?) negative," or more sharply formulated, the "limiting" "condition" which set the "boundaries," within which the infinite possibilities of historical development lie, while the question as to which of these possibilities becomes a "reality"[14] depends on the "higher (?) individual factors of historical life." Thereby, the "general" (das "Allgemeine") — i.e., not the "general milieu" which is wrongly confused with the "general" ("generellen") but rather the rule which is an abstract concept—is hypostasized into an effective force operating

---

[13] It would lead too far afield to examine this problem here in more detail. Cf. my "Roscher und Knies."

[14] This formulation recalls certain modes of thought which were common in the Russian sociological school (Mikhailowski Kareyev, et al.), which are reviewed in Kistiakowski's essay in the "Problems of Idealism" (edited by Novgorodzev, Moscow, 1902) concerning the "Russian sociological school" and the category of possibility in the problems of the social sciences. We shall return to this essay later.

behind the historical scene, and this ignores the elementary fact —
which Eduard Meyer stresses clearly and sharply at other places
— that reality is constituted only by the concrete and particular.
This dubious formulation of the relations between the "general"
and the "particular" is by no means peculiar to Eduard Meyer and
it is by no means confined to historians of his stamp. On the contrary,
it lies at the basis of the popular conception which is nonetheless
shared, by many "modern" historians — but not by Eduard Meyer
— which maintains that in order to establish the study of history
in a rational manner as a "science of the individual," it is necessary
to establish the similarities and identities of patterns of human development, in which case the particularities and the incomparable and
unanalyzable elements remain as a residue, or as Breysig once said,
"the finest flowers." This conception which comes closer to actual
historical practice represents an advance as contrasted with the naive
belief in the vocation of history to become a "systematic science."
But it, too, is very naive in its own way. The attempt to understand
"Bismarck" in his historical significance by leaving out of account
everything which he has in common with other men and keeping
what is "particular" to him would be an instructive and amusing
exercise for beginners. One would in that case — assuming naturally,
as one always does in logical discussions, the ideal completeness of
the materials — preserve, for example, as one of those "finest flowers"
his "thumbprint," that most specific indication of "individuality"
which has been discovered by the criminal police and the loss of
which for history would be irreplaceable. And if to this argument it
were indignantly countered that "naturally" only "spiritual" (*geistige*)
or "psychological" qualities and events can be taken into consideration as "historical," his daily life, were we to know it "exhaustively,"
would offer us an infinity of expressive traits which would never be
found in this blend and pattern in any other person in the world, and
which would not exceed his thumbprints in their interest. If it is
further objected that quite "obviously," as far as science is concerned, only the historically "significant" constituents of Bismarck's
life are to be considered, the logical answer would be: that that very
"obviousness" involves the decisive problem since it raises the question
as to what is the logical criterion of the historically "significant"

constituent parts.

This exercise in subtraction of the common from the unique —
assuming the absolute completeness of the data — would never be
brought to an end even in the most remote future, and there would
still remain, after subtraction of an infinity of "common qualities,"
a further infinity of constituent parts; even aften an eternity of the
most energetic subtraction from this latter infinity of particular parts,
not a single further step would have been taken to answer the question as to what is historically "essential" among these particularities.
This would be the sole insight which would emerge from an attempt
to perform this exercise.   The other insight is that this operation of
subtraction presupposes such a perfect grasp of the causal course
of events, as no science could aspire to even as an ideal goal.   As a
matter of fact, every "comparison" in the historical sphere presupposes that a selection has already been made through *reference* to
cultural "significances" and that this selection positively determines
the goal and direction of the attribution of causal agency while it
excludes a rich infinity of "general" as well as "particular" elements
in the data.   The comparison of "analogous" events is to be considered as *a* means of this imputation of causal agency, and indeed, in my
view, one of the most important means and one which is not used to
anywhere near the proper extent. We shall deal later with its logical
meaning.

Eduard Meyer does not share, as his remark on page 48 which
is still to be discussed shows, the erroneous view that the particular
as *such* is the subject matter of history and his comments on the significance of the general in history to the effect that "rules" and concepts are only "means" and "presuppositions" of historical work
(p. 29 middle) is as we shall see logically right in the main. It is
only his formulation which we have criticized above that is doubtful
and it reveals the same tendency as the error which we have just
criticized.

Now in spite of all these criticisms the professional historian will
retain the impression that the usual kernel of "truth" is contained
in the views which are here criticized.   That this is the case goes
without saying for an historian of such distinction who discusses his
own procedure.   Indeed, he has come quite close many times to the

logically correct formulation of the elements of truth which are contained in his arguments. For instance, on page 27, top, where it is said of "developmental stages" that they are *"concepts"* which can serve as guiding threads for the *discovery* and ordering of facts, and particularly in the numerous passages where he employs the category of "possibility." It is here however that the logical problem really begins; we must discuss the question of how the ordering of historical events occurs by means of the concept of development, and what is the logical meaning of the "category of possibility" and the way in which it is applied in the elaboration of historical interconnections. Since Eduard Meyer failed to confront these issues he was able to "feel" what is correct in regard to the role which the "laws" governing events play in historical research, but he was not able — as it seems to me — to give it an adequate formulation. This task will be undertaken in a special section of these studies (II). Here we shall concern ourselves, after these necessarily essentially negative remarks against Eduard Meyer's methodological formulation, first with the treatment of discussions of the problem of what is the "object" of history, which is dealt with in the second (pp. 34-44) and third (pp. 54-56) parts of his essay — a question on which the considerations just presented have indeed already touched on.

We, too, may along with Eduard Meyer also formulate the question as follows: "Which of the events on which we have information are 'historical'?" He answers it at first in quite general form: "that is historical which has consequences and which has occurred." This means that the "historical" is that which is causally important in a concrete individual situation. We disregard all other questions which are relevant here in order to point out that Eduard Meyer on page 37 gives up this conception which he has just formulated on page 36.

It is clear to him that —as he says —"even if we were to confine ourselves to that which produces effects," "the number of particular events would still remain infinite." He rightly asks: what governs "the selection which every historian makes among them?" And he answers, "historical interest." He adds, however, after some considerations with which we shall deal later, that there are no absolute norms of historical interest and he elucidates this thesis in such a way that, as we previously mentioned, he once more renounces his restriction of the "historical" to the "effective." On Rickert's illustrative remark "that . . . Friedrich Wilhelm IV turned down the German crown is an 'historical' event but it is entirely indifferent which tailor made his coats" he comments: "the tailor in question might of course always remain indifferent for political history but we can easily imagine taking an historical interest in him in connection for instance with the history of fashions or of the tailoring industry or of prices, etc." This is certainly to the point — although Eduard Meyer can scarcely overlook on further reflection that the "interest" which we take in these different cases involves quite considerable differences in *logical* structure and that the failure to bear these differences in mind leads to the danger of confusing two fundamentally different but often identified categories: the *ratio essendi* and the *ratio cognoscendi*. Since the case of the tailor is not entirely unambiguous, let us make the distinction in question clear with an illustration which exhibits this confusion in a more explicit fashion.

K. Breysig in his essay on "Die Entstehung des Staats . . . bei Tlinkit und Iroskesen"[15] attempts to show that certain events which occur among these tribes, which he interprets as the "origin of the state from the kinship constitution" ("Geschlechterverfassung") are "important as representative of a species"; i.e., in other words, they represent the "typical" form of the formation of the state — and possess on that account "validity . . . of almost universal significance."

Now the situation obviously — on the assumption of the correctness of Breysig's factual assertions — is are follows: the fact of the emergence of these Indian "states" and the way in which it occurred remains of extraordinarily slight significance for the causal nexus of the development of world history. No single "important" fact of the later political or cultural development (*Gestaltung*) of the world is influenced by it, i.e., can be related to it as a cause. For the formation of the political and cultural situation in the contemporary United States, the mode of origin of those Indian states and probably their very existence as well is "indifferent"; i.e., there is no

---

[15] *Schmollers Jahrbuch* 1904, pp. 483 ff.   Naturally I do not enter here in any way into the question of the substantive value of the work; on the contrary, the *correctness* of *all* of Breysig's assertions will be assumed in this as in all the illustrations which I cite.

demonstrable causal connection between the two while the after-effects of certain decisions of Themistocles are still visible today — however disappointingly this may block the attempt to construct an imposing unified scheme of "evolutionary historical development." On the other hand—if Breysig is right—the significance of the *propositions* produced by his analyses concerning the process of the formation of those states would, in his opinion, be epoch-making for our *knowledge* of the way in which states arise *in general*. If Breysig's view of the course of development as "typical" were correct and if it constituted a new addition to knowledge — we would then be in a position to formulate certain concepts which quite apart from their value for the conceptualization of the theory of the state, could at least be applied as heuristic devices in the causal interpretation of other historical developments. In other words, as a real historical factor, that specific development is of no significance, but as supplying a possible "principle of knowledge" his analysis is uncommonly significant (according to Breysig). On the other hand, to have knowledge of Themistocles' decisions, for example, signifies nothing for "psychology" or any other conceptualizing science; the fact that statesman "could" in the situation in question decide in that manner is intelligible to us without the aid of a "science constituted by laws" and our understanding of that fact is indeed the presupposition of our knowledge of the concrete causal nexus but it implies no enrichment of our generalized knowledge.

Let us take an example from the sphere of "nature": those particular X-rays which Roentgen saw flashing from his screen have left certain concrete effects which according to the law of the conservation of energy must still be acting somewhere in the cosmic system. But the "significance" of those particular rays in Roentgen's laboratory does not lie in their character as cosmic real causes. What happened in Roentgen's laboratory, just like every experiment, has importance only as the ground for inferring certain "laws" of the occurrence of events.[16]

---

16 This does not mean that these particular Roentgen rays could not figure as "historical" events: in a history of physics. The latter could concern itself among other things with the "accidental" circumstances which brought about the complex of factors in Roentgen's laboratory on those particular days, which

This is, of course, exactly how the situation stands in those cases which Eduard Meyer cites in a footnote to the passages which we are criticizing here (p. 37, fn. 2). He recalls there that "the most indifferent person whom we come to know by chance (in inscriptions or documents) acquires historical interest becanse *we can come to know the circumstances of the past through them.*" And the same confusion occurs when — if my memory does not fail me — Breysig (in a passage which I cannot locate at the moment) believes that he can completely destroy the argument that the selection of subject matter in historical research is oriented towards the "significant," the individually "important," by reference to the fact that research has achieved many of its most important results from the use of "clay fragments" and the like. Similar arguments are very popular today and their affinity with Friedrich Wilhelm IV's "coat" and the "insignificant persons" in Eduard Meyer's inscriptions is quite apparent — as is that confusion which is once again under discussion here. For as we have said, Breysig's "fragments of clay" and Eduard Meyer's "insignificant persons" are not — any more than the particular X-rays in Roentgen's laboratory — integrated as *causal* links in the historical sequence; rather, certain of their characteristic properties are means of ascertaining certain historical facts which facts in their turn become important for "the elaboration of concepts", i.e., they can

---

occasioned the radiation and which thereby led causally to the discovery of the "law" in question. It is clear that the logical status of those rays would, in this context, be completely changed. This is possible because these events play a role here which is rooted in *values* ("the progress of science"). It might perhaps be asserted that this logical distinction is only a result of having moved into the area of the subject matter of the *"Geisteswissenschaften,"* that the *cosmic* effects of those particular rays have therefore been left out of consideration. It is, however, irrelevant whether the particular "evaluated" object for which these rays were *causally* "significant" is "physical" or "psychic" in nature, provided only that it "means" something for us, i.e., that it is "evaluated." Once we assume the factual *possibility* of knowledge directed towards that object, the particular cosmic (physical, chemical, etc.) effects of those particular rays *could* (theoretically) become "historical facts"— but only if—lines of causation led from them to some particular result which was an "historical individual," i.e., was "evaluated" by us as *universally* significant in its *particular individual* character (*individuellen Eigenart*). Such an attempt would be meaningless merely on the ground that such a relationship of the rays to a universally significant object is in no way discernible even if the causal lines could actually be established.

themselves become heuristic instruments for the establishment of the generic "character" of certain artistic "epochs" or for the causal interpretation of concrete historical interconnections. This division of the logical use of the data given by cultural reality[17] into (1) conceptuaization with the illustrative use of "particular facts" as "typical" instances of an abstract "concept," i.e., as an heuristic instrument on the one hand — and (2) integration of the "particular fact" as a link, i.e., as a real causal factor into a real, hence concrete *context* with the use among other things of the products of conceptualization on the one hand as exemplificatory and on the other as heuristic devices — entails the distinction between what Rickert called the "natural-scientific" and Windelband the "nomothetic" procedure (ad 1) and the logical goal of the "historical cultural sciences" (ad 2). It also implies the only justified sense in which history can be called a science of *reality* (*Wirklichkeitswissenschaft*). For the meaning of history as a *science of reality* can only be that it treats particular elements of reality not merely as heuristic *instruments* but as the *objects* of knowledge, and particular causal connections not as premises of knowledge but as *real* causal factors. We shall, moreover, see how inaccurate is the naive popular view that history is the "mere" description of a pre-existent reality or the simple reproduction of "facts."[18]

Rickert's "tailor" whom Eduard Meyer criticizes is in the same position as the clay fragments and the "insignificant persons" of the inscriptions. The fact that a certain tailor delivered a certain coat to the king is *prima facie* of quite inconsequential causal significance, even for the cultural-*historical* causal interconnection of the development of "fashion" and the "tailoring industry." It would cease to be so only when as a result of this particular delivery historical *effects*

---

[17]Here the author wrote on the margin of the proofs: A step in reasoning has been missed here. Add: that a fact where it is considered as an instance of a class-concept (Gattungsbegriff) is a *heuristic* instrument (*Erkenntnis mittel*). But not every heuristic instrument is a class concept.

[18] The term "science of reality" in the sense in which it is used here is perfectly adequate for the essential nature of history. The misunderstanding which contains the popular interpretation of this term as referring to a simple presuppositionless "description" has been dealt with adequately by Rickert and Simmel.

were produced, e.g., if the personality of this tailor, or the fortunes of *his* enterprise were causally "significant" from some standpoint for the transformation of fashion or industrial organization and if this historical role had been causally affected by the delivery of that very coat.

As an heuristic device for the ascertainment of fashion, etc., on the other hand, the style of Friedrich Wilhelm IV's coats and the fact that they came from certain (e.g., Berlin) workshops can certainly achieve as much "significance" as anything else which is accessible to us as material for the discovery of the fashion of that period. The coats of the king are, in this case, to be considered as instances of a *class*-concept, which is being elaborated as an *heuristic instrument* — the rejection of the Kaiser's crown, on the other hand, with which they are compared, is to be viewed as a concrete *link* in an historical situation as real *effect* and *cause* in a specific real series of changes. These are absolutely fundamental logical distinctions and they will always remain so. And however much these two absolutely distinct standpoints become intertwined in the practice of the student of culture — this always happens and is the source of the most interesting methodological problems — no one will ever succeed in understanding the logical character of history if he is unable to make this distinction in a clearcut manner.

Eduard Meyer has however presented two mutually incompatible viewpoints regarding the mutual relationship of these two logically distinct categories of "historical reality." On the one hand he confuses, as we have seen, the "historical interest" in the historically "effective," i.e., the real causal links in historical interconnections (rejection of the Kaiser's crown) with those facts (Friedrich Wilhelm IV's coat, the inscriptions) which can become important for the historian as heuristic instruments. On the other hand, however— and now we shall speak of this — the distinction of the "historically effective" from all other objects of our actual or possible knowledge is so sharpened that he makes assertions about the limits of the scientific "interest" of the historian, the realization of which to almost any degree in his own great work would necessarily be deeply regretted by its admirers. He says (p. 48), "I have long believed that in the selection which the historian must make, what is *characteristic* (i.e., what is characteristically singular and which distinguishes an institution or an individuality from all other analogous and similar ones) is decisive. This is undeniably the case but it is of concern for history only insofar as we are able to grasp the individuality of a culture by its characteristic features. Thus the historian's selectivity is historically always only a means which renders the culture's historical *effectiveness* . . . conceivable to us." This is, as all the previous considerations show, entirely correct, as are the conclusions drawn therefrom: that the popular formulation of the question of the "significance" of the particular and of personalities for history is poorly put, that the "personality" "enters into" history, by no means in its totality but only in its causal relevance for the historical situation as this latter is established by the science of history, that the historical significance of a particular personality as a causal factor and the general "human" significance of the same personality in the light of its "intrinsic value" have nothing to do with one another, and that the very "inadequacies" of a personality in a decisive position can be causally significant. This is all perfectly right. And yet the question still remains whether — or let us rather say at once — in *which* sense is it right to assert that the analysis of the content of culture — from the historical viewpoint — can aim only to make the cultural events under consideration intelligible in their effectiveness. The logical importance of this question is disclosed as soon as we consider the conclusions which Eduard Meyer draws from his thesis. At first (p. 48) he concludes that "existing circumstances in themselves are never the object of history but rather become such when they become historically effective." A work of art, a literary product, an institution of constitutional law, mores, etc., cannot possibly be analyzed in "all their aspects" in an historical work (including art and literary history); nor is it appropriate — since in doing this, elements must be considered which do "not achieve historical effectiveness"; while on the other hand the historian must include in his work "details which are of quite subordinate status in a system" (e.g., of constitutional law) because of their causal significance. He concludes further from the aforementioned principle of historical selection that *biography* is a "literary" and not an historical discipline. Why? Its object is the particular given personality *in its total* intrinsic nature and not as an historically effective factor — that it was historically effective is here merely the presupposition, the reason for its having a biography devoted to it. As long as the biography is only a biography and not the history of the age of its hero, it cannot fulfill the task of history: the presentation of an historial *event*. To this assertion, one responds with the question: Why is this special status accorded to "personalities"? Do "events" like the Battle of Marathon or the Persian Wars in general "belong" in their "totality" in an historical narration, described in all their *specimina fortitudinis* in the style of the Homeric recital? Obviously even in the case of the instances just mentioned only those events and conditions belong in an historical narration which are decisive for historical causal connections. This has been so in principle, at least, ever since heroic myths and history began to follow divergent paths. And now what is the case with regard to "biography"? It is, whatever one may say, obviously false (or a rhetorical hyperbole) to assert that "all the details . . . of the external and inner life of its hero" belong in a biography, however much the Goethe-research which Eduard Meyer has in mind seeks to give that impression. It is simply a question here of collections of materials which aim to include everything which can possibly acquire significance for Goethe's life-history, be it as a direct link in a causal series — i.e., as an historically relevant fact — or be it as a means of establishing historically relevant facts, i.e., as a "source material." In a Goethe biography which meets high scholarship standards, however, only those facts which are significant obviously belong as elements in the presentation.

Here we of course come up against an ambiguity in the meaning of this word ("significant") which requires logical analysis and which analysis, as we shall see, can disclose the "correct kernel" of Eduard Meyer's views as well as the defect in the formulation of his theory of the historically "effective" as the object of history.

In order to see the various logical standpoints from which the "facts" of cultural life may be scientifically considered, let us take an example: Goethe's letters to Frau von Stein. It is not — let us clear this up in advance — the perceivable "fact" before us, i.e., the written paper, which is treated as "historical." This paper is rather only the means of knowing the other fact, namely, that Goethe had the

sentiments expressed there, wrote them down and sent them to
Frau von Stein, and received answers from her, the approximate
meaning of which can be inferred from the correctly interpreted
"content" of Goethe's letters. This "fact" which is disclosed by an
"interpretation" of the "meaning" of the letters — undertaken ultimately by "scientific" procedures — is in truth what we have in mind
when we refer to these "letters." This fact may (1) be integrated
directly as such in an historical causal context: for example, the
ascetic restraint of those years which was bound up with a passion
of unheard of force obviously left profound traces in Goethe's development which were not extinguished even when he was transformed
under the Southern skies. To investigate these effects in Goethe's
"personality," to trace their influence in his creative work, and to
"interpret" them causally by showing their connection with the events
of those years to the extent that this is possible, are among the least
questionable tasks of literary history. The facts of which those letters are evidence are "historical" facts, i.e., as we have seen, are real
links in a causal chain. Now let us assume — we do not raise here
the question as to the probability of this or any other assumptions
that we may make henceforward — that it may be positively demonstrated in some way that those experiences had no influence whatsoever on Goethe's personal and literary development; that is, that
absolutely none of his traits or productions which "interest" us were
influenced by them. In that case, despite their causal ineffectiveness,
these experiences could (2) gain our interest as *heuristic* means; they
could present something "characteristic"— as it is usually said — of
Goethe's historical uniqueness. This means, however, that we could
perhaps — whether we could really do it is not at issue — derive
from them insights into a type of conduct and outlook on life which
were peculiar to him throughout his life or for a substantial period
and which influenced markedly his literary expressions and personal
traits which interest us historically. The "historical" *fact* which
would then be integrated as a real link in the causal nexus of his
"life" would be that "outlook on life"— a conceptual complex of
grouped qualities constituted by the inherited personal qualities
of Goethe and those which were acquired through education, milieu
and in the fortunes of his life and (perhaps) by the deliberately ac-

quired "maxims" according to which he lived and which played a part in the determination of his conduct and his creations. The experiences with Frau von Stein would indeed in this case — since that "outlook on life" is a collective concept (*begriffliches Kollektivum*) which is "expressed" in *particular* events — be real *components* of an *"historical"* fact. But they obviously would not come up for our consideration—under the assumptions made above—essentially as such, but rather as "symptoms" of that outlook on life, i.e., as heuristic *means*. Their logical relationship to the object which is to be known has therewith undergone a shift.

Let us now further assume that this, too, is not the case. Those experiences contain nothing which would in any respect be characteristic of Goethe in contrast with other contemporaries; instead they correspond completely to something which is thoroughly "typical" of the pattern of life of certain German social circles of that period. In that case they would not tell us anything new for our historical knowledge of Goethe, but they could under certain circumstances probably (3) attract our interest as a conveniently usable *paradigm* of that type, as, in other words, a means of knowing the "characteristic" features of the mental and spiritual attitudes of those circles. The particular features of the attitudes which are "typical"— on the basis of our assumptions — of that group in the past and that pattern of life which was its expression, would, in its contrast with the pattern of life of other epochs, nations, and social strata, be the "historical" fact to be integrated into a cultural-historical causal context as real cause and effect; it would then have to be causally "interpreted" with respect to its difference from the Italian *cicisbéa* and the like in the light of a "history of German morals and manners" or to the extent that such national divergences are considered non-existent, in the light of a general history of the morals and manners of that age.

Let us now suppose further that the content of these letters is not useful even for this purpose, and that on the contrary it is shown that phenomena which are in certain "essential" respects of the *same* sort regularly occur under certain cultural conditions — in other words, that in *these* respects those experiences (of Goethe) reveal no peculiar features of German or Ottocento culture but rather certain features common to all cultures under certain conditions which are capable of being formulated in precise concepts. In this event then it would (4) be the task of a "cultural psychology" or a "social psychology," for instance, to determine by analysis, isolating abstraction and generalization, the conditions under which *these* common components emerge, to "interpret" the basis of the regular sequence and to express the "rule" so achieved as a genetic *class*-concept (*Gattungsbegriff*). These thoroughly general (*Gattungsmässige*) components of Goethe's experiences which are highly irrelevant as regards his particular and unique features would, then, be of interest simply as means of attaining this class-concept (*Gattunsbegriff*).

And finally, (5) it must be regarded *a priori* as possible that those "experiences" contain nothing at all which is characteristic of any stratum of the population or any cultural epoch. But even in the absence of all occasion for a "cultural-scientific" (*Kulturwissenschaftlicher*) interest, it is conceivable — whether it is actually so is once again indifferent here — that a psychiatrist interested in the psychology of love-relationships might view them from a variety of "useful" viewpoints, as an "ideal-typical" illustration of certain ascetic "disturbances," just as Rousseau's *Confessions,* for example, are of interest to the specialist in nervous diseases. Naturally, the possibility here must be taken into account — that the letters are to be considered as serving all these various scientific purposes — of course, the variety does not entirely exhaust the logical possibilities — through the *various* components of their content, as well as serving *various* purposes through the *same* components.[19]

Upon reviewing the foregoing analysis in reverse order, we see that these letters to Frau von Stein, i.e., the content which can be derived from them with regard to Goethe's utterances and experience, acquire "meaning" in the following ways: (a) in the last two cases (4, 5) as instances of a class, and hence as heuristic *means* (*Erkenntnismittel*) to the disclosure of their *general* nature (No. 4, 5); (b) as "characteristic" components of a composite phenomenon (*Kollektivum*) and on that account as a heuristic means to the disclosure of its *particular*

---

[19] This will obviously not prove, for instance, that logic is wrong in rigorously distinguishing these various standpoints which can be found within one and the same scientific presentation. Yet this is the assumption of many wrongheaded objections to Rickert's views.

(*individuellen*) features (No. 2, 3) ;[20] (c) as a causal component of
an historical nexus (*Zusammenhang*) (No. 1). In the cases listed
under (a) (No. 4 and 5), "significance" for history exists only insofar
as the class concept (*Gattungsbegriff*), constructed with the aid of
these particular instances, can become important under certain conditions — to be dealt with later — in checking an historical demonstration.   On the other hand, when Eduard Meyer confines the
range of the "historical" to the "effective"— i.e., to No. 1 (c) of
the foregoing list — it cannot possibly mean that the consideration of
the second category of cases of "significance" under (b) lies outside
the purview of history, that, in other words, facts which are not themselves components of historical causal sequences but which only serve
to disclose the facts which are to be integrated into such causal sequences, e.g., such components of Goethe's correspondence which
"illustrate" for instance those "particular features" of Goethe which
are decisive for his literary production or which "illustrate" those
aspects of the culture of the society of the Ottocento which are essential for the development of morals and manners.   In other words, it
cannot possibly mean that these facts which serve to produce the kind
of knowledge just referred to should be once and for all disregarded
by history — if not (as in No. 2) by the "history" of Goethe, then by
a "history of manners" of the 18th century (No. 3).   Meyer's own
work must be carried on continuously with such heuristic means.
What is meant here can only be that, in any such work, the "components of an historical nexus" (*Zusammenhang*) are a different
thing from an "heuristic means."   But neither "biography" nor "classical studies" uses such "characteristic" details as the aforementioned
components of Goethe's correspondence in any way contrary to this
distinction.   It is obvious that this is not the stumbling block for
Eduard Meyer.

---

[20] The discussion of these special cases will concern us more closely in a subsequent section.   For this reason we deliberately leave untouched here the
question as to the extent to which it is to be viewed as something logically
unique.   We wish to state here, only because of its greater certainty, that it
naturally does not in any way obscure the logical distinction between the historical and nomothetic uses of "facts," since in any case, the *concrete* fact is
not being used here "historically" in the sense adhered to in this discussion,
namely as a link in a concrete causal series.

Now, however, a type of "significance" greater than all of those already analyzed comes before us. Those experiences of Goethe — to adhere to our example — are "significant" for us not only as "cause" or as "heuristic means" but — quite apart from whether we obtain from them some new and hitherto completely unkown knowledge of Goethe's outlook on life, the culture of the 18th century, or the "typical" course of cultural events, etc., and quite apart from whether they have had any sort of causal influence on his development — the uniquely characteristic content of these letters is also an object of valuation (*Bewertung*) for us — just as it is and without and strained search for any "meanings" which lie outside it and which are not contained in it. The letters would be such an object of *valuation* even it nothing else at all was known of their author. Now what primarily interests us here involves two points: first, the fact that this "valuation" is connected with the incomparable, the unique, the irreplaceable literary element in the object and — this is the second point — that this valuation of the object in its characteristic uniqueness (*individuellen Eigenart*) supplies the reason why the object becomes an object of reflection and of — at this point we will deliberately avoid saying "scientific"— intellectual treatment, that is, it becomes an object of *interpretation*. This "interpretation"[21] can take two paths which in actual practice almost always merge but which are, however, to be sharply distinguished from one another logically. Interpretation can and does become first *"value-interpretation"* (*Wertinterpretation*), i.e., it teaches us to "understand" the intellectual, psychological and spiritual (*geistigen*) content of that correspondence; it develops and raises to the level of explicit *"evaluation"* that which we "feel" dimly and vaguely. For this purpose, interpretation is not at all required to enunciate or to "suggest" a *value judgment*. What it actually "suggests" in the course of analysis are rather various possible *relationships* of *the object to values* (*Wertbeziehungen des Objektes*). The "attitude" which the evaluated object calls forth in us need not be a positive one: thus in the case of Goethe's relations with Frau von Stein, the usual modern sexual philistine, for example, just

---

21 Here the German word *Interpretation* is used — and is equated by Weber with *Deutung* which is the term he usually employs in the text and which is always translated here by "interpretation." (E.A.S.)

as well as, let us say, a Catholic moralist, would take an essentially negative attitude, if at all an "understanding" one. Or when we successively consider Karl Marx's *Kapital*, or *Faust*, or the ceiling of the Sistine chapel or Rousseau's *Confessions*, or the experiences of St. Theresa, or Mme. Roland or Tolstoi, or Rabelais, or Marie Bashkirtseff, or the Sermon on the Mount as objects of interpretation, there confronts us an infinite multiplicity of "evaluative" attitudes. The "interpretation" of these very different objects shares — if the interpretation is thought to be worthwhile and is undertaken, which we assume here for our purposes — only the *formal* feature that the meaning of interpretation consists in disclosing to us the *possible* "evaluative standpoints" and "evaluative approaches." Interpretation imposes a certain valuation as the only "scientific" one only where, as in the case of the intellectual content of Karl Marx's *Kapital*, for instance, *norms* (in that case, of thought) come into account. But here, too, the objectively valid "valuation" of the object (in this case, the logical "correctness" of the Marxian forms of thought) are not necessarily involved in the purpose of an "interpretation." And such an imposition of a valuation would be, where it is a question not of "norms" but of "cultural values," a task completely transcending the domain of "interpretation." One can, without any logical or substantive contradiction — that is all that is involved here — reject as inherently without validity all the products of the poetic and artistic culture of antiquity or the religious attitude of the Sermon on the Mount just as well as that mixture — contained in our example of the letters to Frau von Stein — of glowing passion on the one side, asceticism on the other with all those flowers of emotional life which are so superlatively fine from our standpoint. That negative "interpretation" would not, however, be at all "valueless" for the person making it for such an interpretation can despite its negative character, indeed even because of it, provide "knowledge" for him in the sense that it, as we say, extends his "inner life," and his "mental and spiritual (*geistigen*) horizon," and makes him capable of comprehending and thinking through the possibilities and nuances of life-patterns as such and to develop his own self intellectually, æsthetically, and ethically (in the widest sense) in a differentiated way — or in other words, to make his "psyche," so to speak, more "sensitive to values." The "interpre-

tation" of intellectual and mental (*geistigen*), æsthetic or ethical creations has in this respect the effects of the latter, and the assertion that
"history" in a certain sense is an "art" has in this respect its jutifiable
"kernel of truth," no less than the designation of the cultural and
humanistic sciences (*"Geisteswissenschaften"*) as "subjectivizing." In
this function of interpretation, however, we reach the outermost edge
of what can still be called the "elaboration of the empirical by
thought"; there is here no longer a concern with "historical work" in
the proper and distinctive sense of the word.

It is probably clear that by what he called the "philosophical consideration of the past," Eduard Meyer meant *this* type of interpretation which has its point of departure in what are in essence *atemporal*
relations of "historical" objects, i.e., their *axiological* validity (*Wert-
geltung*) and which teaches us to "understand" them. This is indicated by his definition of this type of scientific activity (p. 55) which
according to him, "places the products of history in the present and
hence deals with them as finished" treating the object, "not as becoming and having historical effects but as being," and therefore in contrast with "history," treating it in "all its aspects"; it aims, according
to Eduard Meyer, at an "exhaustive interpretation of particular creations," primarily in the fields of literature and art, but also as he
expressly adds, of political and religious institutions, manners and
attitudes, and "ultimately of the entire culture of an epoch treated
as a unity." Naturally, this type of "interpretation" has nothing
"philological" about it in the sense appropriate to the specialized
linguistic disciplines. The interpretation of the textual-linguistic
"meaning" of a literary object and the interpretation of "mental,
intellectual and spiritual (*geistigen*) content," its "meaning" in this
value-oriented sense of the word may in fact proceed hand in hand,
ever so frequently and with good reason. They are nonetheless logically fundamentally different procedures; the one, the textual-linguistic
interpretation, is the elementary prerequisite — not in regard to the
value and intensity of the mental work which it requires but with
respect to its logical role — for all types of the scientific treatment and
utilization of "source materials." It is, from the historical standpoint,
a technical means of verifying "facts"; it is a "tool" of history (as well
as of numerous other disciplines). "Interpretation" in the sense of

"value-analysis" (*Wertanalyse*) — as we shall designate in *ad hoc* fashion the procedure which has just been described above[22] — does not in any case stand in the *same* relationship to history. Now, since this type of "interpretation" is oriented neither towards the disclosure of facts which are "causally" relevant for an historical context nor toward the abstraction of "typical" components which are usable for the construction of a class concept (*Gattunsbegriff*), since in contrast with these it rather considers its object, i.e., to keep Eduard Meyer's example, the "total culture," let us say, of the high point of Hellenistic civilization as a unity — "for its own sake" and makes it intelligible in its "value-relations." Hence it is not subsumable under any of the other categories of knowledge, the direct or indirect relations of which to "history" were previously discussed. This type of interpretation can not, in particular, be properly deemed as an "auxiliary" to history — as Eduard Meyer (p. 54, bottom) views his "philology"— for it indeed treats its objects from viewpoints quite other than history does. If the distinction between the two kinds of interpretation were to be sought only in this, that the one (i.e., value-analysis) treats its objects "statically" as finished products while the other (history) treats its objects "developmentally," the former cutting a cross section through events, the latter a longitudinal section, then it would assuredly be of quite minor significance. Even the historian, e.g., Eduard Meyer in his own works, must in order to weave his design, take his point of departure in certain "given" beginnings which he describes "satically" (*zuständlich*) and he will, in the course of his exposition, repeatedly group the "results" of "developments" into "static" cross sections. A monographic presentation, for instance, of the social composition of the Athenian *ecclesia* at a certain point of time for the purpose of helping to make clear its own causal-historical conditions on the one hand and its effect on the political "situation" in Athens on the other, is certainly, even according to Eduard Meyer, an "historical" work. The distinction in question seems for Eduard Meyer rather to lie in the fact that "philological" (i.e., "value-analytical") work can and indeed normally

---

[22] This is done essentially to distinguish *this* type of "interpretation" from that which is only texual-linguistic. The fact that this distinction does not invariably actually occur in practice should not impede the *logical* distinction.

will concern itself with facts which are relevant to history but that together with these, it will have occasion to concern itself with facts which are quite different from those dealt with by history. "Value-analysis deals with facts which are neither (1) themselves links in an historical causal sequence, nor (2) usable as heuristic means for disclosing facts of category (1). In other words, the facts of value-analysis stand in none of the relations to history which have been hitherto considered. In what other relations then do they stand, or does this value-analytical approach have no relationship whatsoever to any type of historical knowledge?

To get ahead with our discussion, let us turn to our example of the letters of Frau von Stein and let us take as a second example Karl Marx's *Kapital*. Both can obviously become the objects of interpretation, not only of textual-linguistic interpretation of which we shall not speak here, but also of the "value-analytical" interpretation which enables us to "understand" their relations to values (*Wertbeziehungen*) and which analyzes and "psychologically" interprets the letters of Frau von Stein in the way, for instance, in which one "interprets" "Faust" or investigates Marx's *Kapital* with respect to its *intellectual* content and expounds its *intellectual* but not its historical — relationship to other systems of ideas concerned with *the same problems*. "Value-analysis" treats its objects for this purpose, following Eduard Meyer's terminology, primarily in a "static" (*zuständlich*) way, i.e., in a more correct formulation, it takes its point of departure in their character as "values" independent of all purely historical-causal significance, and to that extent as having a status which is for us, beyond history. But does "value-analytical" interpretation confine itself to such an object? Certainly not! — an interpretation of those letters of Goethe no more than one of *Das Kapital* or of Faust or of Orestes or of the Sistine Chapel paintings. It would rather, precisely in order wholly to attain its own goal, take into account that that ideal value-object (*Wertobjekt*) was historically conditioned, that numerous nuances and turns of thought and sentiment remain "incomprehensible," when the general conditions, e.g., the social "milieu" and the quite concrete events of the days on which those Goethe-letters were written are unknown, when the historically given "problem-situation" of the time in which Marx wrote his book and his development as a thinker remain undiscussed. Thus the "interpretation" of Goethe's letters requires for its success an *historical* investigation of the conditions under which they came into being, including all those very minor as well as the most comprehensive relationships (*Zusammenhange*) in Goethe's purely personal —"domestic"—environment as well as in the total broader cultural environment in its widest sense which were of *causal* significance —"effective" in Eduard Meyer's words — for their particular quality. For the knowledge of all these causal conditions teaches us indeed the psychic constellations in which those letters were born, and thereby it enables us really to "understand" them. [23]

---

[23] Even Vossler, in his analysis of a fable of La Fontaine contained in his brilliantly written, intentionally one-sided *Die Sprache als Schopfung und Entwicklung* (Heidelberg 1905, p. 8 and ff.), provides confirmation of this statement although he does not wish to do so. The only "legitimate" task of "æsthetic" interpretation is, for him, (as it is for Croce, whose position is close to his own) to show that, and to what extent, the literary "creation" is an adequate "expression."

Nevertheless he, too, is compelled to have recourse to a reference to the quite concrete "psychic" characteristics of La Fontaine (p. 93) and beyond these to "milieu" and "race" and yet we cannot discern the reasons why this causal imputation, this inquiry into the origins of what exists, which, by the way, always operates with generalizing concepts (on this point, more later) breaks off at the very point at which this very attractive and instructive sketch does or why the extension of this causal imputation for purposes of "interpretation" is thought to become useless, as Vossler seems to think at this point. When Vossler again retracts those concessions by saying that he recognizes the "spatial" and "temporal" conditionedness "only for the matter" (Stoff) (p. 95) but asserts that the "form" which is alone æsthetically essential, is a "free creation of the spirit," it must be recalled that he is following a terminology like that of Croce. Accordingly, "freedom" is equivalent to "conformity with norms" (*Normgemassheit*) and "form" is *correct* expression in Croce's sense, and as such is identical with æsthetic *value*. This terminology involves the danger, however, of leading to the confusion of "existence" and "norm."

It is the great merit of Vossler's stimulating essay that it once more stresses very strongly, against the pure phoneticists and linguistic positivists, that (1) there exists the entirely autonomous scientific task of the interpretation of the "values" and "norms" of literary creations as well as the physiology and psychology of language, "historical" investigations, and those seeking to establish "phonetic" laws; and that (2) the very *understanding* and "experience" of these "values" and norms is also a *sine qua non* for the *causal* interpretation of the origin and conditionedness of mental and spiritual creations, since the creator of literary productions or of linguistic expressions himself "experiences" them. However, it should be noted that in this *case* where the values and norms are the *means of causal* knowledge and not standards of *value* they come into play in the logical role, not of "norms" but rather in their pure factuality as "possible" empirical contents of a "psychic" *event*. They are in this role, not different "in principle" from the delusions of a paralytic. I believe that

But it still remains true, on the other hand, that causal "explanation," here as elsewhere, undertaken for its own sake, and à la Duntzer, "grasps only part of the matter." And obviously, that type of "interpretation" which we have alone called "value analysis" functions as a guide for this other "historical," i.e., causal type of "interpretation." The former type of analysis reveals the "valued" components of the object, the causal "explanation" of which is the problem of the latter type of analysis. The former creates the points of attachment from which there are to be regressively traced the web of causal connections and thus provides causal analysis with the decisive "viewpoints" without which it would indeed have to operate, as it were, without a compass on an uncharted sea. Now, anyone can — and many will — deny that there is need, as far as they themselves are concerned, to see the whole apparatus of historical analysis straining at the task of the historical "explanation" of a series of "love letters," be they ever so sublime. Certainly—but the same is true, however, disrespecful it seems, of Karl Marx's *Das Kapital,* and for *all* the objects of historical research. The knowledge of the materials out of which Marx constructed his work, the knowledge of how the genesis of his ideas was historically conditioned, and any historical knowledge of today's power relationship, or of the development of the German political system in its particular characteristics can, of course, appear to anyone to be a thoroughly dull and fruitless thing or, at least, one of very secondary importance and one which as an end in itself is indeed quite meaningless. But neither logic nor scientific experience can "refute" him, as Eduard Meyer has expressly conceded, although certainly in a somewhat curt way.

It will be profitable for our purposes to dwell a bit longer on the *logical* nature of value-analysis. The attempt has been made in all seriousness to understand or to "refute" H. Rickert's very clearly

---

Vossler's and Croce's terminology, which tends repeatedly towards the logical confusion of "valuation" and (causal) "explanation" and to a denial of the autonomy of the latter, weakens the cogency of the argument. Those tasks of purely empirical work themselves are and remain, alongside of those tasks which Vossler calls "æsthetics," autonomous, both in substance and in logical function. That such causal analysis is today called "folk psychology" or "psychology" is a result of a terminological fad; but this can not, ultimately, in any way affect the objective justification for this type of analysis.

developed idea that the construction of the "historical individual" is conditioned by "value-relevance" (*Wertbeziehung*) as asserting that this relevance to values is identical with a subsumption under general *concepts*[24] such as the "state," "religion," "art," etc., and similar concepts, which are assuredly, it is said, the "values" in question; the fact that history brings its objects into relation with these values and thereby attains specific "viewpoints" is then equivalent — this is what is added — to the separate treatment of the "chemical," "physical," etc., "aspects" of events in the sphere of the natural sciences.[25] These are remarkable misunderstandings of what is and must be understood by "value-relevance" (*Wertbeziehung*). An actual "value-judgment" concerning a concrete object or the theoretical establishment of the possible "value-relations" of the object does not imply that I subsume them under a certain class-concept: "love letter," "political structure," "economic phenomenon." Rather, the "value-judgment" involves my "taking an attitude" in a certain concrete way to the object in its concrete individuality; the subjective sources of this attitude of mine, of my "value-standpoints" which are decisive for it are definitely not a "concept," and certainly not an "abstract concept" but rather a thoroughly concrete, highly individually structured and constituted "feeling" and "preference"; it may, however, be under certain circumstances the consciousness of a certain, and here again, concrete kind of imperative (*sollens*). And when I pass from the stage of the actual evaluation of an object into the stage of theoretical-interpretative reflection on *possible* relevance to values, in other words, when I construct "historical individuals" from the objects, it means that I am making explicit to myself and to others in an *interpretative* way the concrete, individual, and on that account, in the last analysis, unique form in which "ideas" — to employ for once a metaphysical usage — are "incorporated" into or "work themselves out" in the political structures in question (e.g., in the "state of Frederick the Great"), of the personality in question (e.g., Goethe or Bismarck) or the literary prod-

---

24 This is the view of Schmeidler in Ostwald's *Annalen der Naturphilosophie* III, pp. 24 ff.
25 This view, to my astonishment, was also taken by Franz Eulenberg in the *Archiv fur Sozialwissenschaft*. His polemic against Rickert and "his men" is only possible in my opinion precisely because he *excludes* from his considerations the object the logical analysis of which is at issue, namely, "history."

uct in question (e.g., Marx's *Kapital*). Or in a different formulation
which avoids the always dubious and moreover avoidable metaphysical mode of expression: in constructing historical individuals I elaborate in an explicit form the focal points for *possible* "evaluative"
attitudes which the segment of reality in question discloses and in
consequence of which it claims a more or less universal *"meaning"*—
which is to be sharply distinguished from *causal* "significance." *Das
Kapital* of Karl Marx shares the characteristic of being a "literary
product" with those combinations of printers' ink and paper which
appear weekly in the Brockhaus List — what makes it into an "historical" individual for us is, however, not its membership in the class
of literary products but rather on the contrary, its thoroughly unique
"intellectual content," which "we" find "set down" in it.   In the
same way the quality of a "political event" is shared by the pothouse
political chatter of the philistine having his last drink at closing time
with that complex of printed and written paper, sound waves, bodily
movements on drill grounds, clever or also foolish thoughts in the
heads of princes, diplomats, etc., which "we" synthesize into the individual conceptual structure of the "German Empire" because "we"
turn to it with a certain "historical interest" which is thoroughly
unique for us, and which is rooted in innumerable "values"— and
not just political values either.   To express this "significance"— the
content of the object, for instance, of Faust, with respect to possible
relevance to values, or stated in another way, to think of expressing
the "content of our interest" in the historical individual — by means
of a class-concept is obviously nonsense.   Indeed, the inexhaustibility
of its "content" as regards possible focal points for our interest is
what is characteristic of the historical individual of the "highest"
order.   The fact that we classify certain "important" tendencies in
the ways of relating historical objects to relevant values and that this
classification is then useful as a basis for the division of labor of the
cultural sciences, naturally leaves entirely unaffected[26] the fact that

26 When I investigate the social and economic *determinants* of the emergence
of a concrete "embodiment" of "Christianity," for instance, of the provencal
knightly poetry, I do not thereby turn these latter into phenomena which are
"evaluated" for the sake of their economic *significance*.   The way in which the
individual investigator or the particularly traditionally delimited "discipline"
defines its "sphere" out of purely technical considerations of the division of
labor, is of not logical significance here.

the proposition: a "value" of "general, i.e., universal significance" is a "general," i.e., abstract (*genereller*) concept is just as curious as the opinion that one can express "the truth" in a single sentence or perform "the ethically right" in *one* single action or embody "the beautiful" in *one* single work of art.

But let us return to Eduard Meyer and his attempts to cope with the problem of historical "significance." The foregoing reflections do indeed leave the sphere of methodology and touch on the philosophy of history. From the point of view which stands firmly on the ground of methodology, the circumstance that certain *individual* components of reality are selected as objects of historical treatment is to be justified only by reference to this *factual* existence of a corresponding *interest*. "Value-relevance" cannot indeed mean more for such a view which does not enquire after the *meaning* of this interest. And thus Eduard Meyer, too, is on this matter, content to say — justifiably from this point of view — that the fact of the existence of this interest suffices for history, however lowly one might rate this interest in itself. But certain obscurities and contradictions in his discussion are clearly enough the results of such an imperfect philosophical-historical orientation.

"The selection" (of history) "rests on the historical *interest, which the present* has in any effect, in the results of historic development, so that it feels the need of tracing the causes which have brought it about," says Eduard Meyer (p. 37). He later interprets this to mean (p. 45) that the historian finds "the problems with which he approaches history within himself," and that these problems then give him "the guiding principles by which he orders the material."

This agrees entirely with what has already been said and is, moreover, the only possible sense in which the previously criticized statement of Eduard Meyer about "the ascent from effect to cause" is correct. It is not a question here, as he believes, of utilizing the concept of causality in a way peculiar to history but rather of the fact that only those "causes" are "historically significant" which the *regressus,* which begins with a "valued" cultural component, must incorporate into itself as indispensable components. What is involved here, then, is the principal of "teleological dependence" as it has been designated in a phrase which is sure to be subject to misunderstanding.

But the question then arises: must this point of departure of the *regressus* always be a component of the *present*, as might, on the basis of the quotation cited above, be believed to be Eduard Meyer's view? As a matter of fact, Eduard Meyer does not take an entirely certain position on this point. He provides no clear indication — this is apparent from what has already been said — of what he really understands by his term "historically effective." For — as has already been pointed out to him by others — if only what has "effects" belongs in history, the crucial question for every historical exposition: for example his own *Geschichte des Altertums*: is then: what final outcome and which of its elements should be taken as fundamental, as having been "effected" by the historical development to be described; it must also be decided, in that event, whether a fact bcause it has no causal significance for any component of that final outcome must be excluded as being historically inconsequential. Many of Eduard Meyer's assertions create the impression at first that the objective "cultural situation" of the present — as we shall call it for the sake of brevity — should be decisive here. According to this view, only facts which *still today* are of causal significance, in our contemporary political, economic, social, religious, ethical, scientific, or any other sectors of our cultural life, and the "effects" of which are directly perceptible at present (cf. p. 37) belong in an "History of Antiquity"; on the other hand, however, it would be an entirely irrelevant criterion whether a fact were even of the most fundamental significance for the particular character of the culture of antiquity (cf. p. 48). Eduard Meyer's work would shrink rather badly — think of the volume on Egypt, for instance, if he took this proposition seriously and many would not indeed find precisely that which they expect in a history of antiquity if this were so. But he leaves another path open (p. 37): we can also experience it — i.e., what was historically "effective"— "in the past to the extent that we *treat* any phase of it *as if* it were contemporaneous." In view of this, any cultural component whatsoever can surely be "treated" as "effective" from some standpoint, however chosen, in a history of antiquity — but in that case, the delimitation which Eduard Meyer seeks to establish would dissolve. And there would still arise the question: which feature of events is accepted by an "History of Antiquity" as the criterion of what is of essential importance for the historian? From Eduard Meyer's standpoint, the answer must be: the "end" of ancient history, i.e., the situation which appears to us as the appropriate "end point"— thus, for example, the reign of the Emperor Romulus, or the reign of Justinian — or probably better — the reign of Diocletian. In this event, everything in any case which is "characteristic" of this "final epoch," this "old age" of antiquity would undoubtedly belong, to its fullest extent, in the exposition of the age's close as would all the "facts" which were causally essential ("effective") in this process of "aging." This inclusiveness is necessary because the object of historical explanation is constituted by what is *characteristic* of the epoch. At the same time we would have to exclude, for example, in the description of Greek culture, everything which no longer exercised any "cultural influences" at that time (i.e., during the reigns of Emperors Romulus or Diocletian), and this in the then existing state of literature, philosophy and general culture, would be a terribly large part of those very elements which render the "history of antiquity" valuable to us and which we, fortunately, do not find omitted from Eduard Meyer's own work.

An history of antiquity which would include only what exercised causal influences on any later epoch, would — especially if one regards political relations as the true backbone of the historical,— appear as empty as a "history" of Goethe which "mediatized" him — to use Ranke's expression, in favor of his *epigoni,* which in other words, described only those elements among his characteristics and his actions which remain "influential" in literature; there is no distinction in principle in this regard between scientific (*wissenschaftliche*) "biography" and historical objects which are otherwise delimited. Eduard Meyer's thesis is not realizable in the formulation which he has given to it. Or do we have, in his case, too, an escape from the contradiction between his theory and his own practice. We have heard Eduard Meyer say that the historian derives his problems "from within himself, and he adds to this remark: "the present in which the *historian* works is a factor which can not be excluded from any historical presentation." Are we to regard the "effectiveness" of a "fact" which marks it as "an historical fact" as existing where a modern historian interests himself and is able to interest his readers in the fact in its particular individuality and in those features of its origins through which it has become what it is and not something else? Obviously, Eduard Meyer's arguments (pp. 36, 37, and 45) confuse two quite different conceptions of "historical facts." The first refers to such elements of reality which are "valued," it might be said, "for their own sake" in their concrete uniqueness as objects of our interest; the second, to those components of reality to which attention is necessarily drawn by our need to understand the causal determination of those "valued" components — this second type of "historical fact" is the one which is historically "effective" in Eduard Meyer's sense, i.e., as a "cause" in the causal *regress.* One may designate the former as historical individuals, the latter as historical (real) causes, and, with Rickert, distinguish them as "primary" and "secondary" historical facts. A strict confinement of an historical analysis to historical "causes," i.e., to the "secondary" facts in Rickert's sense, or, in other words, to the "effective" facts in Eduard Meyer's sense is, naturally, only possible for us if it is already unambiguously clear with which historical individual the causal explantion is to be exclusively concerned. However inclusive this primary object might be — it might be, for example, the total "modern culture," i.e., the present-day Christian capitalistic constitutional (*rechtsstaatliche*) culture which "radiates" from Europe and which is a phantastic tangle of "cultural values" which may be considered from the most diverse standpoints — the causal regress which explains it historically must, if it extends back into the Middle Ages or Antiquity, nonetheless omit, because they are causally unimportant, a great wealth of objects which arouse to a high degree our "interest" "for their own sake." These latter facts can become "historical individuals" in their own right from which an explanatory causal regress might have its point of departure. It is certainly to be granted that "historical interest" in these latter facts is particularly slight in consequence of their lack of causal significance for a universal history of contemporary culture. The cultural development of the Incas and Aztecs left historically relevant traces to such a relatively very slight extent that a universal history of the genesis of modern culture in Eduard Meyer's sense could perhaps be silent about it without loss. If that is so — as we shall now assume — then what we know about the cultural development of the Incas and Aztecs becomes relevant to us, in the first instance, neither as an "historical object," nor as an "historical cause" but rather as an "heuristic instrument" for the formation of theoretical concepts appropriate to the study of culture. This knowledge may function positively to supply an illustration, individualized and specific, in the formation of the concept of feudalism or negatively, to delimit certain concepts with which we operate in the study of European cultural history from the quite different cultural traits of the Incas and the Aztecs; this latter function enables us to make a clearer genetic comparison of the historical uniqueness of European cultural development. Precisely the same considerations apply, of course, to those components of ancient culture which Eduard Meyer — if he were consistent — would have to exclude from a history of antiquity oriented towards present cultural situation, because they did not become historically "effective."

Despite all this, it is obviously neither logically nor in the nature of facts, to be excluded in regard to the Incas and the Aztecs, that certain elements of their culture in its characteristic aspects could be made into an historical "individual," i.e., they could first be analyzed "interpretatively" with respect to their "relevance to values," and then they could once more be made into an object of "historical" investigation so that now the regressive inquiry into causes would proceed to the facts concerning the cultural development of those elements which become, in relation to the historical individual, its "historical causes." And if anyone composes an "History of Antiquity" it is a vain self-deception to believe that it contains only facts which are causally "effective" in our contemporary culture because it deals only with facts which are significant *either* "primarily" as evaluated "historical individuals" *or* "secondarily" as "causes" (in relation to these or other "individuals").

It is our *interest* which is oriented towards "values" and not the objective causal relationship between our culture and Hellenic culture which determines the range of the cultural values which are controlling for a history of Hellenic culture. That epoch which we usually — valuing it entirely subjectively — view as the "pinnacle" of Hellenic culture, i.e., the period between Aeschylus and Aristotle, enters with its cultural contents as an "intrinsic value" (*Eigenwert*) into every "History of Antiquity," including Eduard Meyer's. This could change only if, in the event that some future age became only as capable of attaining a direct "value-rapport" (*Wertbeziehung*) to those cultural "creations" of antiquity as we are today in relation to the "songs" and "world view" of a central African tribe, which arouse our interest only as instances of cultural products, i.e., as means of forming concepts or as "causes." The matter then may be put as follows: we human beings of the present day possess "*value*-rapport" of some sort to the characteristic embodiments of ancient culture and this is the only possible meaning which can be given to Eduard Meyer's concept of the "effective" as the "historical." How much, on the other hand, Eduard Meyer's own concept of the "effective" is made up of heterogeneous components is shown by his account of the motivation of the specific interest which history shows in the "advanced cultures." "This rests," he says (p. 47) "on the fact that these peoples and cultures have been 'effective' to an infinitely higher degree and still influence the present." This is undoubtedly correct but it is by no means the sole reason for our decided "interest" in their significance as historical objects; it is especially impossible to derive from this proposition another proposition according to which as Eduard Meyer asserts (ibid.), "the interest becomes greater the more advanced they (i.e., the historically advanced cultures) are." The question of the "intrinsic value" of a culture which we touch on here, has nothing to do with the question of its historical "effectiveness"; — here Eduard Meyer merely confuses "valuable" with "causally important." However unconditionally correct it is that every history is written from the standpoint of the value-interests of the *present* and that every present situation poses or can pose new questions to the data of history because its interest, guided by value-ideas, changes, it is certain that this interest "values" and turns into historical "individuals" cultural components that are entirely of the past, i.e., those to which a cultural component of the present day cannot be traced by a regressive causal chain. This is just as true of minor objects like the letters to Frau von Stein as of major ones like those components of Hellenic culture whose effects modern culture has long since outgrown. Eduard Meyer, has, as we saw, indeed conceded this implicity through the possibility which he proposed: namely, that a moment in the past can be "treated," as he put it, as contemporaneous[27] (p. 47). With this he has, in fact, admitted that even "past" cultural components are historical objects *regardless* of the existence of a still perceptible "effect" and can, e.g., as the "characteristic" values of antiquity, supply the standards for the selection of facts and the direction of historical research in a "History of Antiquity." And now to continue.

When Eduard Meyer cites as the exclusive reason why the *present* does not become the object of "history," the argument that one does not yet know and cannot know which of its components will show themselves to be "effective" in the future, this proposition concerning the (subjective) unhistoricity of the present is right at least to a qualified extent. Only the future "decides" conclusively about the *causal* significance of the facts of the present as "causes." This is not, however, the only aspect of the problem, even after, as is here understood, one disregards such incidental factors as the lack of written sources and records, etc. The really immediate present has not only not yet become an historical "cause," but it has not yet become an historical "individual"— any more than an ' 'experience" is an object of empirical "knowledge" at the moment in which it is occurring "in me" and "about me." All historical "evaluation" includes, so to speak, a "contemplative" element. It includes not primarily, and only, the immediate valuation of the "attitude-taking subject" — rather is its essential content, as we have seen, a "knowledge" of the object's *possible* "relations to values" (*Wertbeziehungen*). It thus presupposes a capacity for change in the "attitude" towards the object, at least theoretically. This used to be expressed as follows: we "must become objective" towards an experience before it "belongs to history" as an object — but this does certainly not imply that it is causally "effective."

But we are not to elaborate further this discussion of the relationship of "experiencing" and "knowing" here. It is enough that in the course of the foregoing extensive exposition, it has become quite clear not only that, but also why, Eduard Meyer's concept of the

---

[27] Which procedure, however, according to his remarks on p. 55, can be done after all, really only by "philology."

"historical" as the "effective" is inadequate. It lacks, above all, the logical distinction between the "primary" historical object, that very valued cultural individual to which attaches the interest in the causal explanation of its coming to be, and the "secondary" historical facts, the causes to which the "valued" characteristics of that "individual" are related in the causal regress. This imputation of causes is made with the goal of being, in principle, "objectively" valid as empirical truth absolutely in the same sense as any proposition at all of empirical knowledge. Only the adequacy of the data desides the question, which is wholly factual, and not a matter of principle, as to whether the causal analysis attains this goal to the degree which explanations do in the field of concrete natural events. It is not the determination of the historical "causes" for a given "object" to be explained which is "subjective" in a certain sense which we shall not discuss here again — rather is it the delimitation of the historical "object," of the "individual" itself, for in this the relevant values are decisive and the conception of the values is that which is subject to historical change. It is therefore incorrect in the first place when Eduard Meyer asserts (p. 45) that we are "never" able to attain an "absolute and unconditionally valid" knowledge of anything historical — this is not correct for "causes." It is, however, also equally incorrect when he then asserts that the situation is "no different" with respect to the validity of knowledge, in the natural sciences from what it is in the historical disciplines. The latter proposition is not true for the historical "individuals," i.e., for the way in which "values" play a role in history, nor does it hold for the mode of being of those "values." (Regardless of how one conceives of the "validity" of those "values" as such,— the "validity" of the values is in any case something which is different in principle from the validity of a causal relationship which is an empirical truth, even if both should in the last analysis also be conceived of philosophically as normatively bound.) The "points of view," which are oriented towards "values," from which we consider cultural objects and from which they become "objects" of historical research, change. Because, and as long as they do, new "facts" will always be becoming historically "important" (*wesentlich*), and they ⁓vs become so in a new way — for in logical discussions such ⁓me once and for all that the source materials will remain unchanged. This way of being conditioned by "subjective values" is, however, entirely alien in any case to those natural sciences which take mechanics as a model, and it constitutes, indeed, the distinctive *contrast* between the historical and the natural sciences.

To summarize: insofar as the "interpretation" of an object is, in the usual sense of the word, a "philological" interpretation, e.g., of its linguistic "meaning," it is a technical task preliminary to the historical work proper. Insofar as it analyzes "interpretatively" what is *characteristic* of the particular features of certain "cultural epochs" or certain personalities or certain individual objects (such as works of art or literature), it aids in the formation of historical concepts. And indeed from the point of view of its logical role, it functions either as an auxiliary insofar as it aids in the recognition of the *causally* relevant components of a concrete historical complex as such; it functions, conversely, as a source of guidance and direction, insofar as it "interprets" the content of an object — e.g., Faust, Orestes, Christianity of a particular epoch — with respect to its possible relations to values. In doing the latter it presents "tasks" for the causal work of history and thus is its *pre-supposition*. The concept of the "culture" of a particular people and age, the concept of "Christianity," of "Faust," and also — there is a tendency to overlook this — the concept of "Germany," etc., are individualized *value-concepts* formed as the objects of *historical* research, i.e., by relations with value-ideas.

If these values themselves with which we approach the facts are made the objects of analysis, we are — depending on the aim of our knowing — conducting studies in the *philosophy* of history or the psychology of "historical interest." If, on the other hand, we treat a concrete object from the standpoint of "value analysis," i.e., "interpreting" it with respect to its particular characteristics so that the possible evaluations of the object are "suggestively" made vivid to us, an "empathic experience" ("*Nacherleben*") as it used to be called (albeit very incorrectly), of a cultural creation is aimed at, this is still not "historical work"— this is the "justified kernel" in Eduard Meyer's formulation. But even though it is not historical work, it is the inevitable "forma formans" of historical "interest" in an object, of its primary conceptualization into an "individual" and of the causal work of history which only then becomes meaningfully possible. In ever so many cases, the adduced evaluations of daily life have formed the object and paved the way for historical research — this occurs even in the beginnings of all historical writing in political communities, especially in the historian's own state. The historian might thus come to believe when he confronts these fixed and firm "objects" which apparently — but only apparently and only in the range of familiar, routine use — do not require any special value-interpretation, that he is in his "proper" domain. As soon, however, as he leaves the broad highway and seeks also to achieve great new insights into the "unique" political "character" of a state or in the "unique character" of a political genius, he must proceed here, too, as far as the logical principle is concerned, as does the interpreter of *Faust*. But, of course — and here Eduard Meyer is correct, where an analysis *remains* at the level of such an "interpretation" of the intrinsic value of the object, the task of the ascertainment of causes is left undone and the question is not even raised in regard to the object, as to what it "signifies" causally with respect to other more comprehensive, more contemporaneous cultural objects. At this point, historical research has not yet got under way and the historian can perceive only the raw materials of historical problems. It is only the way in which Meyer tries to ground his belief that is in my opinion untenable. Since Eduard Meyer perceives especially the "static," "systematic" treatment of data as representative of the opposite principle from that of history, and since, e.g., Rickert too, after having seen the "systematic," which is characteristic of a "natural science" view even in the social and mental sphere, in opposition to the "historical cultural sciences," has more recently formulated the concept of the *"systematic cultural* sciences" — the task then is, to raise the following problem later in another section: what "systematics" can properly mean and in what different sets of relationships it stands to the historical approach and the "natural sciences."[28]

The mode of treatment of ancient, particularly Hellenic culture which Eduard Meyer calls the "philological method," i.e., which takes the form of "classical studies," is indeed primarily actually realiz-

---

[28] With this we really enter into a discussion of the various possible principles of a "classification" of the "sciences."

able through the requisite linguistic mastery of the sources. But it is determined not only by that but also by the particular characteristics of certain outstanding scholars, and above all by the "significance" which the culture of classical antiquity has had for our own spiritual and intellectual discipline. Let us attempt to formulate those standpoints towards ancient culture which are, in principle, conceivable, in an extremely schematic and hence purely theoretical fashion. (1) One point of view would be the conception of the absolute value of ancient culture, the exemplifications of which in humanism, as expressed, for instance, in Winckelmann, and ultimately in all the variants of so-called "classicism" we shall not investigate here. According to this conception, if we follow it to its uttermost implications, the elements of ancient culture are — insofar as neither the Christian components of our culture nor the products of rationalism have "supplemented" or "re-shaped" it — at least virtual elements of *culture as such*. They are such, not because they *have been* "causally" effective in Eduard Meyer's sense of the term, but rather because on account of their absolute value they *should* be causally effective in our education. Hence, ancient culture is primarily an object of interpretation *in usum scholarum,* for purposes of educating one's own people to the level of an advanced state of culture. "Philology" in its most comprehensive meaning, i.e., as the "knowledge of what has been known," perceives in classical antiquity something which is in principle more than merely historical, something timelessly valid. (2) The other, modern point of view stands in extreme contrast: the culture of antiquity, according to this view, is so infinitely remote from us as regards its true individuality that it is entirely meaningless to wish to give the "all too many" an insight into its true "essence." It is rather a sublime valued object for the few who imbue themselves with the highest form of humanity which cannot in any essential features recur and who wish to "enjoy" it in a somewhat æsthetic way.[29] (3) Finally, the methods of classical studies are of service to a scientific interest for which the source materials of antiquity provide primarily an uncommonly rich body of ethnographic data which can be used

---

[29] It could be the reputed "esoteric" doctrine of U. von Willamowitz against which Eduard Meyer's attack is primarily directed.

for the acquisition of general concepts, analogies, and developmental laws applicable in the pre-history, not only of our own culture, but of "every" culture   A pertinent instance is the development of the study of comparative religion — the attainment of its present high level wouid have been impossible without the exhaustive survey of antiquity made possible through strictly philological training.   Antiquity comes into consideration on this view insofar as its cultural content is appropriate as an heuristic means for the construction of general "types." In contrast with the first "point of view," thus one does not regard classical antiquity as providing an "enduring" cultural norm, and in contrast with the second, it does not look on classical antiquity as an absolutely unique object of individual contemplative evaluation.

We quickly see that all three of these "theoretically" formulated conceptions are interested for their own purposes in the treatment of ancient history in the form of "classical studies."   We also do not need a special comment to see that, in each of them, the interest of the historian in fact falls short of exhausting their interest, since all three have something different from "history" as their primary aim.   But when, on the other hand, Eduard Meyer seriously seeks to eradicate from the history of antiquity that which is no longer historically "effective" in the contemporary world, he would be justifiably open to the criticism of his opponents in the eyes of all those who look for more than an historical "cause" in antiquity.   And all the admirers of his great work rejoice that he cannot at all proceed with any fidelity to these ideas, and they hope that he will not even attempt to do so for the sake of an erroneously formulated theory.[30]

---

[30] The breadth of the foregoing discussions is obviously incommensurate with what "comes out" of them in directly practical results for "methodology."   To those who for this reason regard them as superfluous, it can only be recommended that they simply avoid questions bearing on the "meaning" of knowledge and content themselves with the acquisition of "valuable" knowledge by concrete research.   It is not the historians who have raised these questions but those who have put forward the wrong-headed view, and who are still playing variations on the theme, that "scientific knowledge" is identical with the "discovery of laws."   This is definitely a question of the "meaning" of knowledge.

OBJECTIVE POSSIBILITY AND ADEQUATE CAUSATION
IN HISTORICAL EXPLANATION

II

"The outbreak of the Second Punic War," says Eduard Meyer (p. 16), "is the consequence of the willed decision of Hannibal; that of the Seven Years War, of Frederick the Great; that of the War of 1866, of Bismarck. They could all have decided differently and other persons would have . . . decided differently. In consequence, the course of history would have been different." To this he adds in a footnote (p. 10, fn. 2): "By this we do not mean to assert or deny that in the latter case, these wars would not have occurred: this is a completely unaswerable and superfluous question." Disregarding the awkward relationship between the second sentence and his earlier proposition about the relationship between "freedom" and "necessity" in history, we must here question the view that questions which we cannot answer, or cannot answer with certainty, are on that acount "idle" questions. It would go poorly with the empirical sciences, too, if those highest problems to which they can give no answer were never raised. We are not considering here such "ultimate" problems; we are rather dealing with a question which has, on the one hand, been "dated" by the course of events, and which, on the other, cannot in fact be answered positively and unambiguously in the light of our actual and possible knowledge — it is a question which, moreover, viewed from a strictly "deterministic" standpoint, discusses the consequences of that which was, in view of the given "determinants," impossible. And yet, despite all this, the problem: what might have happened if, for example, Bismarck had not decided to make war, is by no means an "idle" one. It does indeed bear on something decisive for the historical moulding of reality, namely, on what causal *significance* is properly to be attributed to this individual decision in the context of the totality of infinitely numerous "factors," all of which had to be in such and such an arrangement and in no other if *this* result were to emerge, and what role it is therefore to be asigned in an historical exposition. If history is to be raised above the level of a mere chronicle of notable events and personalities, it has no alternative but to pose such questions. And so indeed it has proceeded since its establishment as a science. This is the correct element in Eduard Meyer's previously quoted formulation that history considers events from the standpoint of "becoming" and that accordingly its object is not in the domain of "necessity" which is characteristic of what has already "occurred"; that the historian behaves in the estimation of the causal significance of a concrete event similarly to the historical human being who has an attitude and will of his own and who would never "act" if his own action appeared[31] to him as "necessary" and not only as "possible." The distinction is only this: the acting person weighs, insofar as he acts rationally — we shall assume this here — the "conditions" of the future development which interests him, which conditions are "external" to him and are objectively given as far as his knowledge of reality goes. He mentally rearranges into a causal complex the various "possible modes" of his own conduct and the consequences which these could be *expected* to have in connection with the "external" conditions. He does this in order to decide, in accordance with the (mentally) disclosed "possible" results, in favor of one or another mode of action as the one appropriate to his "goal." The historian has, however, the advantage over his hero in that he knows *a posteriori* whether the appraisal of the given external conditions corresponded in fact with the knowledge and expectations which the acting person developed. The answer to this question is indicated by the actual "success" of the action. And with that ideal maximum knowledge of those conditions which we will and may *theoretically* assume here once and for all while clarifying *logical* questions — although in reality such a maximum be achieved ever so rarely, perhaps never — the historian can carry out retrospectively the same mental calculation which his "hero" more or less clearly performed or could have performed. Hence, the historian is able to consider the question: which consequences were to be anticipated had another decision been taken, with better chances of success than, for example, Bismarck himself. It is clear that this way of looking at the matter is very far from being "idle." Eduard Meyer himself applies (p. 43) very nearly this procedure to the two shots which in the Berlin March days directly provoked the outbreak of the

---

31 The correctness of this proposition is not affected by Kistiakowski's criticism (op. cit., p. 393) which does not apply to *this* concept of "possibility."

street fighting. The question as to who fired them is, he says, "historically irrelevant." Why is it more irrelevant than the discussion of the decisions of Hannibal, Frederick the Great, and Bismarck? "The situation was such that *any* accident whatsoever would have caused the conflict to break out." (!) Here we see Eduard Meyer himself answering the allegedly "idle" question as to what "would" have happened without those shots; thus their historical "significance" (in this case: irrelevance) is decided. The "situations" were obviously, at least in Meyer's view, different in the case of the decisions of Hannibal, Frederick the Great, and Bismarck. They certainly were not such that the conflict would have broken out in any case or under the concrete political constellation which actually governed its course and outcome, if the decision had been different. For if otherwise, these decisions would be as insignificant as those shots. The judgment that, if a single historical fact is conceived of as absent from or modified in a complex of historical conditions, it *would* condition a course of historical events in a way which would be different in certain *historically important* respects, seems to be of considerable value for the determination of the "historical significance" of those facts. This is so even though the historian in practice is moved only rarely — namely, in instances of dispute about that very "historical significance"— to develop and support that judgment deliberately and explicitly. It is clear that this situation had to call forth a consideration of the logical nature of such judgments as assert what the effect of the omission or modification of a single causal component of a complex of conditions would have been and of their significance for history. We shall attempt to secure a clearer insight into this problem.

The poor condition of the logical analysis[32] of history is also shown by the fact that neither historians nor methodologists of history but rather representatives of very unrelated disciplines have conducted the authoritative investigations into this important question.

The theory of the so-called "objective possibility" which we deal

---

[32] The categories to be discussed subsequently find application, as may be expressly remarked, not only in the domain of the usually so-called *specialist* discipline of "history" but also in the "historical" ascertainment of causes of *every* individual event, including even the individual events of "inanimate nature." The category of the "historical" here considered is a logical category and not one restricted to the technique of a single discipline.

with here rests on the works of the distinguished physiologist v. Kries[33] and the common use of the concepts in the works which follow him or criticize him. These works are primarily criminological but they are also produced by other legal writers, particularly Merkel, Rümelen, Liepmann, and most recently, Radbruch.[34] In the methodology of the social sciences von Kries' ideas have hitherto been adopted only in statistics.[35]

---

33 *Über den Begriff der objektiven Möglichkeit und einige Anwendungen desselben.* (Leipzig 1888.) Important bases for these discussion were first set forth by Von Kries in his *Prinzipien der Wahrscheinlichkeitsrechnung.* It should be noted here in advance that, in accordance with the nature of the historical "object," only the most elementary components of Von Kries' theory are significant for the methodology of history. The adoption of the principles of the so-called "calculus of probability" in the strict sense obviously not only is not to be considered for the work of causal analysis in history but even the attempt to make an analogical use of its points of view demands the greatest caution.

34 The most deeply penetrating criticism of the use of von Kries' theory in the analysis of legal problems has been made by Radbruch (*Die Lehre von der adequaten Verursachung Bd I. NF. Heft 3 of Abhandlungen des von Lisztschen Seminars* in which references to the most important other literature are to be found. His analytical articulation of the concept of "adequate causation" can be taken into account only later, after the theory has been presented in the most simple possible formulation (for which reason, as we shall see, the formulation will be only provisional and not definitive).

35 Of the theoretical statisticians, L. von Bortkiewicz stands in a very close relationship to von Kries' theories. Cf. his "Die erkenntnistheoretischen Grundlagen der Wahrscheinlichkeitsrechnung" in Conrads' *Jahrbucher*, 3rd Series, vol. XVII, (Cf. also vol. XVIII), and "Die Theorie der Bevolkerungs—und Moralstatistik nach Lexis" (ibid. vol. XXVII). The von Kries' theory is also basic for A. Tschuprow, whose article on "Moral Statistics" in the Brockhaus-Ephron Encyclopœdic Dictionary, was unfortunately inaccessible to me. Cf. his article "Die Aufgaben der Theorie der Statistik" in Schmoller's *Jahrbuch* 1905, p. 421 f. I cannot agree with Th. Kistiakowski's criticism (in the essay, cited earlier, in *Problems of Idealism*, p. 378 ff.) which for the time being is, of course, presented only in the form of a sketch with the understanding that a more detailed presentation is reserved for later publication. His central charge (p. 379) is that the theory uses a false concept of cause, based on Mill's *Logic*; in particular the category of "complex" and "partial cause" which itself rests on an anthropomorphic interpretation of causality (in the sense of "efficacy" (*Wirkens*). (Radbruch also adumbrates the latter point, op. cit., p. 22 ff.) But the notion of "efficacy" (*Wirkens*), or as it has been called more neutrally but with identical meaning, the "causal bond" is entirely inseparable from any study of causes which deals with series of individualized qualitative changes. We will discuss later the point that the notion of efficacy need not and must not be encumbered with unnecessary and dubious metaphysical presuppositions. (Cf. concerning causal plurality and elementary causes, Tschuprow's exposition, op. cit. p. 436.) We shall only remark here that "possibility" is a "moulding" "*formende*" category, i.e., it functions in

It is natural that it was precisely the jurists and primarily the jurists specializing in criminal law who treated the problem since the question of penal guilt, insofar as it involves the problem: under what circumstances can it be asserted that someone through his action has "caused" a certain external effect, is purely a question of causation. And, indeed, this problem obviously has exactly the same logical structure as the problem of historical "causality." For, just like history, the problems of practical social relationships of men and especially of the legal system, are "anthropocentrically" oriented, i.e., they enquire into the causal significance of *human* "actions." And just as in the question of the causal determinateness of a concrete injurious action which is eventually to be punished under criminal law or for which indemnity must be made under civil law, the historian's problem of causality also is oriented towards the correlation of concrete effects with concrete causes, and not towards the establishment of abstract "uniformities" (*Gesetzlichkeiten*). Jurisprudence, and particularly criminal law, however, leaves the area of problems shared with history for a problem which is specific to it, in consequence of the emergence of the further problem: if and when the *objective* purely causal imputation of an effect to the action of an individual also suffices to define the actions as one involving his own *subjective* "guilt." For this question is no longer a purely causal one, soluble by the simple establishing of facts which are "objectively" discover-

---

such a way as to determine the selection of the causal links to be incorporated into an historical exposition. The historical material once formed, on the other hand, contains nothing of "possibility," at least, ideally. Subjectively for the mind of the historian himself the historical exposition only very seldom attains judgments of necessity but objectively the historical exposition undoubtedly is governed by the assumption that the "causes" to which the "effect" is imputed have to be regarded as unqualifiedly the sufficient conditions for its occurrence. (It is, of course, to be clearly noted that an infinity of conditions which are only summarily referred to as scientifically "without interest" are associated with the causes which are deemed the sufficient conditions of the effect.) The use of the category of objective possibility does not in the least involve the conception, long overcome by the theory of causality, that certain links in real causal connections were, so to speak, "hovering about without effect" up to the time of their entry into the causal chain. Von Kries himself has shown the contrast between his theory and John Stuart Mill's (op. cit., p. 107) in a way which is entirely convincing to me. (Concerning this, cf. infra.) Still it is true that Mill, too, discussed the category of objective possibility and in doing so, upon occasion also constructed the concept of "adequate causation." (Cf. Werke, III, p. 262, Gomperz edition.)

able by perception and causal interpretation. Rather, is it a problem of criminal policy oriented towards ethical and other values. For it is *a priori* possible, actually frequent, and regularly the case today, that the meaning of legal norms, explicitly stated or elicited by interpretation, inclines to the view that the existence of "guilt" in the sense of the applicable law should depend primarily on certain *subjective* facts in regard to the agent (e.g., intent, *subjectively* conditioned capacity of foresight into the effects, etc.). Under these circumstances, the import of the logically distinctive characteristics of pure causal connection will be considerably modified.[36] It is only in the first stages of the discussion that this difference in the aims of investigation are without significance. We ask first, in common with juristic theory, how in general is the attribution of a concrete effect to an individual "cause" possible and realizable in principle in view of the fact that in truth an *infinity* of causal factors have conditioned the occurrence of the individual "event" and that indeed absolutely all of those individual causal factors were indispensable for the occurrence of the effect in its concrete form.

The possibility of selection from among the infinity of the determinants is conditioned, first, by the mode of our historical *interest*.

When it is said that history seeks to understand the concrete *reality* of an "event" in its individuality causally, what is obviously not meant by this, as we have seen, is that it is to "reproduce" and explain causally the concrete *reality* of an event in the totality of its individual qualities. To do the latter would be not only actually impossible, it would also be a task which is meaningless in principle. Rather, history is exclusively concerned with the causal explanation of those "elements"

---

36 Modern law is directed against the agent, not against the action (cf. Radbruch, op. cit., p. 62). It enquires into subjective "guilt" whereas history, as long as it seeks to remain an empirical science, inquires into the "objective" grounds of concrete events and the consequences of concrete 'actions'; it does not seek to pass judgment on the agent. Radbruch's criticism of von Kries is rightly based on this fundamental principle of modern — but not of all — law. He himself thus concedes, however, the validity of von Kries' theory in cases of so-called unintended damage, of compensation on account of the "abstract possibility of an interfering effect," (p. 71) of profit insurance and of the insurance of those incapable of "responsibility," i.e., wherever "objective" causality comes clearly into question. History, however, is in exactly the same *logical* situation as those cases.

and "aspects" of the events in question which are of "general significance" and *hence* of historical *interest* from general standpoints, exactly in the same way as the judge's deliberations take into account
not the total individualized course of the events of the case but rather
those components of the events which are pertinent for subsumption
under the legal norms.   Quite apart from the infinity of "absolutely"
trivial details, the judge is not at all interested in all those things
which can be of interest for other natural scientific, historical and
artistic points of view.   He is not interested in whether the fatal
thrust leads to death with incidental phenomena which might be
quite interesting to the physiologist.   He is not interested in whether
the appearance of the dead person or the murderer could be a suitable object of artistic representation; nor, for instance, in whether the
death will help a non-participating "man behind the scene" to gain
a "promotion" in a bureaucratic hierarchy, i.e., whether from the
latter's standpoint it would therefore be causally "valuable."   Nor is
the judge interested in whether the death became, say the occasion
of certain security measures by the police, or perhaps even engendered
certain international conflicts and thus showed itself to be "historically" significant.   All that is relevant for him is whether the causal
chain between the thrust and the death took such a form and the
subjective attitude of the murderer and his relation to the deed was
such that a certain norm of criminal law is applicable.   The historian,
on the other hand, is interested in connection, for example, with
Cæsar's death, neither in the criminal-legal, nor in the medical problems which the "case" raises, nor is he interested in the details of the
event — unless they are important either for the "particular characteristic features" of Cæsar or for the "characteristic features" of the
party situation in Rome, i.e., unless they are of import as "heuristic
instruments" or lastly unless they are important in relation to the
"political effect" of his death, i.e., as "real causes."   Rather, is he
concerned, in this affair, primarily with the fact that the death occurred under concrete political conditions, and he discusses the question related thereto, namely, whether this fact had certain important
"consequences" for the course of "world history."

Hence, there is involved in the problem of the assignment of
historical causes to historical effects as well as in the problem of the

imputation of actions under the law, the exclusion of an infinity of components of a real action as "causally irrelevant." A given circumstance is, as we see, unimportant not only when it has no relationship at all with the event which is under discussion, so that we can conceive it to be absent without *any* modification in the actual course of events being introduced; it is indeed sufficient to establish the causal irrelevance of the given circumstance if the latter appears not to have been the co-cause of that which alone interests us, i.e., the concretely essential components of the action in question.

Our real problem is, however: by which logical operations do we acquire the insight and how can we demonstratively establish *that* such a causal relationship exists between those "essential" components of the effects and certain components among the infinity of determining factors. Obviously not by the simple "observation" of the course of events in any case, certainly not if one understands by that a "presuppositionless" mental "photograph" of all the physical and psychic events occurring in the space-time region in question — even if such were possible. Rather, does the attribution of effects to causes take place through a process of thought which includes a series of *abstractions*. The first and decisive one occurs when we *conceive* of one or a few of the actual causal components as modified in a certain direction and then ask ourselves whether under the conditions which have been thus changed, the same effect (the same, i.e., in "essential" points) or some other effect "would be expected." Let us take an example from Eduard Meyer's own work. No one has set forth the world historical "significance" of the Persian Wars for the development of western culture as vividly and clearly as he has. How does this happen, logically speaking? It takes place essentially in the following way: it is argued that a "decision" was made between two *"possibilities."* The first of these "possibilities" was the development of a theocratic-religious culture, the beginnings of which lay in the mysteries and oracles, under the ægis of the Persian protectorate, which wherever possible utilized, as for example, among the Jews, the national religion as an instrument of domination. The other possibility was represented by the triumph of the free Hellenic circle of ideas, oriented towards this world, which gave us those cultural values from which we still draw our sustenance. The "decision" was made by a contest of the meager dimensions of the "battle" of Marathon. This in its turn was the indispensible "precondition" of the development of the Attic fleet and thus of the further development of the war of liberation, the salvation of the independence of Hellenic culture, the positive stimulus of the beginnings of the specifically western historiography, the full development of the drama and all that unique life of the mind which took place in this — by purely quantitative standards — miniature theater of world history.

The fact that that battle "decided" between these two "possibilities" or at least had a great deal to do with the decision, is obviously — since we are not Athenians — the only reason why we are historically interested in it. Without an appraisal of those "possibilities" and of the irreplaceable cultural values which, as it appears to our retrospective study, "depend" on that decision, a statement regarding its "significance" would be impossible. Without this appraisal, there would in truth be no reason why we should not rate that decisive contest equally with a scuffle between two tribes of Kaffirs or Indians and accept in all seriousness the dull-witted "fundamental ideas" of Helmolt's *Weltgeschichte,* as has indeed actually been done in that "modern" collective work.[37]   When modern historians, as soon as they are required by some inquiry to define the "significance" of a concrete event by explicit reflection on and exposition of the developmental "possibilities," ask, as is usual, to be forgiven their use of this apparently anti-deterministic category, their request is without logical justification. Karl Hampe, for example, in his *Conradin,* presents a very instructive exposition of the historical "significance" of the Battle of Togliacozza, on the basis of weighing the various "possibilities," the "decision" between which was made by the battle's entirely "accidental" outcome ("accidental" meaning here: determined by quite individual tactical events); then he suddenly weakens and adds: "But

---

[37] It goes without saying that this judgment does not apply to the individual essays contained in this work, some of which are quite distinquished achievements, although some are thoroughly "old fashioned" methodologically. The notion of a sort of "social" justice which would — finally, finally! — take the contemptibly neglected Kafir and Indian tribes at least as seriously as the Athenians and which in order to make this just treatment really explicit and pronounced, resorts to a geographical organization of the data, is merely childish.

history knows no possibilities." To this we must answer: that process (*Geschehen*) which, conceived as subject to deterministic axioms, becomes an "objective thing," knows nothing of "posibilities" because it "knows" nothing of concepts. *"History,"* however, does recognize possibilities, assuming that it seeks to be a science. In every line of every historical work, indeed in every selection of archival and source materials for publication, there are, or more correctly, must, be, "judgments of possibility," if the publication is to have value for knowledge.

What, then, is meant when we speak of a number of "possibilities" between which those contests are said to have "decided"? It involves first the production of — let us say it calmly — "imaginative constructs" by the disregarding of one or more of those elements of "reality" which are actually present, and by the mental construction of a course of events which is altered through modification in one or more "conditions." Even the first step towards an historical judgment is thus — this is to be emphasized — a process of *abstraction*. This process proceeds through the analysis and mental isolation of the components of the directly given data — which are to be taken as a complex of possible causal relations — and should culminate in a synthesis of the "real" causal complex. Even this first step thus transforms the given "reality" into a "mental construct" in order to make it into an historical fact. In Goethe's words, "theory" is involved in the "fact."

If now one examines these "judgments of possibility" — i.e., the propositions regarding what "would" happen in the event of the exclusion or modification of certain conditions — somewhat more closely and inquires: how are we really to arrive at them — there can be no doubt that it is a matter of isolations and generalizations. This means that we so decompose the "given" into "components" that every one of them is fitted into an "empirical rule"; hence, that it can be determined what effect each of them, with others present as "conditions," "could be expected" to have, in accordance with an empirical rule. A judgment of "possibility" in the sense in which the expression is used here, means, then, the continuous reference to "empirical rules" (*Erfahrungsregeln*). The category of "possibility" is thus not used in its *negative* form. It is, in other words, not an expression of our ignorance or incomplete knowledge in contrast with the assertative or apodictic judgment. Rather, to the contrary, it signifies here the reference to a positive knowledge of the "laws of events," to our "nomological" knowledge, as they say.

When the question whether a certain train has already passed a station is answered "it is possible," this assertion means that the person who answered the question subjectively does not know the facts, which would exclude this belief, but that he is also not in a position to argue for its correctness. It means, in other words, "*not* knowing." If, however, Eduard Meyer judges that a theocratic-religious development in Hellas at the time of the Battle of Marathon was "possible," or in certain eventualities, "probable," this means, on the contrary, the assertion that certain components of the historically given situation were *objectively* present; that is, their presence was such as can now be ascertained with objective validity, and that they were, when we imagine the Battle of Marathon as not having happened or as having happened differently (including, naturally, a host of other components of the actual course of events), "capable" according to *general empirical rules,* of producing such a theocratic-religious development, as we might say in borrowing for once from criminological terminology. The "knowledge" on which such a judgment of the "significance" of the Battle of Marathon rests is, in the light of all that we have said hitherto, on the one hand, knowledge of certain "facts," ("ontological" knowledge), "belonging" to the "historical situation" and ascertainable on the basis of certain sources, and on the other — as we have already seen — knowledge of certain known empirical rules, particularly those relating to the ways in which human beings are prone to react under given situations ("nomological knowledge"). The type of "validity" of these "empirical rules" will be considered later. In any case, it is clear that in order to demonstrate his thesis which is decisive for the "significance" of the Battle of Marathon, Eduard Meyer must, if it is challenged, analyze that "situation" into its "components" down to the point where our "imagination" can apply to this "ontological" knowledge our "nomological" knowledge which has been derived from our own experience and our knowledge of the conduct of others. When this has been done, then we can render a positive judgment that the joint action of those facts — including the conditions which have been conceived as modified in a certain way — "could" bring about the effect which is asserted to be "objectively possible." This can only mean, in other words, that *if* we "conceived" the effect as having actually occurred under the modified conditions we *would* then recognize those facts thus modified to be "adequate causes."

This rather extensive formulation of a simple matter, which was required for the sake of clearing away ambiguity, shows that the formulation of propositions about historical causal connections not only makes use of both types of abstraction, namely, isolation and generalization; it shows also that the simplest historical judgment concerning the historical "significance" of a "concrete fact" is far removed from being a simple registration of something "found" in an already finished form. The simplest historical judgment represents not only a categorially formed intellectual construct but it also does not acquire a valid content until we bring to the "given" reality the whole body of our "nomological" empirical knowledge.

The historian will assert against this, correctly, that the actual course of historical work and the actual content of historical writing follows a different path. The historian's "sense of the situation," his "intuition" uncover causal interconnections — not generalizations and reflections of "rules." The contrast with the natural sciences consists indeed precisely in the fact that the historian deals with the explanation of events and personalities which are "interpreted" and "understood" by direct analogy with our own intellectual, spiritual and psychological constitution. In the historical treatise it is repeatedly altogether a question of the "sense of the situation," of the suggestive vividness of its account report which allows the reader to "empathize" with what has been depicted in the same way as that in which it is experienced and concretely grasped by the historian's own intuition, for the historian's account has not been produced by "clever" ratiocination. Moreover, it is further asserted, an objective judgment of possibility regarding what "would" have happened according to the general empirical rules, when a causal component is conceived as excluded or as modified, is often highly uncertain and often cannot be arrived at at all. Hence, such a basis for the attribution of causes in history must in fact be permanently renounced, and thus it cannot be a constitutive element in the logical value of historical knowledge.

Arguments such as these confuse, basically, problems of distinct character. They confuse the psychological course of the *origin* of scientific knowledge and "artistic" form of presenting what is known, which is selected for the purpose of influencing the reader psychologically on one hand, with the *logical structure* of knowledge, on the other.

Ranke "divines" the past, and even the advancement of knowledge by an historian of lesser rank, is poorly served if he does not possess this "intuitive" gift. Where this is so, he remains a kind of lower rung-bureaucrat in the historical enterprise. But it is absolutely no different with the really great advances in knowledge in mathematics and the natural sciences. They all arise intuitively in the intuitive flashes of imagination as hypotheses which are then "verified" *vis-a-vis* the facts, i.e., their validity is tested in procedures involving the use of already available empirical knowledge and they are "formulated" in a logically correct way. The same is true in history: when we insist here on the dependence of the knowledge of the "essential" on the use of the concept of objective possibility, we assert nothing at all about the psychologically interesting question which does not, however, concern us here, namely, how does an historical hypothesis arise in the mind of the investigator? We are here concerned only with the question of the logical category under which the hypothesis is to be demonstrated as valid in case of doubt or dispute, for it is *that* which determines its logical "structure." And if the historian's mode of presentation communicates the logical result of his historical causal judgments to the reader with reasoning in a manner which dispenses with the adduction of the evidence for his knowledge, i.e., if he "suggests" the course of events rather than pedantically "ratiocinating" about it, his presentation would be an historical novel and not at all a scientific finding, as long as the firm skeletal structure of established causes behind the artistically formed facade is lacking. The dry approach of logic is concerned only with this skeletal structure for even the historical exposition claims "validity" as "truth." The most important phase of historical work which we have hitherto considered, namely, the establishment of the causal regress, attains such validity only when, in the event of challenge, it is able to pass the test of the use of the category of objective possibility which entails the isolation and generalization of the causal individual components for the purpose of ascertaining the possibility of the synthesis of certain conditions into adequate causes.

It is, however, now clear that the causal analysis of personal actions proceeds logically in exactly the same way as the causal analysis of the "historical significance" of the Battle of Marathon, i.e., by isolation, generalization and the construction of judgments of possibility. Let us take a limiting case: the reflective analysis of one's *own* action of which logically untrained sentiment tends to believe that it certainly does not present any "logical problems" whatsoever, since one's action is directly given in experience and — asuming mental "health"— is "understandable" without further ado and hence is naturally "reproducible" in memory directly. Very simple reflections show that it is not, however, so, and that the "valid" answer to the question: why did I act in that way, constitutes a categorially formed construct which is to be raised to the level of the demonstrable judgment only by the use of abstractions. This is true even though the "demonstration" is in fact here conducted in the mind of the "acting person" himself.

Let us assume a temperamental young mother who is tired of certain misdeeds of her little child, and as a good German who does not pay homage to the theory contained in Busch's fine lines, "Superficial is the rod — only the mind's power penetrates the soul," gives it a solid cuff. Let us further assume that she is sufficiently "sicklied o'er with the pale cast of thought" to give a few moments of reflection after the deed has been done to the question of the "pedagogical utility," of the "justice" of the cuff, or at least of the considerable "expenditure of energy" involved in the action. Or still better, let us assume that the howls of the child release in the paterfamilias, who, as a German, is convinced of his superior understanding of everything, including the rearing of children, the need to remonstrate with "her" on "teleological" grounds. Then "she" will, for example, expound the thought and offer it as an excuse that if at that moment she *had* not been, let us assume, "agitated" by a quarrel with the cook, that the aforementioned disciplinary procedure *would* not have been used at all or would not have been applied "in that way"; she will be inclined to admit to him: "he really knows that she is not ordinarily in that state." She refers him thereby to his "empirical knowledge" regarding her "usual motives," which in the vast majority of all the generally *possible* constellations would have led to another, less irrational effect. She claims, in other words, that the blow which she delivered was an "accidental" and not an "adequately" caused reaction to the behavior of her child, to anticipate the terminology which we shall shortly employ.

This domestic dialogue has thus sufficed to turn the experience in question into a categorially formed "object." Even though, exactly like Molière's philistine who learned to his pleasant surprise that he had been speaking "prose" all his life, the young woman would certainly be astounded if a logician showed her that she had made a causal "imputation" just like an historian, that, to this end, she had made "judgments of objective possibility" and had "operated" with the category of "adequate causation," which we shall shortly discuss more closely — yet such is precisely and inevitably the case from the point of view of logic. Refletive knowledge, even of one's own experience, is nowhere and never a literally "repeated experience" or a simple "photograph" of what was experienced; the "experience," when it is made into an "object," acquires perspectives and interrelationships which were not "known" in the experience itself. The idea formed in later reflection, of one's own past action is no different in *this* respect from the idea so formed of a past concrete natural event in the external world, which had been experienced by one's self or which was reported by someone else. It will probably not be necessary to elucidate further[38] the universal validity of this proposition

---

[38] We will here consider briefly only one more example which K. Vossler (op. cit., p. 101 ff.) analyzes in order to illustrate why there must be failure in the construction of "laws." He mentions certain linguistic idiosyncrasies which, within his family, "an Italian linguistic island in the sea of German speech," were developed by his children and imitated by the parents in their conversations with the children; its origin goes back to quite concrete stimuli which are still completely clear in his memory. He then asks: What does folk psychology, and we may add in accordance with his outlook, any "law-seeking science," still wish to explain in these cases of linguistic development? The event, considered in and of itself, is in fact *prima facie* fully explained and nonetheless, this does not imply that it cannot be an object for further elaboration and use. First, the fact that the causal relationship is

with complicated examples, or to state expressly, that we proceed logically in the same way in the analysis of a decision of Napoleon or Bismarck as we did in the example of our German mother.

The distinction that the "inward aspect" of the action which is to be analyzed is directly given to her in her own memory, whereas we must "interpret" the action of a third party from the "outside," is, despite the naive prejudice to the contrary, only a gradual continuous

---

definitely discoverable could (at least conceivably—we are only arguing the possibility) be used as an heuristic means in order to test *other* events of linguistic development in order to see whether the same causal relationship can be confirmed as probable in their case. This requires, however, from a logical standpoint, the subsumption of the concrete case under a general rule. Vossler himself has also formulated the rule as follows: "the more frequently used forms attract the less frequently used ones." But that is not enough. We have said that the causal explanation of the case in question was *prima facie* inadequate. But it must not be forgotten that every individual causal complex, even the apparently "simplest," can be infinitely subdivided and analzyed. The point at which we halt in this process is determined only by our causal *interests* at the time. And in the present case, nothing at all is said to the effect that our causal need must be satisfied with the "objective" process enunciated in the rule. Precise observation would possibly, for example, show that the very "attraction" which conditioned the children's linguistic innovations and similarly the parental imitation of this juvenile linguistic creation took place to a very different extent for different word-forms. The question could then be raised whether something might not be said about why for given word-forms, the attraction or the imitation did not happen more frequently or less frequently or did not appear at all. Our need for causal explanation would be satisfactorily met only when the conditions of this frequency of occurrence were formulated in rules and the concrete case could be "explained" as a particular constellation arising from the "joint action" of such rules under concrete "conditions." At this point Vossler would have the repulsive search for laws, isolation, generalization in the very intimacy of his home. And what is more, through his own fault. For his own general conception, "Analogy is a question of psychic power," compels us quite inescapably to ask the question whether absolutely nothing general can be discovered and stated about the "psychic" conditions of such "psychic power relations." And at first glance it forcibly draws in — in this formulation — what appears to be Vossler's chief enemy, namely, "*psychology,*" into the question. Whenever in the concrete case, we content ourselves with the simple presentation of what concretely occurred, the reason for this may be twofold—: first: those "rules" which could be discovered, for instance, by further analysis would, in the given case, probably not afford any new insights for science — in other words, the concrete event is not very significant as a "heuristic means"; and second, that the concrete occurrence itself, because it became effective only in a narrow circle, had not universal significance for linguistic development, and thus remained "insignificant" as a "real historical cause." Only the limits of our interest, then, and not its logical meaninglessness account for the fact that the occurrence of the formulation of linguistic idiosyncrasies in Vossler's family presumably remains exempt from "conceptualization."

difference in the degree of accessibility and completeness of the "data."

We are indeed always inclined to believe that if we find the "personality" of a human being "complicated" and difficult to interpret, that he *himself* must be able to furnish us with the decisive information if he really honestly wished to do so. We will not discuss further at this point either the fact that or the reason why this is not so — or, indeed, why the contrary is often the case.

Let us turn rather to a closer examination of category of "objective possibility" which we have thus far dealt with only very generally in respect to its function. We shall examine in particular the question of the modality of the "validity" of the "judgment of possibility." The question should be asked: whether the introduction of "possibilities" into the "causal enquiry" implies a renunciation of causal knowledge altogether; whether in spite of all that has been said above about the "objective" foundation of the judgment of possibility — in view of the relegation of the determination of the "possible" course of events to the "imagination"— the recognition of the significance of this category is not equivalent to the admission that the door is wide open to subjective arbitrariness in "historiography." Is not the "scientific" status of historiography therefore destroyed by the very use of this category? In fact, what "would" have happened if a certain conditioning factor had been conceived of or modified in a certain way — this question, it will be asserted, is often *not* answerable definitely with any degree of probability by the use of general empirical rules even where the "ideal" completeness of the source materials exists.[39] However, that ideal completeness of source materials is not unconditionally required. The assessment of the causal significance of an historical fact will begin with the posing of the following question: in the event of the exclusion of that fact from the complex of the factors which are taken into account as co-determinants, or in the event of its modification in a certain direction, could the course of events, in accordance with general empirical rules, have taken a direction in any way different in any features which would be *decisive* for our interest? For we are indeed concerned only with

---

[39] The attempt to hypothesize in a positive way what "would" have happened can, if it is made, lead to grotesque results.

this, namely, how are those "aspects" of the phenomenon which interest us affected by the individual co-determinant factors? It we *cannot*
obtain a corresponding "judgment of objective possibility" to this
essentially negatively posed question, or — what amounts to the same
thing — if in the case of the exclusion or modification of the aforementioned fact, the course of events in regard to historically important features, i.e., those of interest to us, could in accordance with
the state of our present knowledge, be expected to occur, in the light
of general empirical rules, in the way in which it had actually occurred,
then that fact is indeed causally insignificant and absolutely does not
belong to the chain which the regressive causal analysis of history
seeks to establish and should establish.

The two shots fired in Berlin on that March night belong, according to Eduard Meyer, almost entirely in this class of causally insignificant facts. It is possible that they do not belong there completely
because even on his view of the matter, it is conceivable that the
moment of the outbreak might at least have been con-determined by
them, and a later moment might have led to a different course of
development.

If, however, in accordance with our empirical knowledge, the
causal relevance of a factor can be assumed in regard to the points
which are important for the concrete study which is under way, the
judgment of objective possibility which asserts this relevance is capable
of a whole range of degrees of *certainty*. The view of Eduard Meyer
that Bismarck's "decision" "led" to the War of 1866 in a sense quite
different from those two shots, led to the events of '48, involves the
argument that if we were to disregard this decision from our analysis,
the other remaining determinants of the situation in '66 would force
us to accept as having a "high degree" of objective possibility a development which would be quite different (in "essential" respects!).
This other development would have included, for instance, the conclusion of the Prussian-Italian Treaty, the peaceful renunciation of
Venice, the coalition of Austria with France, or at least a shift in the
military and political situation which would have, in fact, made Na-
polean the "master of the situation."

The judgment of "objective" possibility admits *gradations of degree* and one can form an idea of the logical relationship which is

involved by looking for help in principles which are applied in the analysis of the "calculus of probability." Those causal components to the effect of which the judgment refers are conceived as isolated and distinguished from the totality of all the conditions which are at all *conceivable* as interacting with them. One then asks how the entire complex of all those conditions with the addition of which those isolatedly conceived components were "calculated" to bring about the "possible" effect, stands in relation to the complex of all those conditions, the addition of which would *not* have "foreseeably" led to the effect. One naturally cannot in any way arrive by this operation at an estimate of the relationship between these two possibilities which will be in any sense "numerical." This would be attainable only in the sphere of "absolute chance" (in the logical sense), i.e., in cases where — for example, as in the throwing of dice, or the drawing balls of various colors from an urn, unaffected in composition by the drawings therefrom — given a very large number of cases, certain simple and unambiguous conditions remain absolutely the same. Also, all the other conditions, however, vary in a way which is absolutely inaccessible to our knowledge. And, those "features" of the effects concerning which there is interest — in the throwing of dice, the number of eyes which are uppermost, in the drawing from the urn, the color of the ball — are so determined as to their "possibility" by those constant and unambiguous conditions (the structure of the dice, the composition of the urn), that all other conceivable conditions, show no causal relationship to those "possibilities" expressible in a *general empirical proposition*. The way in which I grasp and shake the dice box before the toss is an absolutely determining causal component of the number of eyes which I concretely toss — but there is no possibility whatsoever, despite all superstitions about the "bones," of even thinking of an empirical proposition which will assert that a certain way of grasping the box and shaking it is "calculated" to favor the toss of a certain number of eyes. Such causality is, then, wholly a "chance" causality, i.e., we are justified in asserting that the physical style of the thrower has no influence *"stateable in a rule"* on the chances of tossing a certain number of eyes. With *every* style the "chances" of each of the six possible sides of the dice to come out facing upwards are "equal." On the other hand, there is a general empirical proposition which asserts that where the center of gravity of the dice is displaced, there is a "favorable chance" for a certain side of these "loaded" dice to come out uppermost., whatever other concrete determinants are also present.   We can even express numerically the degree of this "favorable chance," of this "objective possibility," by sufficiently frequent repetition of the toss.   Despite the familiar and fully justified notice which warns against the transference of the principles of the calculus of probabilities into other domains, it is clear that the *latter* case of favorable chance or "objective probability," determined from general empirical propositions or from empirical frequencies, has its analogues in the sphere of *all* concrete causality, including the historical.   The only difference is that it is precisely here in the sphere of concrete causality that ability to assign a numerical measure of chance is wholly lacking since this presupposes the existence of "absolute chance" or certain measurable or countable aspects of phenomena or results as the sole object of scientific interest. But despite this lack, we can not only very well render generally valid judgments which assert that as a result of certain situations, the occurrence of a type of reaction, identical in certain respects, on the part of those persons who confront these situations, is "favored" to a more or less high degree.   When we formulate such a proposition, we are indeed also in a position to designate a great mass of possible circumstances which, even if added to the original conditions, do not affect the validity of the general rule under which the "favoring" of the occurrence in question is to be expected.   And we can finally estimate the *degree* to which a certain effect is "favored" by certain "conditions"— although we cannot do it in a way which will be perfectly unambiguous or even in accordance with the procedures of the calculus of probability.   We can, however, well enough estimate the relative "degree" to which the outcome is "favored" by the general rule by a comparison involving the consideration of how other conditions operating differently "would" have "favored" it.   When we carry through this comparison in our imagination by sufficiently numerous conceivable modifications of the constellation of conditions, then a considerable degree of certainty for a judgment of the "degree" of objective possibility is conceivable, at least in principle,— and it is only its conceivability in principle which concerns us here primarily.   Not only in daily life but also and indeed in history we constantly use such judgments regarding the degree to which an effect is "favored"— indeed, without them, a distinction of the causally "important" and "unimportant" would simply not be possible. Even Eduard Meyer in the work which we are discussing here has used them without hesitation. If both of those shots, which have been frequently mentioned, were causally "irrelevant" because *"any* accident whatsoever" according to Eduard Meyer's view, which we shall not criticize for actual correctness here, *"must* have caused the conflict to break out," this means, at any rate, that in the given historical constellation certain "conditions" are conceptually isolatable which would have led to that effect in a preponderantly great majority of instances given even the co-presence in that constellation of other possible conditions; while at the same time, the range of such conceivable causal factors, that given their addition to the original constellation, *other* effects (i.e., "other" with respect to aspects decisive for our interest!) would seem to us to be probable, appears as relatively very limited. We will not accept Eduard Meyer's view that the chance of any other effect was indeed equal to zero, despite his use of the words "must have" in view of his heavy emphasis on the irrationality of historical events.

We shall designate as cases of *"adequate"* causation[40] in accordance with the linguistic usage of the theorists of legal causality established since the work of von Kries, those cases in which the relationship of certain complexes of "conditions" synthesized into a unity by historical reflection and conceived as isolated, to an "effect" that occurred, belongs to the logical type which was mentioned last. And just like Eduard Meyer — who, however, does not define the concept clearly — we shall speak of "chance" causation where, for the historically relevant components of the result, certain facts acted to produce an effect which was *not* "adequate," in the sense just spoken of in relation to a complex of conditions conceptually combined into a "unity."

To return to the examples which we used above, the "significance" of the Battle of Marathon according to Eduard Meyer's view is to be stated in the following logical terms: it is not the case that a Persian victory *must* have led to a quite different development of Hellenic and

---

[40] Of such and such components of the effect by such and such conditions.

therewith of world culture — such a judgment would be quite impossible. Rather is that significance to be put as follows: that a different development of Hellenic and world culture "would have" been the "*adequate*" effect of such an event as a Persian victory. The logically correct formulation of Eduard Meyer's statement about the unification of Germany, to which von Below objects, would be: this unification can be made understandable, in the light of general empirical rules, as the "*adequate*" effect of certain prior events and in the same way the March Revolution in Berlin is intelligible on the basis of general empirical rules as the "adequate" effect of certain general social and political "conditions." If, on the contrary, for example, it were to be argued convincingly that *without* those two shots in front of the Berlin Castle, a revolution "would," in the light of general empirical rules, have been avoidable with a decidedly high degree of probability, because it could be shown in the light of general empirical rules that the combination of the other "conditions" would *not,* or at least not considerably, have "favored"—in the sense explained before the outbreak—*without* the intervention of those shots, then we would speak of "chance" causation and we should, in that case—a case, to be sure, very difficult to envisage—have to "impute" the March Revolution to those two shots. In the example of the unification of Germany, the opposite of "chance" is *not,* as von Below thought, "necessity," but rather "adequate" in the sense, which, following von Kries, we developed above.[41]   And it should be firmly emphasized that in this contrast of "chance" and "adequate," it is never a matter of distinction pertaining to the "objective" causality of the course of historical events and their causal relationships but is rather always altogether a matter of our isolating, by abstraction, a part of the "conditions" which are embedded in "the raw materials" of the events and of making them into objects of judgments of possibility. This is done for the purpose of gaining insight, on the basis of empirical rules, into the causal "significance" of individual components of the events. In order to pene-

---

41 We shall deal later with the question of whether and to what extent we have the means of assuring the "degree" of adequacy, and whether so-called "analogies" play a role here, and if so, which role they play particularly in the analysis of complex "total causes" into their "components"—since no "analytical key" is objectively given to us. The present formulation is necessarily provisional.

trate to the real causal interrelationships, *we construct unreal ones.*

The fact that abstractions are involved in this process is misunderstood especially frequently and in a quite specific way which has its counterpart in theories of certain writers on legal causality who base their views on John Stuart Mill's views and which has been convincingly criticized in the previously cited work of von Kries.[42]

Mill held that the fraction numerically expressing the degree of probability of an expected result indicated the relationship between causes which act to bring about the result and those which act to "prevent" the same, both kinds of causes existing objectively at the given moment of time. Following Mill, Binding asserts that between those conditions "which act for the realization of a given result" and those "resisting" it, there is in some cases a numerically determinable relationship, (or, in any case, one which can be estimated) which *objectively* exists; under certain conditions, in a "state of equilibrium." The process of causation occurs, according to Binding, when the former kind of condition outweighs the latter.[43] It is quite clear that here the phenomenon of the "conflict of motives" which presents itself as an immediate "experience" in *deliberation* concerning human "actions" has been transformed into a basis for the theory of causality. Whatever general significance may be attributed to this phenomenon,[44] it is, however, certain no rigorous causal analysis, even in history, can accept this anthropomorphism.[45]

---

[42] I scarcely mention the extent to which here again, as in so much of the preceding argument, I am "plundering" von Kries' ideas. While at the same time the formulation thereof is often necessarily inferior in precision to von Kries' own statement. But both of these deficiencies are unavoidable in view of the purposes of the present study.

[43] Binding, *Die Normen und ihre Ubertretung,* I, p. 41 ff. Cf. also von Kries, op. cit., p. 107.

[44] H. Gomperz, *Uber die Wahrscheinlichkeit der Willensentscheidungen,* Vienna, 1904. (Off-print from *Sitzungsberichten der Wiener Akademie, Philosophisch-Historische Klasse,* vol. 149), has used the phenomenon referred to as the basis of a phenomenological theory of "decision." I will not take it upon myself to pass a judgment on the value of his presentation of the process. Nonetheless, it seems to me that apart from this, Windelband's — intentionally, for his own purposes — purely conceptual-analytical identification of the "stronger" motive with the one which ultimately "precipitates" the decision in its favor is not the only possible way of dealing with the problem. (Cf. *Uber Willensfreiheit,* p. 36 ff.)

[45] Kistiakowski is right to this extent. Op. cit.

Not only is the conception of two "opposed" working "forces" a spatial and physical image which can be used without self-deception only in discussing events — particularly those which are mechanical and physical in nature — which involve two physical "opposite" results, each of which can be realized only by the one or the other of the "opposed" forces. Rather it is to be emphasized once and for all that a concrete result cannot be viewed as the product of a struggle of certain causes favoring it and other causes opposing it. The situation must, instead, be seen as follows: the totality of *all* the conditions back to which the causal chain from the "effect" leads had to "act jointly" in a certain way and in no other for the concrete effect to be realized. In other words, the appearance of the result is, for every causally working empirical science, determined not just from a certain moment but "from eternity." When, then, we speak of "favoring" and "obstructing" conditions of a given result, we cannot mean thereby that certain conditions have exerted themselves in vain in the concrete case to hinder the result eventually realized, while others, despite the former ultimately succeeded in bringing it about, rather the expression in question must always and without exception mean only this: that certain components of the reality which preceded the result in time, isolated conceptually, *generally* in accordance with general empirical rules, favor a result of the type in question. This means, however, as we know, that this result is brought about by those previously mentioned components of reality in the majority of the conceivably possible combinations with other conditions which are conceived of as possible while certain other combinations generally do not produce this result but rather another. When Eduard Meyer, for example, says of cases where (p. 27) "Everything *pressed* towards a certain result," it is a question of a generalizing and isolating *abstraction* and not of the reproduction of a course of events which in fact occurred. What is meant, however, if correctly formulated logically, is simply that we can observe causal "factors" and can conceptually isolate them, and that expected rules must be *thought* of as standing in a relationship of *adequacy* to those factors, while relatively few combinations are *conceivable* of those conceptually isolated "factors" with other causal "factors" from which another result could be "expected" in accordance with *general empirical rules*. In instances where the situation is in our conception of it just as it is described by Eduard Meyer, we speak[46] of the presence of a *"developmental tendency"* oriented toward the result in question.

This, like the use of images such as "driving forces" or the reverse "obstacles" to a development, e.g., of capitalism — no less than the usage which asserts that a certain "rule" of causal relationship is "transcended" in a concrete case by certain causal linkages or (still more imprecisely) a "law" is "overruled" by another "law"— all such designations are irreproachable if one is always conscious of their conceptual character, i.e., as long as one bears in mind that they rest on the abstraction of certain components of the real causal chain, on the conceptual generalization of the rest of the components in the form of judgments of objective possibility, and on the use of these to mould the event into a causal complex with a certain structure.[47] It is *not* sufficient for us that in this case one agrees and remains aware that all our "knowledge" is related to a categorially formed reality, and that, for example, "causality" is a category of "our" thought. Causality has a special character[48] when it is a question of the "adequacy" of causation. Although we do not in so doing intend to present an exhaustive analysis of this category of adequate causation, still it will be necessary at least to present one briefly in order to clarify the strictly relative nature of the distinction between "adequate" and "chance" causation which is determined by any of the possible goals of knowledge. This will have to be done in order to make understandable how the frequently very uncertain content of the proposition included in a "judgment of possibility" harmonizes with the claim to validity which it nonetheless asserts and with its usefulness in the construction of causal sequences which exists in spite of the uncertainty of the content.[49]

---

[46] The unattractiveness of the words does not affect the existence of the logical matter in any way.

[47] It is only where this is forgotten — as happens, of course, often enough — that Kistiakowski's criticisms (op. cit.) concerning the "metaphysical" character of this causal approach are justified.

[48] Here, too, the decisive viewpoints have been in part explicitly presented, and in part touched upon by von Kries (op. cit.) and by Radbruch (op. cit.).

[49] A further essay was to have followed.